Beyond Market Value

A MEMOIR
OF BOOK
COLLECTING
AND THE
WORLD OF
VENTURE
CAPITAL

Annette Campbell-White

Harry Ransom Center
Distributed by Tower Books
An Imprint of the University of Texas Press

Requests for permission to reproduce material
from this work should be sent to:
  Permissions
  University of Texas Press
  P. O. Box 7819
  Austin, TX 78713-7819
  utpress.utexas.edu/rp-form

♾ The paper used in this book meets the min-
imum requirements of ANSI/NISO Z39.48-1992
(R1997) (Permanence of Paper).

Library of Congress Cataloging-in-
Publication Data

Names: Campbell-White, Annette, author.
Title: Beyond market value : a memoir of book
collecting and the world of venture capital /
Annette Campbell-White.
Description: First edition. | Austin : [University
of Texas Press], 2019. | Includes index.
Identifiers: LCCN 2019003997
  ISBN 978-1-4773-1935-2 (cloth : alk. paper)
Subjects: LCSH: Campbell-White, Annette. |
Book collectors—Biography. | Book collecting. |
Women capitalists and financiers—Biography. |
Women in finance.
Classification: LCC Z989.C16 C36 2019 |
DDC 002.075—dc23
LC record available at https://lccn.loc.
gov/2019003997

doi:10.7560/319352

Contents

TO MY PARENTS,
WHO SACRIFICED TO GIVE ME
THE GIFT OF EDUCATION

Foreword

In *Beyond Market Value: A Memoir of Book Collecting and the World of Venture Capital*, Annette Campbell-White weaves together three interconnected stories. One is about a British colonial's search for home across four continents; another is about a pioneering career in venture capital investing just as the biomedical field began to boom in the 1980s and 1990s; and the third is about the development of a book collector and her collection. In Campbell-White's telling, these separate threads are, in fact, tightly intertwined.

Campbell-White's first steps as a collector were an effort at recreating a home, which proved fleeting for a recent transplant to London in the early 1970s. Her story is a reminder of the kinds of reassurances, comforts, and pleasures reading can provide. Later, as a successful career enabled collecting on an entirely different level, she spent years following in the footsteps of Cyril Connolly and assembling a collection of his one hundred key works of Modernist literature. That direction was inspired by the Harry Ransom Center's 1971 exhibition *Cyril Connolly's One Hundred Modern Books*.

If the story stopped with the completion of that collection, it would be a remarkable achievement, but *Beyond Market Value* is also a story about the loss of that collection and Campbell-White's recommitment to collecting on an entirely new scale. Her story of personal and professional achievement is punctuated by one remarkable acquisition after another. The great works of modernism are here—James Joyce's *Ulysses*, F. Scott Fitzgerald's *The Great Gatsby*, Ernest Hemingway's *The Sun Also Rises*—but, over time, her attention turned to important association copies and unique manuscripts. The latter included James Joyce's explanatory schema of *Ulysses*; original manuscripts of Joseph

Conrad's short stories "The Sisters" and "Falk"; Saint-Exupéry's corrected proofs of *Vol de nuit*; and the Clive Bell–Lytton Strachey letters.

Great collections are built on an idea, and, as this memoir recounts, Cyril Connolly's idea slowly gave way to Campbell-White's own idea, focusing on networks of friendship and association. In this way Campbell-White takes her place in a long line of great collectors of Modernist literature beginning with John Quinn and extending to the present. One thinks of T. E. Hanley or Carlton Lake, whose collections formed the basis for the Ransom Center's own Modernist holdings.

As we approach the one hundredth anniversary of that *annus mirabilis* of Modernism, 1922—the year that saw the publication of both *Ulysses* and *The Waste Land*—the Ransom Center marks the occasion with an exhibition of the Annette Campbell-White Collection and with the publication of that collection's origin story. The collection that she has assembled is rich in research value, and many of the items have only been on public view briefly, as they were sold at auction and dispersed. Unlike Cyril Connolly's list of one hundred titles, Annette Campbell-White's collection has no predetermined end, no completion point; instead, it continues to expand in delightful ways. The Ransom Center is a fitting place to exhibit this remarkable collection to a new audience, and we are honored to share, as well, this personal account of its making.

Stephen Enniss,
Director of the Harry Ransom Center,
The University of Texas at Austin

Prologue

This writing of this memoir resulted from a chance remark overheard at the exhibition of the sale of my first collection at Sotheby's in 2007 that was later reported to me. Two very noted literary agents were looking at the sale catalog as they walked around the exhibition.

"I see that she copyrighted the introduction," said one to the other.

"Maybe she wants to write a memoir about collecting."

At the time I didn't, but I filed the remark away in the back of my mind for nearly ten years until after I gave up control of my business and retired. And then the words came back. Write a memoir about book collecting? Why not? Beyond *Confessions of a Literary Archaeologist*, published in 1990, I had not read any memoirs written by bibliophiles, although there must have been numbers of these. That memoir was written by Carlton Lake, curator of the French collection at the Humanities Research Center at the University of Texas at Austin in the 1970s. The collections of the Ransom Center were one of my personal lodestars. Being now retired meant having time to create, which was a novelty, and I now made use of this unaccustomed free time and set to work. As I proceeded, I found myself often reflecting on the lives of collectors and the curious process of collecting itself. And this, in turn, resulted in the random reflections presented in the prologue to this book, which have little to do with the narrative of the book, but everything to do with my enduring curiosity about the world of collecting and the collectors who make up that world.

Who was the first collector in history? Nobody knows, of course. Perhaps it all started long ago in prehistory with an early human's fascination with unique and interesting seashells found lying on an ancient shore. All through history, there have been collectors of greater and lesser importance—without them, many of the world's museums would be empty. My own curiosity about those who develop the collecting bug started, I think, when I stumbled on the great collections of the Grünes Gewölbe, or "Green Vault," in Dresden, just after the Berlin Wall had come down. I hadn't expected to find such a collection of treasure in the ruins of the Dresden palaces. It quite took my breath away, consisting as it does of some of the finest examples of objets d'art made from precious materials ever to be seen together.

Who was this man responsible for creating not only the Grünes Gewölbe but so much else besides? The Elector Augustus the Strong, or Augustus II, lived a full life (1670–1733). His armies waged seemingly constant war, he had many mistresses, he loved entertainment, and yet he still found time to collect some of the finest examples of jeweled artifacts to be found anywhere in Europe—probably in all of the world as it was then. And so it was that my curiosity about collectors was born. What was the special instinct, occupied as he was in warlike endeavors, that made collecting, art, and culture so prominent a part of his life, and, in particular—gave him the wisdom to create a museum when, in 1723, he opened the collection to the public for viewing? The Grünes Gewölbe lays claim to be one of the first—if not the first—museums of artifacts open to the public, even predating the British Museum.

After I left the museum, I couldn't stop thinking about it, because I, too, was and am a collector. It seemed to me that I shared some predisposition with Augustus. Owing to his limitless resources, he had collected this fabulous treasure trove of jeweled objets d'art. I merely collected books. But at the root of it, the passion was the same: that passion, that desire, to assemble together as many examples of the thing that attracts as possible. What is this instinct that urges collectors to spend money that could otherwise be used for practical purposes on specialized collections?

Without the advent of museums, we may never have learned about the importance of collectors and their collections, but because museums relied so heavily on private collections for their acquisitions, collectors themselves began to receive recognition. From the Middle Ages onward, especially in Europe, many of those who had means assembled what became known as "cabinets of curiosities," the creation of which was a popular diversion among the class of people wealthy enough to assemble and maintain them. In German-speaking lands, these were known as *Kunstkabinetten*, and some of the great museum collections of Central Europe have their basis in the *Kunstkabinetten* inheritance. There was no collecting mandate, so the contents of any cabinet of curiosities reflected the particular interests of that collector, and the size of collections varied from a small display cabinet to whole rooms of artifacts. Anything was collectible—specimens of natural history being of special interest—and cabinets of curiosities could contain jewels, porcelain, objets d'art, medallions, or even collections of grotesqueries. Originally the name was given to rooms of artifacts that contained collections built around particular themes, whether they were natural history items, scientific curiosities, archeological treasures, or whatever else might have taken the fancy of the collector. Each collection reflected the taste and wealth of the collector and was designed to create a feeling of wonder in the observer. Owing to the personal nature of the collections displayed in different cabinets of curiosities, it is clear that most owners who assembled these had a passion for collecting, but it's equally true that many of the collections were assembled merely as a display of power, rather than to demonstrate the level of the owner's passion for collecting per se.

Some collectors had the means to assemble treasures on a heroic scale. What would the Hermitage Museum in Saint Petersburg be today without the insatiable collecting of Catherine the Great? Catherine freely admitted that she collected not for the love of the art itself, but for the sake of acquiring ever-larger collections, which accounts for the construction of whole palaces to contain the works of art she acquired. In modern times, where would the Metropolitan Museum of Art or the Frick Collection in New York be without donations of art by major collectors? Or the Wallace Collection in London? What about Napoleon, ransacking the collections of Europe and sending cartloads of treasure for display at the Louvre? But was that really collecting? Maybe it was just an expression of power.

In my field of interest, which is collecting books and manuscripts, notable collectors and collections have been celebrated from the times of the Romans up to the present day, and many important national libraries, as well as libraries of religious and educational institutions have benefited from donations and legacies from these collectors. Some public libraries, such as the Harry Ransom Center at the University of Texas in Austin, contain great collections owing to the collecting passion and insight of a succession of enlightened directors. Most of the great private libraries today, such as the Morgan Library in New

York or the Huntington Library in Pasadena, California, exist owing to the collecting passion of a single bibliophile. At Wormsley in Buckinghamshire, the collection that has been assembled in the Library of Sir Paul Getty, with particular help from dealers such as Bryan Maggs of the venerable firm of Maggs Brothers in London, contains one of the best collections of fine bindings to be found anywhere in the world, and this library may be today the greatest library still to exist in private hands.

None of the early collectors who assembled cabinets of curiosities were, unless incidentally and as part of their wider collecting, dedicated collectors of rare books and manuscripts—however, great and scholarly libraries, dedicated solely to the collection and maintenance of manuscripts and books, existed as both private and institutional repositories of knowledge from the dawn of early writing. Maybe the distinction between private and public collections is incidental. John Leland, who styled himself as antiquary to Henry VIII of England, assembled a great collection of manuscripts and books of his own while in the service of the king, ostensibly salvaging great works on the king's behalf from monastic libraries after the Dissolution of the Monasteries.

In the centuries following the invention of the printing press, which made books widely available, the amateur collector of books and manuscripts was able to indulge his or her fancy freely; by that time, the idea of collecting rare books merely because the idea of owning books was an end in itself was feasible. In contrast to the early book collectors, these amateur collectors were just that—knowledgeable, but not specialized scholars. Among this category of amateurs, the life of the English collector William Beckford, who lived between 1760 and 1844, caught my attention. He was the first collector of books and manuscripts in whom I took a significant interest, because up until I encountered Beckford, most of the book and manuscript collectors I had read about, however worthy, appeared stuffy—and even boring. Beckford was neither of those things. Today, he is best known as the creator of Fonthill Abbey, whose outlandish design inspired the craze for Gothic architecture in nineteenth-century England. About Beckford it could be safely said that he was, as Lady Caroline Lamb said about Lord Byron—"Mad, Bad and Dangerous to Know." The trajectory of his life is nevertheless important, because he was a wealthy commoner who spent his fortune acquiring and disposing of several major collections of art and books. Despite his unconventional personal life, Beckford was an intellectual and a voracious reader, who undoubtedly read most, if not all, of the volumes he acquired over the years.

Heir to a great fortune made in Jamaican sugar plantations and factories, Beckford, who inherited this fortune at the age of ten, seems never to have understood self-discipline in any of his undertakings. Shunned by polite society owing to his scandalous way of living, which was protected by his wealth, and self-exiled to the Continent from time to time, he nevertheless preferred to stay in England rather than slink off to live a life in shadows on the Continent. Fonthill Abbey was his greatest and most foolhardy achievement: a Gothic-inspired country house, it was designed to be a spectacular showcase for Beckford's extensive collections, most particularly of his art and book collections. The abbey had doors that were over one hundred feet high and a central tower that reached to three hundred feet. Owing to a faulty mixture of timber and stucco in its construction, the tower collapsed several times, finally nearly destroying the entire abbey when it collapsed for the third time in a great storm, but Beckford had sold the property before the final catastrophe, largely to pay debts. In fact, in his lifetime, he managed to squander nearly all of his inherited wealth.

Despite his rackety personal life, Beckford was one of the great English collectors. He assembled his great library after purchasing the library of Edward Gibbon, but he also created important collections of art, porcelain and ceramics, furniture, and tapestries. All of these, including the book collections, are now dispersed among museums and private collections in many countries. It was probably the lack of self-discipline that enabled him to achieve his great collections, because his spending on them was so extravagant that it was ultimately the root cause of the collapse of his fortunes. Like Augustus II, Beckford acquired only the finest and best examples of works; unlike Augustus, his purse was, in the end, limited by the twin follies of his insatiable spending on his collections and his spending on Fonthill Abbey.

Owing to his financial profligacy, Beckford had to sell his treasures off from time to time even during his lifetime when funds were running low. The record that remains from the sale inventories of these various collections shows the extent of Beckford's collecting passion. It is said that the sale of his effects from Fonthill Abbey before he moved to his final residence in Bath was one of the great sales of the early nineteenth century. Beckford was certainly one of the greatest collectors, and definitely the most colorful collector, of his time. He collected ravenously and passionately, and ultimately, what he collected enhanced the collections of many major British museums and libraries, for which we should be grateful.

Many years ago, at Sotheby's, I bought one of the books from Beckford's library. The history associated with the book fascinated me. Like most of his books, this one is bound between thick boards; the spine is backed with—and the corners tipped by—red half morocco. It's impossible to know whether any of the various small gilt crests that decorate the spine and the corners were designed by or for Beckford, or if they represent the Beckford crest. The books from Beckford's library are full of commentary. The book I own is actually about travel in Russia and Sweden, and was written by Lord Robert Ker Porter. Published in 1809, the chief interest in this copy lies in two pages of comments that Beckford had bound in with his copy of the work. He habitually wrote dismissive handwritten comments in the margins of his books in tiny, crabbed handwriting whenever he disagreed with the opinions or manner of expression of the author, or if he felt he had something to add to what had been written. The comments were seldom kindly, and this is certainly the case with his comments on Porter's *Travelling Sketches in Russia and Sweden During the Years 1805, 1806, 1807, 1808.*

For me, Beckford stands as an epitome of sorts of that curious subset of humanity—the true and instinctive collector. He collected wildly and carelessly, and when he was forced by lack of funds in later times to sell various collections, he participated in his own sales, buying back some of the items at prices exceeding what he had originally paid for them. How to explain this? Not everyone collects like Beckford did. Some people collect solely with a profit motive in mind, and the collection is sold when complete. In my opinion, this is not really collecting; this is investing. In other words, it's just business. Such collectors treat the act of assembling their collections in the same way they would go about creating a portfolio of stocks and shares.

I truly believe that a committed collector is not someone who just has a list to complete, or who benefits from a curated collection assembled mostly by someone other than the person footing the bills. Finding themselves with one or two treasured items of something, anything—books or china ornaments or model trains—natural collectors become so entranced with what they have discovered that they seek more and more of the same thing. And with that sort of collecting comes expertise in the topic, which itself encourages the collection further. Whatever the field and however significant, trivial, or even objectionable the goal of the collection, these are true collectors—people whose passion leads them to assemble as many examples of their particular interest or folly as they can find or can afford or have space to keep.

There's something a little obsessive about the quest to build a collection. Why spend money that could be spent on a holiday buying a book or a print or a toy soldier? Why search for other toy soldiers to add to the growing collection, and why feel such satisfaction as the list of collected items grows? There is no expectation of financial gain in the mind of a true collector, and if gain accrues, it's merely a happy accident. For some reason, for a collector, it is just generally more satisfying to have a group of related items than just one example of something that attracts—even if that one of something is of significant value and interest as a stand-alone item. Some psychologists have posited that collecting is an addiction, like an addiction to drugs or alcohol, but nobody really has more than an opinion on the matter.

I was a collector from my earliest years, although my first collection of note was not of books, but of stamps. Many children of my generation collected stamps. Stamp collecting was very rewarding in the 1950s for children living, as we did, in the countries of the Commonwealth. There were always letters arriving with colorful stamps affixed to them, and these I steamed off the envelopes and mounted with corner transfers into albums labeled with names of countries that no longer exist. It was an enlightening pastime for a child—one could spend hours looking at the stamps, making sure the pages aligned and the stamps were placed in order, that a series was complete. Trading stamps was a social activity. There were colorful stamps from far-off African countries with names that have disappeared from the lexicon, such as Northern and Southern Rhodesia, Nyasaland, South West Africa, Belgian Congo—all the names that represented the historical Scramble for Africa undertaken by the great European powers in the nineteenth century. There were stamps from Palestine and the Straits Territories—now Jordan, Israel, Singapore, and Malaysia. In fact, my old collection, were it still assembled in order, would be a combined geography and history lesson covering the last days of British colonialism. I also had many "first day" covers in that collection—stamps franked on the first day of issue. My New Zealand grandparents would send me every first day cover that accompanied the issue of a brightly colored new stamp issued by the New Zealand Post Office. I was so assiduous a collector that my father and my paternal grandfather gave me their collections to preserve alongside my own sets of stamps and first day covers. But in the end, stamp collecting did not follow me as an avocation into the world of grown-ups, and the remnants of the collection now are stored in boxes, unsorted.

I discovered my true collecting vocation in my early twenties, when the world of rare books opened up before me, although it took some time as a book collector before I understood that my real interest lay in collecting the books and manuscripts of important Modernist authors, along with related ephemera, such as photographs, portraits, and autograph letters written by or to them. This is now and has been for many years my chief collecting preoccupation. But, like all instinctive collecting activity, my collecting focus evolved. I did not direct it; I did not will it. Over time, it became exactly what I knew was right for me, and I believe that, in all probability, the true collector has no choice in the matter of what and how to collect—he or she must follow that collecting instinct along the path that it takes them. Like William Beckford and others before me, I find that I have the willingness to spend more money than I can reasonably afford at times in order, in my case, perhaps to own a page of scribblings written in faded ink, and that I am prepared to forgo sleep in order to bid live online or by telephone for some desired item in a London or Paris auction.

But I have also been lucky in that for me, the prerequisites for becoming a dedicated book collector came together naturally through upbringing and circumstance. I grew up in a family that encouraged reading and appreciation of literature, and that in its turn was at least partly responsible for my own early love of books. Later, the demands of a strict English syllabus in a colonial boarding school broadened my literary knowledge and interests into the worlds of French and American literature. Significant collecting requires financial means, but serendipitously, I finally embarked on a career that gave me the financial wherewithal to create the sort of book and manuscript collections I had only dreamed of when I first started collecting. What this book is about is just that—the story of my collections, and how they came into being over almost a lifetime of seeking out rare Modernist books and manuscripts while at the same time I was engaged in a career of investing in the early years of the Silicon Valley technology boom.

An Auction at Sotheby's

Bond Street in London is always crowded at lunchtime. Legions of cars and black taxis forge their way toward Piccadilly, a stampede of traffic controlled only by the lights at each intersection. The pavements are choked with people, and the expensive designer labels filling the windows of the boutiques adorn the toned physiques of many of the tourists and upmarket shoppers who crowd the pavements. I've walked this street more times than I can count—first as an impecunious window shopper, newly arrived in London in the early 1970s with scarcely a penny to my name. In those days, I was even concerned that someone—I couldn't say who, but someone—would notice that I didn't belong there and ask me to leave. There was the thrill, about ten years later, in coming to London as part of an investment banking road show, staying at Claridge's with our group, and venturing along Bond Street secure in the knowledge that my American Express card would clear the way for me in those same glamorous shops and boutiques. A few years after this was the joy of taking my mother along Bond Street, looking for the sales. Even later, there was a day when, walking along Bond Street in the early morning with my husband, Ruedi, celebrating the end of chemotherapy for a recurrent breast cancer, I saw a diamond ring in the window of the French jeweler Chaumet. Ruedi had always told me that he would buy me a beautiful diamond to complement my tiny engagement ring with its row of pavé diamonds—but only once his ship had come into port.

"Ruedi," I said, "look at that ring. Has your ship come in yet?"

"Nearly," he told me. "Let's go in and try it on." The ring fitted me as if it had been made for me. Ruedi had it put in the safe at Chaumet until, six months later, his ship came in and he paid for the ring. Just in time, too, because Chaumet in London closed shortly after that owing to a great financial mismanagement and corruption scandal, although it reopened some years later with new owners. I always wondered what had happened to the company's private museum, which occupied the floor above the Chaumet headquarters on the Place Vendôme in Paris, the place where Chopin died. Its collection held tiaras that had adorned many of the crowned heads of Europe in the nineteenth century.

Yet, of all that Bond Street has meant to me over the years, my closest association with the area arose from my relationship with Sotheby's, which produced some of the most intense moments I have experienced as a collector. As I walk down Bond Street from Piccadilly, or up the street from the tube exit on Oxford Street, I always experience a little flurry of anticipation when I see, halfway down New Bond Street, the understated green canopy that stands above the entrance to the famous premises of Sotheby's auction house, with the company's blue flag, bearing its characteristic logo, fluttering limply above the doorway, stirred by any passing shallow breeze. I love Sotheby's, and the reason for this is that I have bought and sometimes sold through Sotheby's many of the key works of Modernist literature and poetry that have enabled me to assemble over time not one, but two significant collections in that field of literature. The auction houses of Sotheby's, Bonham's, and Christie's are the Big Three of the auction business for books and manuscripts, but it's been Sotheby's where I have developed the most personal of relationships, although I have been a happy customer over the years of both Christie's and Bonham's.

I say this, but surprisingly, although I had been a collector of rare books since my first rare book purchase in 1972, it took nearly twenty-five years until I finally had the confidence and courage to buy directly in a book auction on my own behalf. This was the 1996 sale of significant works from the library of the noted collector Anthony Hobson, the former head of the Rare Book Department at Sotheby's. There was so much of interest in the catalog of that sale, and I had a limited budget, so I had to pick and choose among items, which made for difficult decisions—hardly the sort of task one could leave to an agent. The intricacies of choice in that Hobson sale provided the final impetus I needed to buy without an intermediary. After that, I never looked back. Buying or selling in the premises of a major auction house is a pivotal experience in the life of a collector.

Sotheby's foyer is not just about the café, which is, however, one of the best places for lunch in Bond Street. The air conditioning keeps the temperature mild in any weather, and there is just enough of a faint odor of expensive perfume floating in the air to remind you that you are in a temple of sorts—a temple devoted to the religion of fine art. For more than two hundred years, Sotheby's has made a business of assembling and selling collections of exquisite objects—the kind that nobody needs, but everybody wants. The faint scent that hovers in the air is like the ingrained smell of incense you find in old cathedrals, which makes sense, because this is a temple of luxury, devoted to the sale of the most important and exquisite objects to be found among the various categories of the fine arts. Strategically placed in the Sotheby's foyer are large television monitors that present a silently moving display of current sales activity for your review, if you care to look at what treasures are currently for sale. In these premises are sold important paintings, ranging from the Old Masters through to the Modern art bought and sold in the frenzied auctions that have become the norm in recent years, as well as fine gems and jewelry, wine, automobiles, fashion, furniture, and objets d'art. And books. Rare books, manuscripts, and autographs, all described in fine catalogs that make one long to own what is offered within the pages.

I'm now going to fast-forward to a particular day, June 7, 2007, when I found myself shuffling gloomily down Bond Street toward Sotheby's in a completely different frame of mind. Normally, I felt a frisson of anticipation when I walked through the heavy front door of Sotheby's, but on this day, I could scarcely summon anything other than a nod to the doorman as I entered the building. The previous evening, I had been to a cocktail event at the auction house, and there, viewing the exhibition of the books on display, it had sunk in for me with a thud that the following afternoon, my treasured collection of Cyril Connolly's titles, a selection of Modernist works discussed in his book *The Modern Movement: One Hundred Key Books from England, France, and America, 1880–1950*, was about to go under the auction hammer. What had I done? What madness had possessed me to offer this collection for sale? It was the end result of years of assiduously chasing down titles, trading lesser copies for better copies, meeting dealers, writers, and other people who had become part of my world, and learning, all the time, more and more about the books and poetry and manuscripts that I had bought. If books had a soul, these books and manuscripts were my family, and I was now set to divorce them that very afternoon.

As I entered, I noted without really focusing on it that the screen in the foyer displayed a succession of carefully curated images of the fine and rare books that were to be sold. The sale was of a collection of Modernist literature, billed as Modern Movement books. The screen images dwelt lovingly on pictures of first editions of works written by important authors of the Modernist movement in literature, such as Ernest Hemingway, F. Scott Fitzgerald, Evelyn Waugh, Joseph Conrad, James Joyce, Marcel Proust, Guillaume Apollinaire, and many of their contemporaries. High-definition pictures of the fine bindings and the inscriptions contained in various of these books flicked by, and automatically, that inscrutable desire possessed me, that same desire which seems to kick in whenever I see beautiful books in fine bindings and first editions, or letters and manuscripts written by or corrected by or annotated by writers whom I revere, which manifests as a longing to touch the items, to handle them, perhaps to own them. The items looked strangely familiar, and now I started to pay attention. Wait a minute—these were my books, this was my collection. The monitors were showing works from my collection. Again that awful truth, revealed the previous evening, became evident. Yes, it was my collection. I took no pride in the fact that it had been deemed important enough to have a bespoke sale devoted to its dispersion, but I shook myself out of my stupor. Concentrate, I told myself. This was the reason that I was at the Sotheby's premises that day. To watch my beloved books and manuscripts go under the auction hammer.

I looked at the items sliding by in succession on the monitor display, experiencing both regret and longing. I must have been mad to do this, I thought, feeling vaguely ill, because it was too late to go back. The contracts had been signed, the buyers were gathering, the catalog had been widely dispersed, and the items in the collection had been shown in a series of public viewings. The knot in the pit of my stomach tensed into a leaden ball of anxiety; I felt almost as if I were about to put my children up for sale.

That collection of Modern Movement books was deeply personal. The separate items in the collection were a parallel record of the course of my life and career up until the day when I sold it. Over the course of more than thirty years leading up to that day in June 2007, I had devoted myself to collecting rare examples of books that appealed to me. After a first rash purchase of a rare book in the early 1970s, I began to buy books seriously, starting with the earnings from my first job in London. Over those thirty-plus years, I used any spare money to buy books, not just books for reading, but rare books and first editions. Initially, I bought works of English poetry from the World War I era, but within ten years, the collecting passion had turned into a focused search for first editions, inscribed editions, and association copies of works by leading authors of a broader period spanning the years before and after that war, and even literary letters, portraits, and related items. What had attracted me was the Modernist movement, the movement that changed the course of literature in the twentieth century just as decisively as the revolution in the visual arts changed how artists drew, painted, and sculpted. The roadmap for my collection had been that selection of Modernist authors whose key works were discussed in my personal collecting guidebook, the influential catalog from an exhibition on the works discussed in Connolly's 1965 book, *The Modern Movement*, which Connolly curated, and which was held for some months in 1971 at the Humanities Research Center at the University of Texas in Austin. Connolly's book was not meant to be a work of scholarship, but since Connolly was one of the most influential and well-connected literary critics of his day, the book and the related exhibition catalog were the best guides one could find on the subject, and I followed Connolly's choices in assembling my own collection. Over a twenty-year period, I had succeeded in creating my own version of his list by assembling what I could find of beautiful examples of all the items he had included. And now this prized collection was about to go under the auctioneer's hammer.

There had been objective reasons for making the decision, practical reasons—at least I had convinced myself that this was true. The collection was complete, and my collecting was now no longer a treasure hunt, but more of a duty. The caretaking of the collection was becoming onerous. The increased value of some of the items meant that handling them was a matter of concern, and some of the items were in need of conservation, owing to the fragility of the paper or the backing. And it had to be said that not all of the items in the collection were precious to me. There were items on the Connolly list that I had acquired only owing to their presence on the list, not because they held special meaning for me. There were items whose significance I questioned as arbiters of Modernist thought. Against that, there were authors who had been left off the Connolly list whose exclusion from the list I also questioned.

Still, it's one thing to be objective. Subjectively, I had a completely different and altogether unanticipated reaction. I'd had absolutely no idea how much that collection meant to me, personally, until I sent it to Sotheby's to be sold. I had never considered how, over the many years in which I had assembled the collection, I'd almost begun to consider the authors of many of the works to be personal friends. And, in addition, I felt a deep connection to Connolly himself, particularly on those occasions when I disagreed with some of his choices, not only of authors on his list but also of exclusions from it. I could even imagine myself in debate with Connolly, arguing for or against inclusion of particular works and particular authors as key examples of Modernism. But by the time that realization bore in on me, it was already too late for subjective analysis.

In hindsight, I am sure that, even without considering the practical reasons I used to convince myself, such a sale had to happen. Perhaps I already knew this intuitively the day I called Sotheby's to discuss a sale. The sale was a sort of catharsis, a trial by fire, to force a change in my collecting direction, since collecting in such a narrow range had clearly become stale. My collecting activities had become confined by the Connolly list, and I no longer wanted my interests to be defined by Connolly's choices. It was time to move ahead on my own, to throw away the roadmap. In other words, objectivity aside, it was a response to the urging of that small, intuitive voice, a voice which lives inside the head of every collector, telling me that the collection was complete, that it was time to move on. That's the real reason. But against that logic, I often, even today, hear a different voice suggesting that it might have been possible to keep the collection in safe custody and add to it according to my own growing and changing interests. But it's too late for this sort of retrospection, just as it was already too late on that June morning in 2007. The sale was about to happen.

First Acquisition

I became a bibliophile quite by accident and in an unusual way. In the early 1970s, I was living for a time at Olave House, the Girl Guide hostel in Earl's Court. Like Dick Whittington, I had come to London to seek my fortune, but fortune was eluding me. I was twenty-five years old—alone, lonely, and with very little money, so the fact that the hostel was open to me was a salvation of sorts. I was actively looking for work, but completely unaware that London in the early 1970s was no place for a young Colonial to try to start a career; the country was depressed and on the brink of financial ruin. However, since I had no money for newspapers, and the day-to-day necessity of finding work didn't leave a lot of time to study newspapers and magazines in any case, I didn't know and hadn't learned that Britain was broke. I kept on unsuccessfully answering advertisements, while in the evenings, to keep at bay the perpetual anxiety that comes from being out of work, I would sit in the common room of the hostel and pass away the time by sewing appliqué flowers onto my jeans. Flower Power was over, but flower patterns on our jeans and long, flowing peasant blouses were still de rigueur.

What made me choose England as my home? All my life, it seemed, had led up to that point. England, and London in particular, drew in young Colonials like me because we had been taught that London was the lodestar, so I was sure that it would be in England that I would find roots. Yet, here I was after my first months in the capital, nearly out of money and sharing a room in the Girl Guide hostel.

Near the hostel, in Abingdon Road, very near to Kensington High Street, was a shop whose windows drew me ineluctably toward them every time I walked past. At first, I was too shy to enter the shop itself, but finally, curiosity overpowered me and I took my courage in both hands and found myself inside. The interior was dim and crowded with books—books on shelves, books in glass display cabinets—yet everything was orderly. I looked around me, not daring to touch anything, overwhelmed by the sight of the crowded shelves, which seemed to be on the point of overflowing with books. But not ordinary reading copies of books. There were numerous elegantly bound volumes with covers of tooled leather, some chipped and rubbed, showing the wear of time. I loved the intermingled smell of paper and old leather, an aroma exuding the implicit promise that the stories contained within, bound by those rich, leather bindings, could introduce me to the new and unknown.

It was very quiet in that shop, dim and cool. As I looked around, I was overcome by the thought that I could be alone with these thousands of rare volumes. It was a defining moment, but I quickly discovered that I wasn't alone after all. As my eyes became accustomed to the shadows, I saw, standing to one side, toward the back of the showroom and behind a counter, the figure of an elderly man who was obviously the owner of the shop. He had been standing for some time, partly hidden behind the counter, watching me with a mixture of amusement and curiosity. And no wonder. With my flowered jeans and my cork platform clogs, I did not look in the least bit like his usual customer.

I don't remember his name, but I do remember that he was a connoisseur and vendor of incunabula, the early texts printed before 1500. In fact, his shop windows were full of such early texts, as well as several old books relating to his other specialties: early atlases and medical texts, the latter replete with exact but garish drawings and engravings of human anatomy. It was these old medical books that had finally given me the courage to enter the shop, because I wondered, in my naïveté, if I could perhaps afford one of them as a birthday present for my sister, a physician living in South Africa. To his credit, the book dealer was kind to me, because he could sense that I was a lover of books. He didn't dismiss me, nor did he laugh at my ambition. He loved his books and loved showing them off, and he took out item after item and let me open these rare books and handle them. I was entranced, and I like to think that this was the day that I became a real bibliophile. Of course, the price of the anatomy text that had attracted me was an astronomical £600, so a purchase was out of the question.

I might have left the shop as one might leave a museum after a satisfactory visit, and never thought further about owning and collecting rare books, but as it happened, almost incidentally, the dealer also had, perched on his topmost shelves, some Modern first editions and some beautiful illustrated books on botany. I wanted to return to take a closer look. In fact, after that first visit, for some while, I haunted this little shop, and again to his credit, the elderly dealer let me do that. For me, it was a respite from the outside world, from the constant struggle to find work and housing. Inside the shop, I felt safe, among friends. There wasn't much Modern literature, but there were some books of poetry, mostly valuable, I suppose, for the richness of the bindings. Until then, I had known nothing about books as artifacts and collectibles, and the prices of some of the items, especially the ancient medical texts, seemed to me astronomical. But the world of bibliophilia came together at that shop in Abingdon Road, where for the first time, I learned about books as collectible items.

I was, even from that first encounter with the world of rare books and manuscripts, more interested in the Modern first editions than the other books that were for sale. This was the world of literature that I had known in the years when, growing up in various Commonwealth countries, I had lost myself in books and poetry. As I opened the volumes in the Abingdon Road shop, I could scarcely believe that writers whom I revered had actually touched and signed and written words in these pages. I felt strongly a connection to the books, perhaps because in some way, their antiquity and provenance linked me to the authors themselves and to the past, because these were rare and first editions of works by writers with whom I had communicated as a child, in an imaginary world of my own creation. In this world of imagination, I had placed a different sort of home for my childhood, and this invented world of home, so much more satisfying than the real world, was somehow the one where these writers had lived and about which they had written. Generally speaking, the location of this imaginary home was England, and in time, it existed in the early years of the twentieth century. And that was perhaps what had driven me toward seeking a new home in England in the first place. About the time period, I couldn't be sure. One can't live in the past. Anyway, it was all daydreaming. I had no money and I could not realistically afford to buy anything for myself, so, after some time, I would reluctantly close whichever volume I was studying and place the book back on the high shelves and return to the street and the everyday world.

Then one day a *coup de foudre* overcame me and I bought a book. It was the first book I ever collected. It was an edition of what are known as the Ariel poems, and this was T. S. Eliot's "A Song for Simeon" in the limited edition, hardback copy of 1928. This was a poem that I had learned and loved while at boarding school in Cape Town in the early 1960s, and these were the years when Eliot was, to young people, one of the gods, if not the god, of poetry. Milton and Keats were passé, Pound was still suffering the loss of reputation caused by his Italian broadcasts during World War II, but *The Waste Land* was a bible for young adults, even if most of us who read it could scarcely understand what it was about. Eliot was for earnest conversation late at night, while listening to the music of Bob Dylan and the folk singers Peter, Paul and Mary. Perhaps because of the impenetrability of so much of Eliot's poetry, you could assign any meaning to the words and everyone would nod sagely. My personal favorite among Eliot's poems was "Burnt Norton," the first of the *Four Quartets*; it was a strangely metaphysical poem and I felt very sophisticated trying to understand it. I'm not sure that what I have written describes accurately the immediate excitement I felt on seeing the little book that contained the first printing of "A Song for Simeon" in the shop on Abingdon Road. After I took the book down from the shelf, for a time I just gazed at the back page, which showed that the book was number 158 of a limited edition of 500 printed books. But that didn't mean a lot—of most importance was that, below this listing, was the signature; this book had been actually signed by T. S. Eliot. It didn't matter that the copy was one of several hundred signed books in that edition; I knew that the book I held in my hands was a magic book, meant just for me. The signature spoke to me; it was like receiving a letter from an ancient relative who lived in that home I dreamed about but somehow couldn't seem to find in reality, a letter that held the key to finding the roots for which I was searching. In the midst of my uncertainty, the terrible loneliness I had felt since arriving in London, and, most of all, my fear about the future, a hand, Eliot's hand, reached out from the past. The signature and the fact of its being a limited edition made the book personal. It wasn't just any little book that happened to contain a poem that I had studied and enjoyed. It was a special book that had been waiting for me to discover it, so that I could connect immediately with the hidden realm that, in all of my life up until that time, I had assigned as my spiritual home of sorts, even if it was a world that didn't really exist.

Finding that copy of one of Eliot's more popular poems was a sign—I knew that it was a sign—that everything was going to turn out well in the end. My sojourn with the Girl Guides was a temporary interlude, I was going to find a job and a place to stay, and someone was looking over me. Just as Eliot had expressed his doubts for the future by writing "A Song for Simeon," the discovery of this signed and limited edition was, I felt, meant to tell me that the friends of my imagination were still there and looking out for me. I have always been superstitious, so the notion that the book represented that Everything Was Going to Turn Out All Right meant that I had to buy it.

The poem was published on handmade paper, and the book contained a lithograph by the American artist Edward McKnight Kauffer, which had been commissioned to accompany the poem. The book cost £45. The purchase was an act of monumental folly, because I was still unemployed and my funds were significantly depleted. To put this price in perspective, my first proper job in London paid me £2,400 annually, of which the government took half in tax. I lived on £100 a month. So, this purchase took half of a month's salary of a job which I had yet to find. But I wanted that book so badly that I threw caution to the winds and paid the full price. It was more than a book, more than a collectible—for me, it was a talisman that held a message; if I only hung on long enough, all would be well. Only once I returned to my lodging did it sink in that I had spent so much of my rapidly dwindling cash on a slim book of verse that I was going to have to live on cereal for a while. But it didn't matter—I had the book.

Time has shown that as a financial investment, the purchase was a bust, but as a treasure, for me, it was of incalculable value. Personally, I think collectors and scholars alike have sadly underrated the Ariel poetry series. Between 1928 and 1931, the firm of Faber and Gwyer, which became Faber and Faber after 1928, produced fine examples of thirty-eight of these poems by different poets in hardbacked limited and signed editions printed on handmade paper. Each poem in the series was also produced in a larger pamphlet series intended for wider distribution. The poems of the limited series, each printed in numbers ranging between 200 and 500 copies, were originally sent to patrons of the firm as Christmas gifts, which consequently means that they are very hard to find. Over the years, I have collected all but two of the series, and in addition, most of a small softcover series that Faber and Faber produced in 1954. The lithographs that accompany each poem of the series are almost as interesting as the poetry. Eric Gill illustrates a poem by G. K. Chesterton; Stephen Tennant illustrates poems written by his lover Siegfried Sassoon; as mentioned, T. S. Eliot chose his friend Edward McKnight Kauffer to produce most of the Modernist, almost vorticist illustrations for the works he contributed to the series.

Of course, I learned most of what I know about the Ariel poems later, but it was that first book, "A Song for Simeon," that started the collecting passion that continues to the present day.

The signature was the miracle. I could imagine all sorts of circumstances in which T. S. Eliot had actually sat down and signed 500 of these books! There was also the special paper and the lithograph. Every time I opened the book and looked at that signature, I felt I was, however obscurely, linked to Eliot and to the poets who were his contemporaries. No purchase I have ever made subsequently has had the same impact.

I sometimes wonder if I would have become a collector if that first book had not been the T. S. Eliot Ariel poem, or if it had been an item of fantastic value, such as Eliot's *The Waste Land*, instead, which I could never have afforded in those days. What if that book had contained an Ariel poem to which I was not as attached? I have no concrete answer to these questions, yet I assume that my early passion for books and reading, together with my avocation for works of early twentieth-century writers, would sooner or later have found a connection with the world of rare book collecting, and from there to collecting works of Modernism.

During my childhood and adolescence, I read poetry widely, but without much comprehension, and being a solitary child, at my boarding school in Cape Town I continued a tradition from early childhood and imagined myself in the worlds and lands of the authors whose works I was engaged with at the time. T. S. Eliot had been only the first poet among a number of imaginary literary friends. I loved his poetry, even though I didn't understand a lot of what he wrote; this may be the reason why, contrary to what might be expected, it wasn't *The Waste Land*, or "The Love Song of J. Alfred Prufrock," that caught my imagination—but that little poem written in 1928 for the first of the Faber and Gwyer Ariel poem series—"A Song for Simeon." The poem speaks of the moment in the temple when the prophet Simeon sees the infant Jesus, who has been brought to the temple for a blessing. God has told Simeon that he will not die until he has seen the young Messiah with his own eyes.

It's hard to understand why certain words, books, or lines of poetry find resonance for someone. The poem really didn't relate at all to my struggle to adapt to life in Africa, trapped in the confines of an Anglican girls' boarding school. Yet, I think that poetry lives on several levels— there is the meaning intended by the author, the meaning ascribed to the words by the reader, and, above all, the rhythm of the words that hum along each line of the text, like electrons buzzing down a wire. I didn't understand exactly what Eliot had in mind, but I loved the words and the imagery of the poem itself.

> Lord, the Roman hyacinths are blooming in bowls and
> The winter sun creeps by the snow hills;
> The stubborn season has made stand.
> My life is light, waiting for the death wind,
> Like a feather on the back of my hand.
> Dust in sunlight and memory in corners
> Wait for the wind that chills towards the dead land.

I would recite that part of the poem to myself each morning, mantra-like, when we had to run twice around the school perimeter for exercise before breakfast, come rain or come shine. Because I hated that school, I suspect that reciting the poem was a catharsis of sorts, because I was secretly hoping for an Apocalypse of total destruction to be rained down on Herschel School, with the hurling down of deadly thunderbolts onto the school buildings in order to set me free. Back then, in my early teens and feeling abandoned at boarding school, I endowed the words of the poem with my own interpretation and chose it to mean that as long as I persisted in moving forward, all would be well; school would finally end and I would be free to get on with my life. And the poem also spoke to me in other ways. As I read it through for the first time, I actually felt that T. S. Eliot was talking directly to me through his poetry. I felt that he had reached out from the lines on the page to show me his personal path and his struggle with faith and circumstance.

I later learned that critics and scholars have focused on the fact that Eliot wrote the poem at the time of his conversion to Anglo-Catholicism, which, they infer, accounts for the religiosity of the work. Nothing in the construct of anything Eliot wrote is ever that simple, however. In later years, as I grew into my collection over time and learned more about the writers of the early twentieth century, I wondered if Eliot, with his new religious insights, could have been thinking back to the tragedies of the war of 1914–1918 as he wrote those lines. I speculated that perhaps because twentieth-century English literature had lost so many of its promising poets in that conflict, Eliot might have felt the guilt of a survivor, because he had taken no active role in the Great War, as it had become known to subsequent generations. Poets with huge potential, such as Rupert Brooke, Julian Grenfell, and Wilfred Owen, never came back from that war. Siegfried Sassoon and Robert Graves returned, but they were cynical and disillusioned by the tragedies and the suffering they had seen in the trenches. Eliot never saw a theater of war.

So now I had the book, but I was far from being a collector. I knew nothing about collecting, I had no money, and my knowledge of literature was limited to what I had learned in my schooldays. Not a promising start! There's a large difference between the act of reading, bibliophilia, and actually assembling a meaningful book and manuscript collection. Even though I had been a voracious reader all of my life, as a young person, bibliophilia was not a word that even registered in my vocabulary. I had no idea that rare books existed outside of libraries and museums; as far as I was concerned, manuscripts were things that one viewed, if at all, with difficulty through the dusty glass of ancient cabinets. The idea of collecting rare books had never occurred to me, although by the time I left university, I had assembled a huge collection of Penguin paperbacks, because I never stopped reading and I always kept every book that I bought in case I wanted to read it again.

Indeed, when I look back, it's clear from my pattern of reading and hoarding those treasured and dog-eared paperback books I owned that one way or another, I was bound eventually to be a collector of books and manuscripts. I just needed an introduction to that rarefied world. I loved books so much that, once I was introduced to the existence of books as collectible items, it was only going to be a matter of time before I became a bibliophile. I can see that if it hadn't been that first purchase from the bookshop in Abingdon Road, there would have been another first purchase in some other bookshop that would have set me on my way. Some other book in some other shop would have struck a chord, and the process would have started. As a psychologist would say—there was just too much synchronism between my love of books, the world of literature, and, most importantly, my habit of aligning my life and circumstances with whichever author I happened to be fixated on at the time. I started collecting, and although there have been natural ebbs and flows in activity, once on my way, I have never stopped.

Although my subsequent baby steps into the world of collecting actually started with cautious purchases of World War I poetry, the copy of "A Song for Simeon" remained for many years my most treasured and valuable possession.

Books of Childhood

I had a rootless childhood. My father's profession in the world of mining meant that our family was constantly moving among the countries of the mid-twentieth-century British Commonwealth. Sometimes, I wonder if it was the strictly British education I received during those years of travel that later caused me to set my collecting interests so firmly in the Modern Movement. The curricula of the English and French lessons to which we were subjected in school, in whichever country we happened to reside at the time, were mostly focused on literature of that period. Yet, I think my focus on the writings of that period also relates to my experiences as a very young child in the wondrous garden created in New Zealand by my English grandmother: the gardens at Merrilea in the tiny farming town of Blenheim in the South Island made an enormous impression on me at a time when I was trying to imagine a place in the world where I truly belonged. The gardens and the house of my grandmother were living embodiments of the worlds I read about in my children's books. Most children's classics written by English authors include or center around a garden, and these gardens are always beautiful: green and filled with flowers. Books such as *The Wind in the Willows*, the Beatrix Potter books, the red, blue, yellow, and green fairy books of Enid Blyton—and on and on—all have a bucolic country setting of some sort, usually an English garden.

Although removed by distance and time from England, Merrilea and its gardens had been created in a faithful simulation of an English country household. My maternal grandmother grew up in Tunbridge Wells, which is all that I know about her early life. She married my grandfather after the end of World War I and emigrated with him to make a new home in New Zealand, where he became a country schoolmaster. She never returned to England. I wish we did know more about her, but she never spoke of how she grew up; nor did she express any longing to return to England, despite maintaining an air of superiority over the neighbors, because she never forgot her English heritage. I remember her as a stern late Victorian, a believer in the maxim that "children should be seen and not heard." I am sure she had an upper-middle-class upbringing, because she had never learned to cook, and she inherited some money later in life, which she used to assemble a small but perfect collection of antique furniture and china.

As children, we were not allowed into the rooms where my grandmother kept her precious antiques, unless accompanied by her. There was a particular parlor where the collection was housed, on the left at the end of a corridor that bisected the house from its front door to the kitchen at the back. The room was always cool and shaded under the drawn blinds. I had never seen anything as exquisite as the objects hidden away in this treasure trove where the air smelled like camphor in the dim shade. Even though it was forbidden, I would steal away to this room to drink in the splendor of the tall Chinese vases that stood on each side of the fireplace, and to gaze in awe at the polished and embroidered cottons of the sofas and the green of the carpet, so fine and woolly. My grandmother took down the china ornaments every evening and rested them among the cushions of the sofas and laid the Chinese vases on their sides on the carpet, because she had earlier lost a number of her porcelain pieces to the earthquakes that shake New Zealand at very regular intervals. I inherited a little eighteenth-century chocolate cup with a lid, whose legs have been glued back on in an irregular fashion. I am sure that this piece was damaged in one such earthquake.

Merrilea. There was a cow for milk, and chickens in a pen across a paddock, where exactly six sheep grazed. In the garden, there was a fishpond, at one end of which stood a thatched summerhouse and an aviary full of chirping budgies. The summerhouse was a magnet for grandchildren, with child-sized tables and chairs where it was possible to dream away an afternoon, watching the fish and the flashing bright colors of the budgies' wings, fluttering behind the mesh of their enclosure. I learned to play chess with my grandfather, just the two of us sitting at one of the little tables in the sunshine. At the back of the house was a small dairy, where my grandfather churned milk into fresh butter and cream and sorted the eggs. Behind the little dairy was a stand of nut trees, mostly walnuts, which dropped so many nuts that they lay rotting on the ground unsorted.

On one side of the house, my grandmother created a formal rose garden, and on the other, perennial borders, where dahlias blazed in the late summer sunshine. A lavender-bordered path led under an arbor of trees from the street to the house. It was a magical place for a child to play, and even today, I can recall the scent of the flowers, can see the sunshine flickering on the waters of the pond, and the goldfish nosing quietly among the lily pads, and I can recall the musty odor under the walnut trees and the smell of grain in the little barn where my grandfather kept his old Willys Whippet sedan, which had given up the ghost many years previously but, much loved, still had pride of place among the sacks of grain.

I appropriated this garden in my imagination. It was mine, and it was just as I had read about in my fairy books and my Noddy books. Even though I was growing out of Pooh, I could imagine him with Christopher Robin in the summerhouse. In fact, so thoroughly did I appropriate the garden that, throughout the rest of my childhood, I never felt as if I had any other home than Merrilea, and I carried its image, burning brightly in my imagination, wherever we went after that visit. The idyllic setting of Merrilea coincided so exactly with what I imagined of the worlds I read about in my children's books that reality and imagination collided. Throughout my childhood, I believed that the fictional worlds created in books had an analogue somewhere in reality, and therefore reading was only the way to discover this reality. Having this imaginary home as my spiritual locus centered what might have otherwise been a strangely unfocused way of existing, so often were we on the move to new and distant countries and climates. But not having any real idea of geography, I just assumed that all English gardens were in England itself, and that settled the matter for me.

My upbringing was a child's experience of the colonial extension of Britain's Empire from the Arctic to the tropics. In those days, vast swaths of the map were still painted the pink of Britain's waning Colonial Empire, and the British flag still flew over those pink areas, which were now largely the countries of the emerging British Commonwealth, where English was the universal lingua franca. Yet the fact that the British Empire really didn't exist anymore had not been made known to the priests in those colonial outposts, who prayed for England and the Queen; or to the headmasters and headmistresses of the schools, where we dutifully sang "God Save the Queen" and again prayed for England and the Queen. For very young children, it was a bit of a puzzle; those of us who moved around to different countries of the Commonwealth had to imagine everything. We knew that where we were living wasn't home; for me, New Zealand, which we had left behind when I was only three, clearly wasn't home either, because we didn't live there. So where was home? Where were we—where was I—rooted? I had no real idea. Only the worlds contained within the covers of books remained constant. You could read Enid Blyton books in the heat of Africa or in the snows of northern Canada, and the words on the page and the worlds they invoked always stayed the same. There was comfort in knowing you could read A. A. Milne's poems in Australia and Canada just as well as in Zambia—which in those far-off days was still called Northern Rhodesia—knowing that the worlds they conjured would always be consistent.

I first learned to read in the deserts of New South Wales in Australia, in the mining town of Broken Hill. It was not a lovely place to live; my abiding memory of Broken Hill is of sand, rocks, heat, and ugly tin-roofed buildings. Our family was very poor. My father had returned from six years of training and combat as a fighter pilot in the Royal Air Force, and then the Royal New Zealand Air Force, during World War II; immediately thereafter, he had set out to achieve a professional education in mining and metallurgical engineering, studying at the University of Otago in Dunedin, where later I was born. Despite my father's war service, all of this had to be paid for with borrowed money. He worked as a laborer on the railroads of the South Island of New Zealand during university vacations to earn money to support my mother and my older sister, who had been born at the end of the war.

My first memories are of the tiny flat where we lived in Broken Hill, where my father had taken his first professional position after graduating from university. Family lore has always had it that the reason we left New Zealand after my father graduated from university was that he had forgotten to check on employment opportunities in New Zealand before starting out on that course in mining and metallurgical engineering, and indeed, it was true that the last of the New Zealand gold mines that used the sort of mineral extraction procedures in which my father came to specialize had closed during the war period. Thus, we had to leave New Zealand and never lived there permanently again.

I once asked my father why he had undertaken such a profession when employment opportunities in his own country were not going to be available.

"Oh," he replied, casually, "but I never intended to live in New Zealand. I shared a tent in Malaya with a silver mining engineer during the war, and he told me that life in Malaya on a silver mine was splendid and paid really well. But obviously, after the war, with your mother and sister being around, it wasn't going to be possible to head out to Malaya."

So that was how our small family ended up living in Broken Hill on a street named, appropriately enough, Oxide Street. The little flat had two rooms, a roof of corrugated iron, and not much else. It was a dreary little place, with no garden and dust everywhere. The flat was one of several in the building, each leading off a dark hallway, where I was too terrified to linger, even had I been allowed to do so. Although my mother tried her best to make the flat habitable for a family of four, home it was not, although we lived there for nearly four years. I hated the heat, the corrugated iron roof, which kept the interiors stifling in the still air, and the fact that we were looked down on because we were so obviously poor—even by the standards of Broken Hill. My mother took a part-time job teaching, but it didn't change anything in our living standard.

My older sister owned a book called *Peg's Fairy Tales*, to which I was devoted, largely because it was illustrated with pages of magnificently colored pictures of those magical fairies and elves and pixies, who lived under leaves and in the inevitable mushroom houses of such stories. Of course, the homes of the little goblins, who built tiny houses in the roots of old trees, received similar scrutiny. But I could only look at the pictures, even though I knew there were stories attached to them. If only I could read them! I longed to read. With the obscure reasoning of early childhood, I recognized that books held the key to a world I longed to inhabit, a world far away from Oxide Street and the dust of Broken Hill. My sister could read, and she took just enough interest in me to help me sort out the fact that the combinations of letters of the alphabet, which I already knew, were the same letters that made up words. I would sit for hours with any book that my older sister had been reading and trace out the letters on the page, following them line by line, and I would try to sort the words into patterns and the patterns into meaning. Any illustrations in a book were helpful. I still remember the moment when, like the etchings on the Rosetta Stone yielding to the scrutiny of a linguist, the letters on the page slowly resolved into words I could understand—and just like that, I could read. I'm sure it must have been more complicated than that, but this is how it appears in memory. I must have been a peculiar child, because I remember that I kept secret for some time the fact that I could actually read, and took great satisfaction in discovering the content of books for myself. I didn't want anyone telling me what was in those books, or "helping" me to understand, which led to some conundrums. One of those was Robert Louis Stevenson's poem "Bed in Summer":

In winter I get up at night
And dress by yellow candle-light.
In summer, quite the other way,
I have to go to bed by day.

I couldn't make head or tail of that poem. Was the child sick? Why did the parents make the poor child go to bed in the daytime? It took many years before I understood that the poem related to the changing of the seasons. Eventually, I revealed my secret. Fortunately for me, because my mother was teaching at the primary school, once my academic precocity had revealed itself, I was able to counteract some of the dreariness of day-to-day life by actually going to a real school.

Books became my constant companions and I read everything I could find, even things that I didn't fully understand. I stole books from my sister, because I preferred hers to my kiddie books. She had a copy of Hilaire Belloc's *Cautionary Tales for Children*, which offered the sort of bloodthirsty poetry that appealed to children in the days before Xbox and *Grand Theft Auto* took over, and the imagination of childhood yielded to the passive imagery of the small screen. I happily read about Matilda, who told Dreadful Lies and was consequently Burned to Death, and there was Jim, who Ran Away from his Nurse and was, as a result, Eaten by a Lion. Knowing of my obsession with this book, our neighbor Miss Farnie, who lived at the end of the dark hallway in the building where our flat was located, gave me a copy of Belloc's *The Bad Child's Book of Beasts*, but this gift was not successful. I wondered what I had done so wrong to be given this book about "bad children"; I put it away and returned to *Cautionary Tales* and Winnie-the-Pooh books. Interestingly enough, despite my early obsession with Winnie-the-Pooh and Milne's poetry, I have never been more than mildly interested in collecting any of those childhood classics: I simply outgrew them. By chance, I have collected some works of Hilaire Belloc, but not his writing for children.

Over the years, there were other countries and other schools and other friends, from whom one parted with little regret when either their families or ours moved on. In Africa, we arrived by boat in Cape Town and left on a train, traveling to the north, following the route of Cecil Rhodes until the train stopped at the railhead in Lusaka. We were transported by car the rest of way along the red, dusty roads of Africa until we arrived at our new destination—Chingola on the copperbelt of Northern Rhodesia, right on the border of what was then known as the Belgian Congo, which is now the Democratic Republic of Congo.

From the outset of his career, my father's professional focus became the design and optimization of the chemical plants that leached pure concentrate from crushed ore from the mine. He had a restless character, probably created by unresolved mental trauma from his experiences as a fighter pilot during the war. My mother, devoted, never questioned his desire to move on to yet another position on yet another mine in a new country, but even without his apparent need to be peripatetically on the move, it would probably have happened anyway, because the mining world itself is notoriously fickle. The fate of any mine is hostage to world prices of metals and minerals, and mining areas are always under threat of mineral depletion—the veins of copper, tin, lead, zinc, or any other mineral can become depleted, and when that happens, the mine will close.

Life in Africa was as different from life in Australia as it could possibly be. We went from the desert to the lush vegetation of the tropics, from a tiny flat with a roof of corrugated iron to a brick house with a wide front porch. This was the Africa of Joseph Conrad and David Livingstone. Still, in most respects it was just the same as anywhere else. I did what I was told and went to school, kept out of the sun between noon and 3:00 p.m., and, although curious about the sights and sounds of Africa, spent most of my free time either planting lantana in the garden, climbing the mango trees, or reading. I had now graduated to adventure books, and my Enid Blyton obsession had advanced to include her series featuring the intrepid young detectives called the Famous Five. Some of my classmates would even lend me ancient copies of *The Beano*, a series of comic books. Even in the tropics, Britannia's influence was undiminished. We children still sang "God Save the Queen" each morning before class, and of course we prayed for the health of the Royal Family. Probably no other family in the history of the world can have had so many people constantly praying for their health and well-being. (And as some members of the Royal Family have proven over time to have extraordinary longevity, perhaps the cumulative effects of all those prayers have been salutary!) I accepted that we were now living in another extension of England, and so nothing felt out of place at all.

It's hard in today's world to explain what it was like to live in the last stages of colonial Africa. For instance, we had servants. We moved from being poor in Broken Hill to living in a brick house owned by the mining company, at 71 Eighth Street in Chingola. The house had a tropical garden full of flowers and fruit trees—mango, banana, pawpaw, avocado—and a driveway fringed with fragrant frangipani and tall jacarandas, whose heavy blossoms leaned toward the street. The hedges that surrounded the property blazed with the bright orange flowers of tropical lantana. We now had a gardener, who laughed to watch me climb the mango trees to pick ripe mangos, and helped me with my first commercial venture of selling mangos from a perch high on the stone wall at the back of the property. Our meals were prepared by a cook, who also shined the floors, which were of a red concrete designed to keep away the foraging red ant tribes that marched across the property. Africa was dangerous—during a thunderstorm, lightning leaped out of a socket in the dining room where I was doing homework and jumped between my legs, which were twined around the legs of my chair, and on into the socket across the room. I looked down at the blue flash, which disappeared before I had time to be terrified. There were snakes and poisonous insects, and the grownups feared that Mau Mau was on the march across the continent, which concern kept them constantly on the alert. (Mau Mau itself was an ideology stemming from the armed rebellion in Kenya in the 1950s against British colonial rule, which became known as the Mau Mau Uprising.) In hindsight, it all seems like a dream; the only constant was that Northern Rhodesia, like Australia and New Zealand, was part of England's dwindling Empire. We lived in a bubble of Englishness surrounded by the jungles of Africa. The young queen was on our stamps and on our currency. At 6:00 p.m. every evening, my father would turn on the shortwave radio to listen to BBC News. In those days, the service was called the General Overseas Service (GOS); the prelude to the news was the march "Lilliburlero," at the end of which Big Ben would chime, following which a portentous voice would announce over the crackling of the airwaves: "This is the BBC. Here is the news."

That voice broadcasting on the GOS obviously represented home, but I still didn't know where that was. At that stage of my life, I had a number of books about "the little princesses," about Princesses Eliza-

beth and Margaret as children. We were all ardent Royalists, so we followed news of the Queen's growing family with interest on the shortwave of the Overseas Service. The Queen and her family appeared to
me as some kind of distant relatives, familiar yet far away. We knew
them, but they didn't know us. The Queen was married to a handsome
prince, and there was a young prince and a princess. The books about
the Royal Family were boring, but the pictures were pretty, and these
distant relatives of ours dressed in elegant clothes, lived in lovely palaces, and smiled a lot. No wonder that I preferred England, which was
where they all lived. It was clear to me that the prosperous land inhabited by this family, who lived in such grand palaces in a world that was
home to Pooh and Christopher Robin, the same one invoked by the
books of Enid Blyton, was home.

It was entirely natural that, as a young child, my virtual lodestar
became the house and garden of Merrilea, because I grew up feeling
as if I were continually perched on a suitcase en route to somewhere
else, never entirely sure of where that was. The fact that Merrilea, with
its many garden rooms and features, corresponded so exactly to the
descriptions of England—and especially the English gardens—that I
had read about in my books accounts for why I assumed it was a part
of England, and why, in just the same way, I was sure the setting for
The Wind in the Willows was the Pukaka Valley Stream in Marlborough
in New Zealand, where we went to pick blackberries for tea. Because
the concept of Merrilea and its garden was so inextricably bound to
England, wherever that was, I assumed that being a Colonial English
girl and being an English girl were one and the same thing. We just
lived under a different sun—ours was from time to time the hot and
burning sun of the tropics, or the wintery, watery sun of northern Canada, in the snow—but our influences, ethics, and teachings were one
and the same. England, I concluded, was obviously where home was.
And nothing that I read during my early childhood conflicted with that
conclusion.

The fact was that, in the outposts of the fading days of colonial Britain, as it transitioned to becoming the Commonwealth of Nations, the
difference between England itself and its various colonial outposts was
too difficult for a young child to understand, so I didn't even try. No
matter that the Christmas tree might be a thorn bush decorated with a
few sad silver glass ornaments and a plaster Father Christmas on top:
we read *A Christmas Carol* and imagined ourselves in a snowy landscape with red-breasted robins scratching in the snow, the red berries

of holly ready to be picked to decorate the plum pudding. The view from the living room window didn't matter at all—one could be anywhere. Real life was what we celebrated, and that came from books. Several generations of Commonwealth citizens, brought up as I was, went eagerly to England only to realize that it was all a myth after all, and that England didn't want Colonials with their funny accents claiming to be like the English. Henry Higgins was right—the accent is all—and we had no claim to be English. We were British subjects, but Commonwealth citizens, and that difference was as wide as the oceans that separated the countries of the former British Empire. But I only learned that many years later.

Palgrave's Golden Treasury

On my ninth birthday, we left Chingola and returned to New Zealand. For me, this meant that the time of that magical period at the house and in the garden of my grandmother was at hand, the time that cemented my earlier, faint memories from infancy into the creation of the imagined home of memory that sustained the rest of my childhood. Yet the idyll ended after only six short months, and we were on the move again, this time to Northern Ontario in Canada. It's hard to imagine today that the mining boomtown of Elliot Lake in Northern Ontario came into being in the late 1950s only as a result of the Cold War paranoia that gripped the Western world after the end of World War II. Elliot Lake's mines were busy excavating and processing uranium for the US military; the concentrated uranium from Elliot Lake went to Oak Ridge, Tennessee, to be stockpiled for the manufacture of nuclear bombs and warheads. It was a strange time. Citizens of the United States built bomb shelters in their basements and their gardens, and schoolchildren in the United States regularly participated in practice air-raid drills.

In Canada, things were not quite as politically paranoid as elsewhere in the Western world, or perhaps I was still too young to register these things. I swam in the lakes in the summer and took water from the streams for my goldfish without knowing that the waters were tainted with uranium effluent from the mines, where men were working night and day to extract uranium from the alluvial soil. Nobody protected the environment from pollution then, and the nearby copper and nickel mines of Sudbury and Coppercliff had stripped the earth bare for miles around. Nothing grew, and people lived among bare black rocks in a fog of polluted smoke. The poisons were not all obvious, but it was the invisible ones that were the most insidious. In later life, the instances of childhood and adult cancers among children of our generation who had lived among the Elliot Lake mines proved to be far above average compared to the population at large. But, knowing nothing about the fact that I was being invisibly poisoned, I enjoyed life in Canada, even though our family was still living with those semi-packed suitcases. Although we had crossed oceans to our new destination of Canada, however, neither of my parents particularly enjoyed life there. They were frugal people, conditioned by the deprivations of both the Great Depression and the war, which had hit the economy of New Zealand particularly hard. Being patriotic, New Zealand loaded up its best butter and meat during the Depression and the war and sent them out of the country, to Britain, creating a hardship for New Zealand families that lasted nearly a decade after the war was over. Canada, with its open way of life, scared my parents, I think. They feared the loss of their values, and the fact that Canadians were generally relaxed, and their children were given a lot of freedom, disturbed them. We were never going to make a permanent home in Canada, which was a pity, from my perspective.

Never mentioned in our family was the fact that my father suffered frequent nightmares, probably owing to the aftereffects of his six years of service as a fighter pilot. His time in the war had left many other intangible scars as well, and they caused him to erupt from time to time in unreasonable rages. Today, it would be called posttraumatic stress disorder, or PTSD, but in those days, the syndrome was not recognized. I felt it my childish duty to try to make my mother happy, because she seldom seemed happy. I didn't know what went on behind closed doors and knew better than to ask. I liked it best when my mother and I were alone together, and she would tell me about many things—about music and literature, for example—as well as old family stories.

It was in Canada that I began to be aware of the power of poetry, a power stronger than that of mere rhyming stories such as I had read in my sister's copy of Belloc's *Cautionary Tales*, and it was my mother who instilled in me the love of poetry that informed my choices when I later began to collect Modern first editions. She carried with her wherever we traveled a battered copy of *Palgrave's Golden Treasury of English Songs and Lyrics*. I read many of the poems without understanding a fraction of the content. My mother did her best to encourage me, but I was still only nine or ten at the time, so I often had little understanding of the verses selected. Being a trained teacher, my mother tried to direct me to poems that I might grasp. I remember well John Masefield's "Cargoes." The first two verses are dreamy and evocative, almost soporific:

> Quinquireme of Nineveh from Distant Ophir
> Rowing home to haven in sunny Palestine,
> With a cargo of Ivory
> And apes and peacocks,
> Sandalwood, cedarwood, and sweet white wine.

Who reads Masefield today? I have in my collection copies of various of his works, which I purchased before he finally disappeared from view. The reading public is fickle and generational. Anyway, "Cargoes" is really not much of a poem, and the third stanza completely destroys the quiet romance of the first two verses. Masefield might have been trying to make a point about industrialization and its ills, but to my childish way of thinking, he destroyed a perfectly wonderful picture and so ruined the poem. We got to that third stanza on a day when my mother was busy ironing, and I retain a mental picture of her stabbing at the ironing board while intoning:

> Dir-ty British coa-ster with a salt-caked smoke-stack,
> Butt-ing through the Chan-nel in the mad March days. . . .

I don't think she liked that verse much either.

I was lucky my mother was a teacher and that she loved poetry and was willing to share her love of it with me. I have her copy of *Palgrave* beside me as I write. The index has a series of faint markings indicating poetry she and I studied together. Henry Newbolt's "Drake's Drum," which she expounded in a fake piratical accent, her best imitation of a Devonian:

> Drake he's in his hammock an' a thousand mile away,
> (Capten, art tha sleepin' there below?)

Alfred Lord Tennyson was a favorite, and among his works my personal favorite was "The Lady of Shalott":

> On either side the river lie
> Long fields of barley and of rye . . .

Even at a young age, I found Percy Bysshe Shelley and John Keats too precious to enjoy, but I loved Samuel Taylor Coleridge, and developed a special fondness for "Kubla Khan." In general, I gravitated to the narrative, but the sound of the words of a poem has always meant nearly as much to me as the meaning. It was important that my mother read with me and to me, which enabled me to find the beauty and meaning in what might otherwise have been dull rows of words in lines, had I encountered poetry first in any other setting. I felt proud that she wanted to spend time with me this way, and I think she enjoyed our sessions together, because she had a sensitive nature, and poetry was important to her. I think perhaps it allowed her to experience vicariously those emotions that had been denied outlet by her own upbringing—with a stern Edwardian mother, a father who rarely stood up for his own beliefs, and an early life that had been shaped by the Depression and war.

Palgrave's Golden Treasury is limiting in its choice of verse: it covers what a professor of poetry at Oxford University in the middle of the nineteenth century selected as representative of the best of English poetry from the early sixteenth century up to his time. Initially, there were four books, which Francis Turner Palgrave conveniently alluded to as aligning closely with the eras of William Shakespeare, John Milton, Thomas Gray, and William Wordsworth. Later on, a fifth book was added to the treasury, with poems selected by the scholar and poet Laurence Binyon. The selections in the fifth book cover not only the Victoria era, but also important poetry written by selected poets of the World War I era and immediately following—poets such as Masefield. This addition was presumably intended to provide a link to the twentieth-century verse of the future.

My imagination was fired by Robert Bridges's poem "London Snow," because it conjured up pictures of Charles Dickens and the world of *A Christmas Carol*. London seemed to be a marvelous place, with children playing in the snow and the winter sun glinting off rooftops and high eaves. I skated over the reference of the rows of workers staggering to their daily toil through the snowdrifts, or perhaps I didn't examine the meaning. Probably, my mother didn't think me old enough to understand.

As the fifth book proceeds, the next poem beyond "Cargoes" became another favorite, and that was James Elroy Flecker's lyrical "The Old Ships":

I have seen old ships sail like swans asleep
Beyond the village which men still call Tyre,
With leaden age o'ercargoed, dipping deep
For Famagusta and the hidden sun
That rings black Cyprus with a lake of fire.

So much better than "Cargoes." Why did Masefield ruin his beautiful poem with that uncomfortable third verse? It was a question I asked myself again and again when we opened *Palgrave*.

Not far beyond "Drake's Drum" in the chronology of the fifth book were two poems that influenced me so greatly that I cannot but think that my first collection of the poetry of the World War I era relates somehow to studying them with my mother in our warm living room, deep in the wilderness of Northern Ontario. The first was Rupert Brooke's "The Soldier," with these magnificent opening lines:

If I should die, think only this of me:
That there's some corner of a foreign field
That is forever England.

Reading these lines as a child made me proud of my heritage, proud that I belonged to that tradition of service and the stiff upper lip that at all times made up the myth of what it was to be truly English. But this sense of pride was rapidly shattered by the next poem, cleverly juxtaposed to follow "The Soldier," and this was Wilfred Owen's devastating "Anthem for Doomed Youth."

What passing-bells for these who die as cattle?
Only the monstrous anger of the guns.
Only the stuttering rifles' rapid rattle
Can patter out their hasty orisons.

The power of Owen's poetry is such that even today, I cannot read those lines without emotion. "What passing-bells for these who die as cattle?" I remember that my mother tried to explain it to me in terms I might understand, but I couldn't grasp the reality of it. Children learn about the inevitability of death in different ways, but here was a poem, by a poet killed in that war about which he wrote, who was writing verse that pointed out how wrong it all was. Even though I knew my parents had suffered in World War II, that they had lost friends and relatives and in fact everyone had endured a great deal of hardship—I hadn't internalized that knowledge. My life up until that time had been so safe and sheltered—children's books and children's classics. In Canada, there was television, but our watching was strictly supervised. My mother realized, I think, that I wasn't ready to study "Anthem for Doomed Youth," so she quietly put away *Palgrave* and we returned to our everyday world.

Yes, thinking back, I am now sure that my choice of World War I–era poetry as my first collecting focus had something to do with those first readings, those first examples of both the idealistic and the realistic in the works produced by World War I poets. Although I went on to study Brooke, Owen, and the others at school, it was the impact of those first readings in my mother's copy of *Palgrave's Golden Treasury* that remains for me the most fundamental emotional connection to those works.

Growing Up

Life in Canada had been too good to last. As the 1950s ended, it was becoming clear that the uranium boom was ending as well. The United States had stockpiled enough uranium to fuel a nuclear capability that could easily destroy the earth, and the technology behind weaponry had rapidly advanced. We were now in a world of Mutually Assured Destruction, which went by the appropriate acronym MAD. Besides, after four years in Canada, my father was growing restless. It was time to move on.

For some reason, my parents also had a desire, not shared by me, to have my sister and me complete our education at a good boarding school of the English system. At the end of the nineteenth century, as the English settled the countries that later formed the core of the English-speaking British Commonwealth, they created in these outposts of Empire a system of private schools that emulated the curricula and the rules and regulations of the public schools they had left behind in Britain. Thus it was that in 1960, we sailed away from Canada, down the St. Lawrence Seaway and then across the Atlantic to the fabled England of my books and imagination, for a short stay there before traveling, again by ship, to South Africa. Interestingly enough, the real England of the early 1960s didn't interest me as much as the imagined one of the 1930s, which I easily conjured up over that long, wet summer from the apt descriptions found in the books of Agatha Christie, which I discovered and devoured all through that holiday, being confined inside by the weather more often than not. In effect, I ignored the experience of visiting the actual England of 1960.

At the end of the summer, we left for South Africa from Southampton, again by ship. We always traveled by ship; it never occurred to me to wonder why we didn't travel by plane. I loved these trips by sea, so exciting for a child. Food was abundant—in addition to ordinary meals, bouillon was available on deck at 11:00 a.m., served in little cups and accompanied by salty crackers. A formal cream tea was served every afternoon in the main lounge by waiters wearing bright white mess jackets. And as if that was not enough, the ultimate pleasure occurred early each morning, when one would be woken by the cabin steward, who would enter the cabin carrying a cup of milky tea accompanied by a hard biscuit. This was luxury for a child—lying back in bed, drinking tea and contemplating the day ahead, which might include a children's play, a fancy dress, or a splash in the salty waters of the ship's swimming pool. In those days, ships were a valid means of transport for families and business people, and the giant tourist cruise ships of today were not even imagined. Travel by sea was for going from one country to another, not for holiday cruising. However, I later learned that the real reason we always traveled by sea was that my father had carried with him from his experiences as a fighter pilot, along with other psychological damage, a horror of the air. Twenty years after World War II had ended, he forced himself to get a private pilot's license again, to get over the psychological barrier; although this enabled him to travel once again by air, his right hand became mysteriously paralyzed, and it remained that way for the rest of his life.

For the journey to South Africa we sailed on the *Pretoria Castle*, one of the fabled Castle Line boats that circumnavigated the African continent for most of the twentieth century. I was thirteen, and my sister was sixteen; we were the only young girls traveling in first class, so we stood out among the elderly English traveling to Cape Town for the Cape summer. We were very popular with the ship's officers, who had to amuse the passengers in the first-class lounge after dinner each night. There was always a band playing in the lounge at that time of the evening, and I learned the foxtrot from the junior second officer. On the morning the ship sailed into Table Bay, the mountain had a thin, white covering of cloud, the famous Tablecloth, and I could smell the fresh bread baking on the shore. The arrival augured well, but I soon found that it wasn't going to be that simple. Boarding school beckoned.

After this sybaritic few months of travel, and the ease of life at school in Canada, the reality of the routine of an Anglican girls' boarding school came as a shock of cold water. I never really adapted, but gritted my teeth and stuck it out for the remaining three-plus years of high school. Unlike my contemporaries, I never went back to the school to visit after the day I graduated. Boarding school, to me, seemed like a prison. We girls who boarded were allowed out of the school grounds a mere three Sundays in an eight-week term. We could leave only after Matins was finished in the late morning, and we had to be back for Evensong at 6:00 p.m. When we left the school premises, we were obliged to wear our shapeless Sunday uniforms, which consisted of a long-sleeved dress of gray watered silk with a white Peter Pan collar, accessorized by white gloves, thick stockings, a Panama hat, and brown lace-up shoes. No wonder I hated it all. In Canada, to the consternation of my mother, I had already sported my first pair of kitten heels, even though I was only twelve.

Herschel School was a High Anglican boarding school that had been one of the four schools established by the Anglican Church in Cape Town in the late years of the nineteenth century. Two of the schools were for boys and two were for girls. Both of the boys' schools were establishments of great education and purpose; in fact, one of the schools, Diocesan College, had been allotted two scholarships by Cecil Rhodes. In contrast, the teachers at Herschel were a patched-together group, largely drawn from a pool of wives of retired Anglican clergyman, but since none of us were expected to go on to higher learning, it didn't matter to the school trustees. In all fairness to the school curriculum, however, I did learn enough literature to help form my tastes. I learned from reading works of the eighteenth and nineteenth centuries, sitting in a nook in the library, that I had no real affection for this period, and I also learned from my school studies that the French and English writers of the early twentieth and late nineteenth centuries drew me in some ineluctable way. Sadly, the school library had few books for reading beyond the period of the eighteenth- and nineteenth-century classics.

Poetry formed a leading part of the English literature curriculum, and World War I poetry, in particular, constituted a significant part of the syllabus. Once again, I met up with Wilfred Owen, Rupert Brooke, and their contemporaries, but now, in addition to reading their poetry, I also learned the context of these poems. I learned how World War I had descended over the course of four years into a charnel house of unspeakable atrocity, because we studied the poetry along with the history of the war. And so it became clear that although these young men had begun their war service at an almost giddy level of patriotism and optimism, the horror of the trenches and the extent of the slaughter that became manifest in the later stages of the war changed their outlook, and their poetry became dark, bleak, cynical, and despairing.

All of this influenced me tremendously, and probably had a lot to do with my later gravitation to the war writings of Robert Graves, the war poetry of Siegfried Sassoon, and the writings of Louis-Ferdinand Céline, in particular his *Voyage au bout de la nuit* (*Journey to the End of the Night*), because I did gain a solid French vocabulary, even if I didn't learn to speak the language properly. In that respect, those three and a half years at Herschel School were not entirely wasted.

And then I went to the University of Cape Town. For those years, my imaginary world was again suspended, since I had decided, for various practical reasons, to become a chemical engineer. There was no poetic reason for the decision other than the fact that I had thought it romantic to walk through the mills of the uranium mines of Elliot Lake, observing the myriad bubbles covered with ore particles in the flotation chambers, which, after ore extraction, ended up as bright yellowcake drying slowly on giant rollers. Being practical, I knew I was going to have to make a living for myself, and I thought a career in engineering would at least be interesting, allowing me to travel and not to be locked away somewhere in a dreary office. It could be adventurous, and I would probably earn decent money.

I had always secretly wanted to be a writer, but since I had to earn a living, writing was out as a vocation from the start. With little training and no literary connections, it seemed an impossible goal, and I was practical enough to realize that. But I was still an avid reader; despite the heavy workload involved in pursuing an engineering degree, I always managed to find time to read. There was a bookshop in the suburb of Rondebosch near the university, and I haunted it. I bought books and I read prolifically and catholically, continuing my habit of devouring everything I could find by any author who interested me. I read all the works of Evelyn Waugh, and some of those several times over; I read Robert Graves and Siegfried Sassoon, Virginia Woolf, Anthony Burgess, Ford Madox Ford, D. H. Lawrence, Graham Greene, Ernest Hemingway, John Updike, and John Steinbeck, and, of course, F. Scott Fitzgerald. In translation, I read all of Honoré de Balzac's *La Comédie Humaine*, as well as works by European and Russian authors such as Émile Zola, Alexander Pushkin, Fyodor Dostoevsky, Albert Camus, and Franz Kafka. I read Goethe's *Faust* several times. I tried and failed to read those Modern masterpieces, James Joyce's monumental *Ulysses* and Marcel Proust's *À la recherche du temps perdu* (*In Search of Lost Time*, or *Remembrance of Things Past*, when published in English translation). I read incessantly and greedily, glad to be liberated from the narrow choices dictated by high school literature classes and the meager collection contained in that barren, but beautiful, Herschel School library where I had passed so many hours, especially during the endless weekends of boarding school confinement. Owing to this habit of incessant reading during the scarce free hours in my university days, I built up what might pass for a first collection—that enormous library of Penguin paperbacks that I bought in my local bookshop in Ronde-bosch.

I was a solitary reader during those university days. I had no one with whom to share my enthusiasm for reading, because my fellow students in chemical engineering were not readers. Even if some had been readers, I would never have discovered this, because, in any case, I had never been in the habit of discussing with others what I was currently reading or learning about in my world of books. We did not sit around after classes discussing world literature; most of our conversations, if not about rugby, cricket, or the latest set of tutorials, were about the latest engineering smoker, and making bets about who could drink the most beer at the next one. Moreover, unlike those students studying in the arts faculty, who might have perhaps one or two lectures daily, we engineering students had five hours of lectures in different subjects each morning, followed by a practical lab of some sort every afternoon. Most evenings, I would return from the campus, make a sandwich, and collapse onto my bed with whatever book or books I happened to be reading at the time.

After seven years of study, I graduated from university with both a bachelor's degree in chemical engineering and a master's degree in physical chemistry. The master's had been a side trip, during which, for a brief time, I had considered a university teaching career. But I had lost interest in what had started as a PhD project, and scraped together only the master's degree, which more or less meant that I now had to leave the world of the university: the real workaday world beckoned. I had trained as an engineer, and now I had to earn a living. Two problems rapidly emerged. One was that most of the companies I applied to were not anxious to employ a woman in a manufacturing plant; the second and more important problem was that I knew I wasn't really interested in engineering after all. In the end, I had no choice: I had to find work quickly. I tried and failed at a series of jobs in South Africa; tried again, also unsuccessfully, to achieve that elusive PhD, this time in the emerging field of biomedical engineering, and I tried and failed even more dismally at a few romantic relationships. Finally, with my fortunes at a supremely low ebb, I decided it was time to go somewhere else. Africa, after all, was not home as I understood it. I would go to England. Of course! So I packed my bags, booked a second-class berth on a ship of the Castle Line, the *Edinburgh Castle*, and headed back to Southampton.

Edward Heath became prime minister of England in 1970, presiding over a sad and impoverished country. It wasn't Heath's fault that the country was in such a state of terminal decay when the Conservatives took power in 1970, but he did very little to improve the situation. London was grim and run down and seedy and very, very expensive. You had to think hard before buying fruit, because an apple could cost sixpence; even then, it might be floury and tasteless. I had very little money and no plan. My first address in London was at a flat rented by the sister of a friend from university days, who agreed to have me stay for a short time. Her name was Sue Levy, and her small flat was in Sussex Gardens near Paddington Station. It was my first experience of putting shillings in a gas meter; I could not believe how rapidly the shillings disappeared, and I was always cold. Strangely enough, despite all the discomforts, I felt immediately at home in London and could find my way around without a map from the beginning.

Sue had been in London long enough to make friends, and she even had a boyfriend. He was much older than Sue, but that meant he was in a position to help her with her rent. She had taken elocution lessons, which I thought rather affected, and she now spoke with a modulated, slightly posh, upper-class English accent. I soon discovered why she might have done that—before long, I learned that young citizens of the Commonwealth were not really welcome in London. This first became apparent at a party I attended with Sue, who, when not with her boyfriend, hung around with a crowd of graduates from minor English public schools. I stood by the fireplace, nervously clutching a glass, not knowing anyone and feeling out of place amid the chatter. A young man came up to me and began a long yarn. I tried to look interested, but said nothing, which meant that he did all the talking. Finally, he stopped his monologue.

"What do you think?" he asked, or something like that. I don't know what I said in reply, but he looked at me with something like horror.

"Oh my God!" he exclaimed. "A Colonial!" And with that, he spun smartly around and moved off, leaving me still standing beside the fireplace, wondering what had just happened.

That was England of the early 1970s. Britain was still a class-ridden society, and perhaps the poverty of the country made it worse. People trying to maintain class status had to find people to look down on. I do know that within a few weeks of arriving in England, I had been made very aware in several minor and some not so minor incidents that, after all, I was not English. I wasn't even Colonial English. I was a Colonial with a Colonial accent that just had to be mocked; on the status ladder, we Colonials ranked lower than South Londoners.

This was not the London I had been expecting. Until I actually began to live in London, I had always been very sure that England was my true and my spiritual home. I had been taught by my books, by my grandparents, and by our way of life that we were English, that we were part of the Empire, dwindling though it might be. My father had fought for six years, partly with an RAF fighter squadron; my maternal grandfather had been at Gallipoli; my family had lived in poverty during the Depression so that the mother country might be fed—but now I found that our feelings of Englishness were manufactured out of Colonial patriotism, and, worse, were not appreciated. The construct of home created during my childish reading and dreaming wasn't true at all. Still, I was in London now and I had burned my bridges, so I had to make the best of it. I had to make it work.

Having been kind enough to take me in, Sue now indicated after a few weeks that it really was time for me to move on. I had a few days to find somewhere else to go, and I had no plan. In desperation, I remembered that I had been a Girl Guide during my adolescence; I even had my Guiding badges with me. I appealed to Olave House, the London Girl Guide hostel, and, to my relief, they took me in. And that, of course, led to the Abingdon Road bookshop and my first book purchase, which I have described previously.

I stayed at Olave House longer than I should have, unsuccessfully applying for jobs and wandering the streets of London by day, while spending most evenings sewing those appliqué flowers onto my jeans. All the while, my little pile of cash was steadily dwindling, especially owing to that first purchase of "A Song for Simeon." I had to take the little book out from time to time from its place in my drawer and turn the pages to reassure myself that it hadn't been so wildly extravagant a purchase after all. I was desperate to find work. I had an idea of pursuing a university career in England, but it turned out that a master's degree—coming from a colonial university such as the University of Cape Town—just wasn't enough. I grew very afraid. I couldn't stay at the Guide hostel forever, but there seemed to be no other place to go.

I had a few contacts, but no friends, and my first encounters with real English people had made me timid. What to do and where to go? My parents, now living in Tasmania, had made it clear they had fulfilled their duty to bring me up and educate me; my mother even wrote me a letter warning me against coming to Australia, and certainly against arriving in Tasmania. As for returning to South Africa, that was impossible. It would be such a loss of face to return that I never considered it for an instant.

I had now been in London for several months, and finding work became such an urgent matter that I stopped looking for a permanent position and found temporary employment through an advertisement in the *New Scientist*. The job was co-creating an encyclopedia of rocks and minerals for a publisher in Soho. I had to write and type out, in clean copy, two hundred mineral descriptions starting with the letters A through K; my coworker was tasked the same responsibility for minerals starting with L through Z. Since the London phone directory then was divided that way, the publisher felt it would be an even distribution of the project. We worked every day in the library of the Geological Museum in South Kensington, sorting through dusty volumes and painstakingly copying out formulas and descriptions.

At the same time that I started work on this project, the Girl Guides finally gave me notice. I had long overstayed my welcome. Lodging was then, as now, extremely expensive for a young person starting out, but I eventually found a place in North London, sharing a house in Wembley Park with six other young people. The house smelled permanently of chip butties (sandwiches made with french fries), and was seldom cleaned, but I had a little room of my own, and the single bathroom was down the hall and usually available. My little Ariel poem sat on a bookshelf, encouraging me when I was lonely, which was often. After a family or a pet, I do believe that books are next in the line of friends in a time of need. The Girl Guide hostel had offered some sanctuary, but now I had to face the world.

The English November nights were long and dismal, but as long as I had a book, everything was all right. I would climb into bed and read for hours until it was time to sleep. I could forget that I was alone in London without a real plan for the future. Nevertheless, that first Christmas in London was the hardest I have known. The house was empty and I had nowhere to go. A motherly friend in South Africa sent me a tiny orange tree in a pot from Fortnum & Mason. I sat on the floor with the orange tree next to me and cried for several hours.

Fortunately, that Christmas was the low point, because with the New Year of 1973, things started to look up. I got a real job, working with the long-range planning division of the medical group at the British Oxygen Company on Hammersmith Broadway. I had three interviews, but I owned only two dresses. When I was asked to return for the third interview, I passed a sleepless night wondering if my prospective employers would notice if I arrived in the same outfit I had worn for the first interview. As it turned out, my qualms were misplaced. I was hired, and my life took a turn for the better. I never knew if the encyclopedia was ever published, because I stopped short of the final entries, glad to be rid of the geology museum and to have the security of a proper job.

Once I was settled at my new job, and had moved from Wembley into a tiny flat in Abbey Road, I had time to begin to find my feet as a nascent bibliophile. I've noticed, looking back, that my collecting periods over the years have gone in spurts of activity. Not that I ever lost interest at any time, but there has been a definite ebb and flow in the process of actual acquisition, and not a little of this rhythm has related to having available funds. Of equal importance is probably having the time and leisure to pursue the search for collectible items. And so it was that after I was finally gainfully employed, my first thought was to begin a serious collection. Of what sort of books, I didn't yet know.

Since I had bought that first Ariel poem from him, my bookseller friend from the Abingdon Road bookshop had decided that I was, after all, a proper customer, in recognition of which he gave me a pass to the London Antiquarian Book Fair of 1973, which in those days was held in the Art Deco ballroom and gallery of the Europa Hotel on Grosvenor Square. It made a dazzling impression. I couldn't believe that so many special books existed. Walking the aisles of the exhibits at that first book fair, I realized there was a whole hidden world full of people who bought, sold, and treasured these other kinds of books, which were not trade copies, but editions and copies of books that could also connect you in some way with their authors. It wasn't only the Abingdon Road bookshop—there was a whole world of such things as limited editions of signed copies; sometimes, in fact, writers signed or dedicated books to friends, lovers, relatives, or, of lesser importance, just to people who wrote asking for dedicated copies. I discovered all of this at that first book fair. I felt like Alice in Wonderland as I walked the aisles of the exhibition. There were dozens of booths laid out around a central stairway, and in each booth were scholarly looking people perusing shelves, talking with dealers, and generally looking very learned. Some people carried parcels sealed with important-looking stickers marked "Sold." It was a revelation. Here was a world where books were treated as fantastic objects, worthy of collection and debate—books were not just for reading. There were special books and volumes that one could collect. The very air smelled of old paper and leather, with that particular musty smell you come across in a room filled with old books and manuscripts. I longed to join the ranks of collectors. I suspected that both collectors and book dealers had secret keys to this hidden book land that I so fervently desired to enter.

I forgot momentarily the pressing fact that I still had little money, and I bought a book for £6. It was a school edition of collected poetry in which Louis MacNeice had signed one of his poems. Probably, Louis MacNeice had given a talk at the school, as it was an anonymous signature. I wasn't overly impressed with the purchase, but it was what I could afford, and I wanted to appear like a collector and sophisticated. I wanted to walk out of the fair with a little package with a "Sold" sticker on it, confirming that I belonged in this new world.

I could see, as I wandered in and out of various booths, that there were select displays of collected World War I poetry in many of them, and some of the volumes seemed not to be outrageously expensive. Perhaps, I decided, I would collect World War I poetry. After all, I knew that period from my early encounters with the World War I poets included in my mother's copy of *Palgrave*, as well as from the history and the further poetry of that era I had studied at school. I was still keenly interested in the poets of the Great War—I actually happened to be reading Robert Graves's semiautobiographical account of his World War I service, *Good-Bye to All That*, at the time. That book had led me to take a fresh look at such writers as Siegfried Sassoon, whom I had encountered previously but not studied in depth.

As I went in and out of those booths, examining works that I could never hope to own, I bought one further book to confirm this new commitment to World War I poetry. It was a better choice than the impulsively acquired poetry schoolbook—a book by Robert Bridges, written in 1920, containing poems written during and after World War I in his capacity as poet laureate. The book, *October and Other Poems*, cost twenty shillings, and I wasn't in love with it. It had a faded olive green dust jacket, it smelled musty, and the stiff pages turned only with difficulty. In addition, I didn't think these poems, written to order in his capacity as poet laureate, had much emotional impact. But it was a book of World War I poetry.

At the end of the afternoon, I left that first book fair with a tiny package carrying that special "Sold" sticker. My copy of "A Song for Simeon" now had companions on my bookshelf. If it achieved nothing else, this volume of Robert Bridges's poetry and the edition of school poetry signed by Louis MacNeice marked the start of a focus for collecting activity for me. I have them still, and although I am still not fond of either volume, I recognize that they were important, because they were the volumes that formed the beginning of my collection. My copy of "A Song for Simeon" wasn't just a treasured talisman anymore; it was part of something larger . . . a real collection, in fact.

Early Collecting

Looking back, I realize how much fun I had in those early collecting days in London. No matter that I had little money—booksellers are generous people and are happy to share their private passions—and I was an eager audience. There was Larry Wallrich in Islington, whose acquaintance I made at that first book fair. I remember Larry in overalls, telling me stories as he sat halfway up a long ladder, which he had been climbing to reach for books he knew I would find interesting and, of most importance, that I could afford. I still own Sassoon's *Poems by Pinchbeck Lyre*, signed by Sassoon, which I bought from Larry. *Pinchbeck Lyre* is a collection of satirical poetry written in the exaggerated style of the poet Humbert Wolfe, which, if nothing else, demonstrates sadly that there was a mean-spirited side to Sassoon's character. I later bought some of the many cartoons that Sassoon drew of the Sitwell siblings, none of them flattering, after he had fallen out with that family.

Larry had a large collection of the work of Ted Hughes, and I bought an anthology called *Spring, Summer, Autumn, Winter*, which I still own, but to this day have not read. It's a beautiful edition in a handsome cork box. For some reason, I was never an aficionado of Ted Hughes—he always seemed to take himself too seriously—and I wasn't a fan of Sylvia Plath either. The main reason I didn't take to the book was, however, that Hughes did not belong in my pantheon. I was now firmly set on the idea of collecting the work of poets of the World War I era, and the purchase of the volume of Ted Hughes's poetry, however beautiful that cork box, was an aberration.

Besides haunting bookshops, I was getting on with creating a life in London. In my first summer there, I was offered the chance to rent a houseboat for several months, and I jumped at the opportunity. The summer on the Mudlark on the Chelsea Embankment, right off Battersea Bridge, was idyllic. The boats are still there, but when I look at them these days, they seem to have lost their glamour—or maybe I've grown old. The boats were primitive—built on the hulls of old landing craft, they floated on the tides. There was no sewage hook-up, so everything had to be collected, and we slopped out our buckets on the fast-moving tide as it receded toward the mouth of the Thames Estuary. No wonder there were no fish in the river in those days. During low tide, the boats sat on the mud; they still do, I have noticed. It was a seedy, bohemian neighborhood, but to me, it was a glamorous adventure. My neighbor on the houseboat adjoining was an American who grew marijuana in an improvised greenhouse on his deck. I spent many evenings sitting on the deck with Joe in the warm summer air, listening to the water lapping the hulls of the landing craft and the creaking of the dock as the tide rushed away to the estuary. I felt very sophisticated; Joe had harvested his plants and we would sample the crop; the marijuana would make us talk expansively of the universe and where we were going and what we wanted from life.

Years later, when I was living in California, I learned that Joe had actually been a fugitive from the law in the United States, as he had often hinted. I still wonder how they found him. I received a letter from him once, written from a federal penitentiary in Philadelphia, so whatever he did must have been a serious crime in the eyes of American law enforcement. I wondered how he had found my address. By that time, I had an expanding career in the world of finance, and I was terrified that Joe might arrive on my doorstep, but I never saw him again after that summer on the river.

Randolph Churchill, the son of Winston Churchill, used to frequent the pub opposite the houseboats on the Embankment, and I often observed him lurching drunkenly up to the King's Road from the Embankment. The pub, however, along with the magic of the Chelsea Embankment, has long since disappeared.

I was still on the hunt for books to build my collection. The Chelsea Bookshop was on the corner of Battersea Bridge Road and the King's Road. I went there often while I was living on the river, but the shop offered little of my personal genre of collecting. I was still looking for work of the World War I poets, although I was interested in the poetry of any English poet of the early twentieth century. I had bought more poetry by Robert Bridges and a first edition of Rupert Brooke's *1914 and Other Poems*, published as a posthumous volume in 1915 by Sidgwick & Jackson. None of these volumes from the era are lovely. Paper was scarce, and although the pages of the book were stiff and thick, the binding was functional rather than beautiful—although the frontispiece did have a rather lovely picture of Brooke, which was protected by tissue paper from the facing page.

Even after I left the river, I continued to haunt the Chelsea Bookshop. One day I walked in to find the floor of the shop full of boxes of books.

"What have you got here?" I asked.

"It's the library of James Pope-Hennessy," I was told. Pope-Hennessy was a travel writer and biographer who, in one of the more lurid of the homosexual scandals in London in the 1970s, had been sensationally murdered in his London flat in January 1974 by three young men; as a result, his library had come to the Chelsea Bookshop to be sorted and sold.

"Take a look," I was advised. "There might be something of interest for you there."

As usual, there was little to see that was of interest, although I wasn't allowed to look into the most important of the boxes. They knew me at the Chelsea Bookshop, so they knew I had little money. In the end, I had to be content with a copy of Francis Thompson's poetry; it was inscribed to Edward Marsh, Christmas 1911, with the ex libris of James Pope-Hennessy on the inside cover. Like all the early books in my collection, this volume is one that I still own. In fact, this book has a wealth of wonderful associations. Edward Marsh was an influential critic and writer as well as a senior civil servant, secretary to a succession of prime ministers and cabinet ministers of the early twentieth century, the most notable of whom was Winston Churchill. "Eddie" Marsh, as he was known, had been a friend of a number of the World War I poets; he had actually introduced Rupert Brooke to Siegfried Sassoon. Marsh was also very influential in the literary homosexual circles of the time. Pope-Hennessy was an acolyte of Marsh's, and had probably received the book from him as a gift, perhaps after writing an appreciation of Marsh in the early 1950s in *The Spectator*: Pope-Hennessy had been, for a time in the late 1940s, the literary editor of that magazine.

By searching in bookshops and attending the occasional book fair, I had now built up a tiny collection. It didn't yet fill a single shelf in a bookcase, so I still kept the books on a little table next to my bed. Even though I now had a few friends in London, my book collection was, of all things, the most important to me. It was mine, and it was unique, and the books were my good friends.

My initial decision in favor of the World War I poets was a good way to begin, because as time went by, and I discovered more dealers and book fairs, it became clear that, fortunately for me, I had been correct in my thinking that the work of a number of the poets from the period were sufficiently out of vogue that I could make some progress—although mostly it seemed that I was ending up with different editions of collected works of Robert Bridges. However, after I had bought Rupert Brooke's poetry in that posthumous edition, I began to feel that I was on my way to starting a collection. I can't really explain why I wanted to build a collection, but whatever the reason, after that first experience at the Antiquarian Book Fair, I was determined to align myself more closely with that magic world of old books and manuscripts, with places where the air smelled of musty paper and old leather, and people talked with familiarity about authors whose works I had absorbed in my solitary reading. I was steadily finding a focus for my collecting activities: when I entered a bookshop, I knew which shelves to select for browsing. I was also beginning to learn which book dealers would not have items for sale in my particular area of interest, and which dealers had inventory that I could not possibly afford. Thanks to the hours spent in conversation with book dealers, I was learning about the collectible books of the World War I poets. Although I couldn't afford to purchase works by most of the writers and poets whose work I was exploring, I was learning about books of interest to read and books of interest that I might one day purchase.

I wanted to buy works by Robert Graves, but couldn't afford anything close to the price of first editions of his poetry or prose. For a long time, Graves stood for me as a literary mentor: although he had emerged cynical and disillusioned from World War I, he had friendships and relationships with many of the important poets of the era, so that he could stand as a kind of literary guide to its pivotal works. In fact, to me, *Good-Bye to All That*, Graves's semiautobiographical account of his experiences in the Great War, appeared not only as an indictment of the mentality of that Empire which encouraged the conflict, but also as a kind of literary Who's Who of the best of the writers created by the war. Reading Graves leads not only to Sassoon, and to Wilfred Owen, but also, further across the Channel into France, to Louis-Ferdinand Céline and his doctrine of nihilism, best expressed in *Voyage au bout de la nuit*. I followed Robert Graves's direction faithfully, even to reading *Voyage* in translation. The book is a difficult read in any language, mainly owing to the subject of the book. Céline believed that man is unable to control his destiny and inclinations, which inevitably leads us to war and pestilence. Céline's work today is not widely read in English; he is considered a controversial writer, as he largely discredited himself with anti-Semitic writings before and during World War II, for which crimes he was sentenced to and spent time in prison in Denmark following the war. Nevertheless, Céline was a great writer, and *Voyage* remains an important book. For me, Céline opened a door that led to a discovery of more of the French poets and writers of the period—Guillaume Apollinaire becoming a particular favorite.

Sassoon popped up everywhere; he seems to have known every literary person in London during the World War I years and afterward. He became a sort of phantom literary uncle to me. I read *Memoirs of a Fox-Hunting Man*, but actually preferred reading Sassoon's war poetry. I read all of these authors, but could not afford to collect their works in first or limited or signed editions. I particularly wanted, but could not afford to buy, a copy of the most important book of World War I poetry—the poetry of Wilfred Owen, in that posthumous edition assembled by Siegfried Sassoon.

This is how the early involvement with collecting went during my London days. Since there was so little that I could actually afford to purchase, it was as much an exercise in learning about the writers of the period as about collecting examples of the literature of World War I. One book or biography led to another, and there was so much to discover that I was never stuck for something to read by these writers. I immersed myself in their writings in my spare time. In hindsight, I realize that all of this early unstructured reading was leading me indirectly to Cyril Connolly and his analysis of Modernist writers, although at that point I had never heard of Connolly; nor did I know that the works I was discovering for myself were some of the most important books of the Modernist period.

Finding connections among authors and poets was somehow thrilling. Since the world was smaller in those days, many of the writers of the period knew one another through university or through social circles in London or Paris, and since they read and critiqued and wrote about each other's work, and their literary circles tended to overlap or align, the same names feature in biographies. As I read about Bloomsbury, for instance, I was introduced to the circle of authors who gathered near Rye—including Joseph Conrad, Ford Madox Ford, and Henry James. To me, they seemed like Grand Old Men of literature—I identified more with the "bright young things" of the novels of Evelyn Waugh. Virginia and Leonard Woolf and their circle seemed too austere—like late-Victorian aunts and uncles; pictures of Virginia Woolf reminded me of my stern English granny in Blenheim. My mythical home still existed in my imagination, and it was beginning to place itself firmly in and around the London of the 1930s. As I went around London, the names of the streets and districts, even the look of the houses, resonated. Bond Street, St. James, and Piccadilly brought to mind the world of Waugh's early novels, while the rows and rows of identical semidetached houses lining the streets that led out of central London conjured the suburban hideousness so well described by Graham Greene, as well as by George Orwell in his novel *Keep the Aspidistra Flying*.

But despite my growing familiarity with London, sadly, London had finished with me by the mid-1970s, and in truth, I was done with London for the time being. The dire situation of the British economy and my limited prospects in general in London finally bore in on me. The country continued its grim decline: Britain was in the grip of the three-day workweek, and strikes were the norm of the day. At work, after only two years, I had reached my personal glass ceiling; it was clear that my lack of connections and my Colonial background, and probably the fact that I was a young woman without real business training, meant that, after a couple of small promotions, I had gone as far as I was likely to go within British Oxygen. I couldn't afford a flat of my own and was never likely to, because I was still living on £1,000 annually after tax. Since my rent was £9 weekly, it didn't leave a lot for other living expenses, and saving was an impossibility. It was time to go. Yet, thanks to those years in London, I took with me more than work experience. Owing to those hours in shops with rare books, those many discussions with book dealers, and all of that focused reading, I had found my feet as a collector and bibliophile, and I knew that avocation would travel with me wherever I next was headed.

California and Collecting Detours

It was a rare, sunny Northern California afternoon. The ocean, freed from its usual blanket of coastal fog, sparkled in the distance, and the air was dry and smelled of the grasses of late summer. Although only recently arrived in California, I had immediately connected into the world of rare books; through a stroke of good fortune, one of my father's contacts in the mining world, Noel Kirshenbaum, lived on Baker Street in San Francisco, and his wife, Sandy, was, by luck and coincidence, one of the premier dealers in fine print material in the United States. On that day, she had taken me north to meet Ralph Sipper of Joseph the Provider Books, who was at that time one of the two or three most important dealers in works of fine print and literary Modernism in California. I spent the afternoon with these new friends, Ralph Sipper the book dealer and Sandy Kirshenbaum, the fine print expert, talking contentedly about books, fine print, and literature, as we relaxed in the shade of a grove of stunted Monterey pines. Ralph was based north of San Francisco in the little laid-back town of Inverness, which was nestled in a bay by the ocean, near the oyster fields. I couldn't believe my luck. I had arrived in California—not to visit, but to work and live.

The world of rare books, which had been such a significant part of my life in London, had transitioned seamlessly into this new environment. Granted that dealers in California were more interested in works by Ernest Hemingway than in works by Ford Madox Ford—to me that didn't matter too much, as all of these writers belonged to my imaginary world, and as far as World War I poets were concerned—well, Hemingway, while not exactly a poet, had been wounded in Italy in that war, and that gave him certain credentials. As the afternoon progressed and the good California wine flowed, Ralph brought out various volumes from his vast inventory, either to illustrate a point about an author whose work we had been discussing or to show off the beauty of a particular Small Press book, a subset of the field of book collecting in which I had taken little interest, but which was thriving in the United States at that time, owing to the numbers of small private presses that had sprung up, particularly along the West Coast. This was now the mid-1970s, and for me, this new life in Northern California was a whole new world. Nothing seemed impossible to achieve.

It had been a challenge, but I had succeeded in my goal to find a professional position in America. In the autumn of 1974, as it became clear to me that I had no real future with British Oxygen—and as it also became clear that I had no desire to face yet another English winter with only a two-bar electric heater to warm my small rented room—I had decided to try to find a way to work in the United States, Northern California in particular. The seed of this ambition had been sown following a business trip to the United States on behalf of British Oxygen. America seemed so open, after the narrow attitudes prevailing in London, that it seemed promising as a next step. In America, I felt that nobody was likely to care that I was a woman, or worry about my accent, or where I had been to school. I felt that the only criterion by which I would be judged would be my energy and dedication.

It wasn't that simple, of course: to get to America, one needed a job offer and a visa, and obtaining these would be no easy task. Luckily, after making several trips to the San Francisco Bay Area, I had made some contacts. British Oxygen subscribed to the Long Range Planning Service of Stanford Research Institute in Menlo Park, colloquially known as SRI. The mission of SRI was largely to provide economic information for corporate contractors; in other words, it was a think tank that lived off government and corporate contracts. At one time, SRI had enjoyed a close relationship with Stanford University, but now, aside from the name, the geographic proximity of the two institutions, and a few joint scientific research projects, barely anything remained of the relationship. Some of the joint scientific research projects that were still funded happened to concern the field of medical imaging, which was then emerging as a technology of huge interest to diagnostic and therapeutic medicine, and thanks to the various projects I had done for British Oxygen, this had become my field of core knowledge. More particularly, I was becoming a specialist in market analysis of the emerging field of diagnostic ultrasound imaging. It so happened that many medical research projects in diagnostic ultrasound were being funded at SRI, and these were usually joint projects with Stanford University.

Through trips to SRI to review some of the institute's scientific work in medical imaging research, I had made contacts in Palo Alto at Stanford University and at SRI who, knowing of my desire to work in the United States, had been on the lookout for me. The result of this was that one day, not too long after I had made my decision to leave England, I received a telephone message: a job had opened up at SRI. The institute was interested in hiring a consultant who not only knew about medical imaging technology but also had commercial knowledge of the numbers of emerging new businesses in the field of medical ultrasound imaging. Max Maginness, a fellow Kiwi, and a postgraduate engineering student at Stanford, had tracked me down at a medical technology meeting in Milan to tell me this news. There were no cellphones in those days, and international calls were inordinately expensive, but I threw caution to the wind and used the telephone at the flat in Milan where I was staying to call Max.

"George von Haunalter is in London." he told me, when I finally reached him. "He's the Head of the Medical Economics Group. You need to meet him if you can. But you have to be fast—I heard that he's returning to California soon. But I know for certain that his group is looking for an economist with expertise in medical imaging."

Medical imaging. Quite by chance, I had spent my time at British Oxygen exploring developments in that field on behalf of the company's Long Range Planning Group, which had a goal of creating a new business area in the emerging field of diagnostic medical ultrasound. From chemical engineer to medical economist—why not? But what to do? Unfortunately, there was a logistical problem, because I happened to be in Milan at the aforementioned medical conference, and I was supposed to be in Milan another three days. I took a deep breath. I was young and determined and I wanted to work in California, so I left the meeting in Milan and booked myself on a flight back to London, without telling anyone what I was doing. The next morning, back in London, I called the hotel where George von Haunalter was staying, and managed to reach him shortly before he took a taxi to Heathrow.

"I really want to talk to you about this job," I told him, when he tried to tell me it was too late—he was leaving for Heathrow shortly. "Please wait a little longer," I begged. "I'll be at your hotel within the hour. I can show you my work."

I didn't waste a minute. I grabbed a number of the reports I had written for British Oxygen from my desk and jumped into a taxi—a wild expense—and headed across London to the hotel where George was waiting, slightly bewildered, in the lobby. He looked a little confused, and probably wondered why he had agreed to meet me. Nevertheless, he courteously offered me lunch, so we proceeded to the hotel dining room for my interview. I wasted no time. I pulled out report after report, earnestly selling my ability and my knowledge. It was a bold move, but I wanted that job and I wanted it very badly. And my persistence prevailed! After several more interviews, I was offered a position at SRI. I got a visa and I left for the San Francisco Bay Area early in 1975 to pursue the American Dream. And if you are going to pursue the American Dream, California was—and probably still is for young people—the place to go.

When I arrived, I knew nobody, but I had that introduction to Noel and Sandy Kirshenbaum, which became all important, merely because it was the only connection I had. Noel worked for the giant Bechtel Corporation, which is headquartered in San Francisco, and is one of the largest engineering, construction, and project management companies in the world. At that stage, Bechtel was working with Phelps Dodge Mining on the construction of a large mining complex at Black Mountain on the edge of the Namib Desert in what was then South West Africa. My father was the consultant metallurgist on that project.

Considering that the introduction to the Kirshenbaums was the only contact I brought with me, it was a stroke of extreme good fortune that Sandy was the founder of *Fine Print*, a small magazine devoted to exploring the role of the book as a work of art. She knew everyone in the book world in Northern California. She was also, in a limited way, a rare book dealer of sorts herself. Through Sandy, I met that most prolific of the rare book dealers in Modern literature of that time—Ralph Sipper, the owner of Joseph the Provider—and that introduction led, in turn, to that first meeting on the blissful afternoon in Inverness, which I remember so fondly.

I loved my new life in Northern California. Despite its reputation for being a boring decade, it was good to be young in Northern California in the 1970s. The state had not yet become overcrowded, and the freeways were still relatively uncluttered. Marijuana, although technically illegal at the time, was easy to obtain; in Berkeley, at any rate, life still adhered to the Timothy Leary principle of "Turn on, tune in and drop out." I loved it! I experimented with several alternative substances, had friends with whom I went to dark and poky clubs late at night to hear transcendent jazz, and started to develop the sort of self-confidence that comes with a growing maturity.

For a young person, nothing could compare with the sense of freedom that came from being young and driving the wide lanes of Highway 280 from San Francisco down to Menlo Park to work while watching the fog spill over the coast range into the sunshine. I arrived long after the Summer of Love, but the spirit of that time lived on among young people in Berkeley, where I moved soon after I had settled, because San Francisco, despite its attractions, was just too expensive. I enjoyed the fact that in Berkeley, I could hang out at the Café Mediterranean on Telegraph Avenue with former hippies, and, of course, book dealers. In Berkeley, Moe's Books and Cody's Books on Telegraph Avenue were legendary, and the talk in the Berkeley cafés was still of Jack Kerouac and the Beat generation, so that being a book collector was a good introduction to Berkeley life, better than being a researcher at a buttoned-up research institute in Menlo Park.

Ralph was a very good book dealer. Rapidly sizing me up as someone who could not afford his choicer items of Modern literature, he steered me toward collecting fine print material. In this, of course, he was supported by Sandy. It was a detour in my collecting activities that continued longer than it should have, but I drifted along with an exploration of fine print because, at that time, my little collection had stalled. I couldn't afford much of significance, and my collection of World War I–era poetry had topped out. The letters and manuscripts from that period were too expensive, and the poetry books I could afford were generally in poor shape and not interesting to look at. The pages of those few first editions of World War I poets in my collection were generally foxed and smelled of musty library shelves. I still read Sassoon, Owen, and Graves, but the fact was that, especially in the United States, there wasn't a lot to buy in the field of actual, published World War I poetry—at least not at my price level. As a result, I was open to considering new directions of collecting. Everyone who collects heads into a blind alley at one time or another, and this brief excursion into the field of fine print was mine.

Ralph Sipper had been one of the strong supporters of the Small Press movement that flourished at that time, and he represented in particular one of the small presses, the Loujon Press of New Orleans, that had started publishing the works of Charles Bukowski, the German-born American poet, in limited, fine print editions. I hadn't heard of Bukowski, but the Loujon Press books were works of art, and I bought them for that. I never read the poetry seriously. I bought a limited edition of Bukowski's first published work from the Loujon Press, *It Catches my Heart in Its Hands.* The book was a thing of beauty. The paper was handmade, each page of a different thickness, color, and consistency. It must have cost the Webbs, the New Orleans–based couple who started the press, more to produce each book than they ever realized in the sale of a copy. I bought other examples of fine print and Small Press books as well over the next few years, spending more than I should have on some items. For example, in the early 1980s, I bought copies of *Alice's Adventures in Wonderland, Through the Looking Glass,* and later, *Moby-Dick* from the Massachusetts-based woodcut artist Barry Moser. They were works of art rather than literature—big, bold items in handmade folding boxes, illustrated with the woodcuts for which Barry is justly famous.

The fact is that I was never really interested in these books, despite the beauty of the illustrations and the fine feel of the handmade paper. I still yearned for books of the period of the World War I poets, even if my notion of being rooted in that mythical home of the early years of twentieth-century England was growing dim as I made my way in the California sunshine. Still, my continuing dedication to early twentieth-century literature and poetry and World War I poets was confirmed on the day that I managed to buy from Ralph a fairly battered copy of Wilfred Owen's posthumously published *Poems.* It had always been for me the definitive World War I poetry book, and as it later turned out, it was also my first collected title from the Connolly Modern Movement list, of which more later.

There was one other purchase I made from Ralph that had the effect of nudging me back to my true vocation as a collector, and that was a limited, signed edition of a work by Robert Graves, produced shortly after he had left England behind and moved to Majorca. In Majorca, Graves founded a private press, which he named the Seizin Press, devoted to the book as a work of fine art. The Seizin Press was never very successful, and Graves seems to have lost interest in it. The book I have, a small collection of poetry called *To Whom Else?,* was largely a broadside at the England Graves had left behind. Most of the copies of this book were stored in premises that were damp, and so there is never a fine copy to be found. Nevertheless, despite the condition, the book served to remind me of Graves and his works, of Sassoon and his friends, and that period of English literature and poetry at the time of and immediately following World War I, the era that was of such interest to me personally.

Yet, by the late 1970s, it was clear that my collection was going nowhere. It had no direction. Only the collection of the Ariel poems of Faber and Gwyer / Faber and Faber was growing, because I had found that they were available from American book dealers and were not too expensive. The collection of Ariel poems naturally built on that first Ariel poem I had bought—"A Song for Simeon." According to Sandy, Ariel poems counted as fine print. But what led to my increasing interest in the series was that the authors of these limited editions of commissioned poetry were poets I admired, or at the very least, with whose names I was familiar—Sassoon, Eliot, G. K. Chesterton, Edith Sitwell, Vita Sackville-West, and so on.

I bought some of these and books by various of the Sitwells from Robert Link, a small bookseller in downtown Oakland. He had a wonderful shop that took up the entire remodeled foyer of an old building, so that the grand front door of his shop was the former front door of the entire building. The floors and the walls up to and beyond picture rail height were tiled with blue-patterned Mexican tiles, and there was actually a working fountain in the center of the large space. I also browsed the scruffy but legendary bookshop of Peter Howard, Serendipity, on University Avenue in Berkeley. Tom Goldwasser, who later set up a successful dealership of his own, worked at Serendipity at the time. I still scoured Moe's Books and Cody's Books on Telegraph Avenue in Berkeley, looking in vain for an overlooked major first edition. Owing to my own ignorance, I bought a lot of rubbish from those two venues. I was still just another scruffy and penniless book lover looking to strike gold from an overlooked important first edition.

In my new life in California, book collecting gave me an identity. California, although exciting, was alien to me. I had been welcomed in California, and for once, my Colonial accent was thought to be "cute," and not a sign of impoverished breeding. Still, I found it hard to be part of California life. I found Americans baffling. They were so hospitable at first glance, but seldom followed up with overtures of true friendship. Just as San Francisco was built on a base of reclaimed and shifting sands, so the population drifted in and out, coming from other places and leaving for other places. California was a state of nomads;

very few of the people I met were actually rooted in San Francisco. My new friends Sandy and Noel were old San Francisco stock, but they were older than me by enough years to make close companionship impossible. They were married and had a growing family. I was single and still trying to find my place in the world.

In my search for new acquaintances, book dealers made solid friends; they were different from the average American. You could walk into Serendipity and browse for hours without even having to buy anything. Book dealers the world over just like to chat about their trade, the works they have in stock, and, if prompted, they can teach one more about literature than a university course could ever accomplish. Generally, if you probe deeply enough, you will find that book dealers lead fascinating and different lives from the rest of us. I am not, and have never been, a literary scholar. In some ways, collecting literature and manuscripts and related material is an exercise designed to make one humble, because many dealers are literary scholars who know the material inside out. Yet dealers can't prevent you from making mistakes. I think today I am a more circumspect collector than when I began, but that has not prevented me from making some hugely misplaced purchases at times. My excursion into fine print was one such misguided activity, although it did have one unforeseen and positive effect on my later collecting activities.

In my early days of collecting, for some reason, I felt that the pursuit of prose as opposed to poetry was not interesting. A collector is almost helpless with respect to his or her passion. If you force the direction of the collection, more likely than not you will make a mistake. You have to let your own interests and instincts take you where you need to go in the end. For this reason, it's forgivable to make a mistake in direction from time to time, because you almost need that momentum in the wrong direction to understand where you need to go. My detour into fine print produced one such good result in that it nudged me into purchasing prose in addition to poetry, even though I was still buying books without a collecting focus in mind. The collection had become a hodgepodge of World War I poetry, fine print material, Ariel poems and bits and pieces from my excursions to lesser booksellers such as Moe's and Cody's. Something had to change. With each purchase of another fine print item, I was starting to dislike my collection as a whole.

The key to finding a new focus for the collection was that expansion of my collecting activities into the realm of prose. Now that my range, so to speak, was broader, I expanded to collecting the prose of other early twentieth-century authors in addition to poetry. Ralph Sipper and Tom Goldwasser, sensing the emergence of an addicted collector, were only too happy to help me. I started timidly to buy lesser works by writers such as E. M. Forster and Ernest Hemingway. None of these early acquisitions proved their worth over the long run, but one has to start somewhere. The collection still had little focus, as even I could see that this selection of random, but minor works by early twentieth-century authors had no center of gravity. Things had to change a lot more.

Finding a Focus

As the early years in California sped by, I became increasingly intent on building a career. One result of this was that book collecting, while still an important part of my life, slipped into the background for some time. Part of this semi-neglect of my collection also resulted from the general dissatisfaction I had developed with the collection as a whole as it then stood, largely because I had not solved the dilemma of focus. Unfortunately, the final result of that excursion into fine print had been that the collection now had no center of gravity.

I had worked for Stanford Research Institute for less than two years when I decided, with the naive self-confidence that only someone not yet thirty years old can muster, that my position there had given me the contacts to leave the institute and start a small consulting firm of my own. This little business, which I named ECCO Consulting, was headquartered in a house that I rented north of the Berkeley campus, on Hearst Street. The name was a play on the word "echo," for ultrasound, and the Italian "eccolo," which, loosely translated, means "that's it!" Because most of the consulting work was with companies anxious to enter the emerging business of medical ultrasound diagnostics, I was pleased with the name, and more pleased to find that, as I had anticipated, I could immediately attract major clients. I began each day, as I felt a good consultant should, reading the *Wall Street Journal*, while occupying a table in a little coffee shop that was only a short distance up the road from my office, on the corner of Hearst and Euclid. The coffee shop was also a favorite hangout of the postgraduate students in the nuclear physics department, since it was just across the road. They played chess for hours, drinking endless cups of strong espresso. Berkeley was a nuclear-free zone, then as now, but there was a particle accelerator installed under the nuclear physics building.

ECCO Consulting offered competitive business analysis of medical imaging markets as well as technology assessments of new medical imaging technology. More particularly, work focused around developments in diagnostic medical ultrasound, a field then entering a period of high growth. Whereas in the years up to and including the 1960s, the terms "medical imaging" and "X-ray" had been largely synonymous, in the heady ten-year period from the mid-1970s to the mid-1980s most of the modern tools of medical imaging beyond those of X-ray technology emerged. Nuclear medicine, the study of organs and their metabolism using short-lived, radioactive isotope tracers, grew apace, owing to the introduction of new and more specific isotopes. Diagnostic ultrasound changed from the depiction of images as green dots on a cathode ray tube to showing detailed images in real time in full gray scale on an image processor. MRI scanning was developed and introduced, as was digital processing of X-rays. Most of the large medical companies wanted to participate in the new technologies, so they were seeking advice, and as a result, my tiny consulting company was soon in demand. I worked largely with giant corporations, such as Siemens and Polaroid, and this part of the business was soon doing so well that I took on projects for a few emerging medical technology companies in Silicon Valley.

In my work for these smaller, emerging companies, I was also becoming aware of the world of venture capital investment, as I worked from time to time on diligence projects for venture capital investors. It had not gone unremarked by the world of venture capital that investment opportunities were emerging in the expanding field of medical imaging, but figuring out how best to take advantage of these opportunities was not easy. To make a good decision, an investor needed to know about the potential competitiveness of a prospective product, and about the robustness of the technology, which meant, in turn, that any diligence project involved technological assessment as well as evaluation of commercial prospects. Since large sums of money were involved in medical imaging product development and introduction, these large companies needed all the good advice they could get, and in the absence of other knowledgeable professionals with expertise and experience in this emerging field, I became, by default, an indispensable source of information. Before long, my business was flourishing.

Diasonics was one of the early ultrasound diagnostic companies that became my client. Founded in 1978, it had been backed by the legendary investors Arthur Rock, who was the first investor in Intel and

Apple, among other companies, and Robert Noyes, the founder of Intel. I knew Dr. Al Waxman, the company's founder, and as the company got off the ground, he offered me a role as the first vice president of marketing for the firm, suggesting that I close ECCO Consulting and join Diasonics. I nearly took the job, and if I had, things might have turned out very differently.

In hindsight, my interviews for the Diasonics position would be the stuff of comedy in today's business world. Having no formal business training, I still had not learned how the world of business really functioned. Despite the fact that my tiny ECCO Consulting was more than holding its own, my business sense was definitely not that of a shiny, newly minted MBA graduate, although perhaps, in its own funky way, it was just as effective. For example, not knowing that it wasn't really professional, I took my mother, who was visiting me, to my final job interview, which was a dinner at the home of Al Waxman and his wife, Anita. Anita was not a born cook, and dinner was delayed until after ten o'clock. During that interminable period of waiting, my mother and I sat stiffly on the couch in the living room, making stilted conversation with Al and, I remember, Anita's business partner at the time, who was a Russian—a blowsy blonde woman who periodically during the evening bounced in and out of the room. Anita had a small executive recruiting firm. I think there was a dog that periodically bounded in and out as well, but perhaps my memory is faulty on that score. It was a very long time ago.

As we drove home, I asked my mother her opinion, because I valued her judgment more than my own. She was a practical woman with good insight into character.

"If you take that job," she said, "you won't last twenty-four hours. And if you do last twenty-four hours, Anita will make certain you don't last forty-eight hours."

I took her advice, and instead of joining Diasonics, became a consultant to and an investor into the company. I believed in the technology so much that I invested every penny I had into Diasonics. It wasn't much, but would have been enough for a down payment on a house. My mother was horrified, as were my lawyer and my accountant.

"You know," I told them, "I won't ever be young enough again to throw away every penny I have for an investment I believe in. If it doesn't work out, I can earn more money. If it does, I'll have a cushion for life."

The result turned out to be halfway between those extremes,

although initially, the business of Diasonics went from strength to strength, with sales that more than doubled each year. My personal investment gave me the first taste of what it could be like to be a professional venture investor, and I started wondering if I, too, could become a venture capitalist. By that time, I had consulted with enough venture capital investors to have learned about the business, and venture capital investing seemed to me to be the key to the modern world of business. It was the place at which science and business met at an inflection point where, if the idea was good enough, new businesses would storm forth that would shape the direction of the modern world. Imagine being one of the small group of wizards who could shape the future! I still didn't know enough to take account of the stark reality that my total business career, including my time at British Oxygen, had by that point lasted no more than six years. And I didn't have an MBA.

In the later 1970s and early 1980s, venture capital investing was still in its relative youth, and there had been little investment in medical technology. Life sciences investment as a separate field of business activity did not yet exist. I had no knowledge of the world of finance and investment banking, but professional investors had begun to hear of me through my work for various small medical imaging technology firms. I thought I'd try to determine whether there might be an opportunity for me in investing, so I went to see Larry Mohr, a member of the venture investing team at Bank of America. He heard me out, but showed no enthusiasm.

"Annette," he said, at the end of my spiel, "there are fewer than seventy professional investors in the venture capital world today. What do you think you could offer that would enable you to be a professional venture capital investor?"

Little or nothing, I supposed, and dejected, I slunk out of his office in the big Bank of America high-rise building on California Street in San Francisco. I was crushed, but not defeated. The following year, I was offered a position at the leading emerging technology investment bank on the West Coast, Hambrecht & Quist, and invited to start a health-care practice for the firm. Knowing next to nothing about the world of investment banking, I decided I could always return to consulting if things didn't work out, and so accepted the offer. I never looked back.

For some idea of the times of the early 1980s, one has to realize that the Dow Jones Index was still barely above the 1,000 level (in 2018, it routinely hovered well above the 20,000 mark). The NASDAQ, created in 1971, had only just found its footing by underwriting the best of the first wave of technology companies to emerge from Silicon Valley. At that time, the first biotechnology company, Genentech, was still an embryonic business—nobody knew if genetic engineering had any chance of creating new pharmaceutical and agritech businesses. With unbelievable luck, I had stumbled, untrained and with a breathtaking lack of financial knowledge and know-how, into the world of investment banking and finance at a pivotal moment. The stock market, which had been moribund for over a decade, was about to take off on a dizzying ride that has continued, with only some setbacks, to the present day. Silicon Valley was in its earliest phases of productivity, and now I became a small part of that world. It was very hard work, but never boring, and every day brought new adventures and discoveries. I threw myself into this new business and along with my colleagues rode the wild breakers of the first technology boom of the 1980s.

I had been entrusted with a large charter at Hambrecht & Quist. The firm had decided to extend its technology focus into the field of health care, and I was the person hired to accomplish that task. As a first exercise, I was to build up a portfolio of diligently updated research reports on a group of publicly traded health-care businesses of my choosing. In addition, which I enjoyed more, I worked with the bankers and the venture capital team on diligence of new deals. I worked seven days a week, had no social life, ate breakfast and lunch at my desk, and loved every minute of every day. Our firm had invested in the first of the biotechnology companies, so I was privileged to be involved as the pioneer among these companies, Genentech, became the first public biotechnology company listed on Wall Street. Life sciences and biotechnology are today household words. It is hard to believe that the business is just over forty years old.

I remember the day, early in my tenure at Hambrecht & Quist, when Bill Hambrecht handed me a slim portfolio containing the material for the firm's investments into each of the first three biotechnology companies—Cetus, Biogen, and Genentech.

"Here," he said. "You're the engineer and the health-care specialist. Maybe you should tell us what we've invested in."

And so I ended up visiting Genentech in South San Francisco and learning about recombinant DNA while eating hamburgers at a picnic table in the sunshine with Bob Swanson, Genentech's cofounder, and his former Harvard roommate Fred Middleton, Genentech's chief financial officer. I knew this was important technology, but nobody except perhaps Bob Swanson understood how much of an impact genetic engineering would have on the future.

My first task at Hambrecht & Quist was to learn financial jargon. The brokers were warned to keep their clients away from me until I had learned the rudiments of financial analysis, but in my first weeks, I was hijacked by one of the more aggressive brokers—Ed Lowe—who brought his best client, Joe McNay of Essex Investment, to my tiny cubbyhole of an office. I didn't know at the time how important Joe's firm was to the technology world.

"What's your best stock pick?" asked Joe, "and what are your estimates for that company?"

The research department had a hideous orange-covered sofa on which I was sitting. I looked at my shoes. I had no idea what he was talking about. Joe persisted.

"What's your best stock pick?" he demanded.

"Um-m-m—New England Nuclear?" I hazarded. This was one of the companies that made diagnostic and therapeutic isotopes. I was still observing my shoes. I remember that they were beige with little checks at the tips.

"Well, what are your estimates for next year?" demanded Joe. I had no idea what he was talking about.

"I think it's going to do really well," I said weakly. "It's the leader in thallium chemistry." (Use of thallium isotopes for cardiac imaging had just been introduced.) Both Joe and Ed were now frowning at me. What to do? What to say? Thankfully, the head of the research department, Cliff Higgerson, came out of his office at that point and rescued me.

I learned finance from a Merrill Lynch investor handbook and a friend's accounting textbook from Harvard Business School. Whenever I was asked a question to which I had no answer, I would go to my office, shut the door, and refer to one or the other of these two guides. I soon realized that the subject of finance was by and large common sense: all one really needed to survive in the field was the ability to translate financial lingo into everyday language. After that, things went better, and I actually began to think I could make it in the world of investor finance.

The financial business can be summed up as the management of the vast river of money that runs through the world, money that is hidden from all but investment professionals. These various professionals, like fisherfolk, stand on the banks of this river and fish from it, and their rewards are manifold, because nobody other than those on the river-bank can see what they take from the river. From time to time, regula-tions are put into place to control the fishing, but soon, the fishermen move to new waters and the fishing continues. Somehow, I had stum-bled upon this river, and now, as the technology boom raced ahead, I began to earn more money than I had ever thought possible. In com-parison to the sums earned today by financial professionals, it was not significant, but it was enough for me to realize that I could now begin collecting in earnest. I had at least begun to earn the sort of money that enabled me to think of my collection in a more serious light. If I could solve the problem of focus for the collection, that is!

There was no doubt that I needed the world of book collecting in this new life, not only because of my continuing passion for books, but also because the world of bibliophilia offered a refuge from the pace and stress of the financial business. So it was with relief that I turned back to book collecting. When I entered a bookshop, things slowed down; everything in the bookshops seemed somehow less materialis-tic than in the world of which I had become a part. Thus, although col-lecting was no longer the central focus of my interests, as it had been previously, I spent many weekends browsing the bookshops of Berke-ley and San Francisco. Occasionally, I would find time to head to Santa Barbara, which had become the mecca for book dealers on the West Coast. Joseph the Provider had now moved to Santa Barbara, and the collector and book dealer Maurice Neville was there, as were a number of smaller dealers.

I went to Santa Barbara one weekend in the early 1980s to visit Ralph Sipper. He had more fine print to show me, but I was tired of fine print. It didn't speak to me; I just wasn't interested. Without the urging of Sandy Kirshenbaum, I might never have been interested. I was at a loss about how to proceed. Even though I had been haunting antiquarian bookshops for years, I still felt that I didn't know enough about book dealers and auctions and catalogs; nor, despite my wide reading, did I have the literary knowledge to be discerning. I was still at the stage where browsing led to finding, which sometimes led to a purchase, which was yet another reason that my collection was then so hodgepodge. Actually, it was worse than hodgepodge; the collec-tion was a mess! Although I still had my tiny collection of World War I poetry, and the list of Ariel poems in my possession was growing, the rest of the collection had been randomly assembled. It included many items of no interest and no value, bought largely from Cody's and

Moe's—books such as collections of the poetry of Ruth Pitter and minor works by major writers.

It was Ralph Sipper who made the crucial suggestion during that weekend visit that started to turn the page for me.

"Why don't you look at the Connolly list?" he asked.

I was now very familiar with Cyril Connolly's list, because in Serendipity Books in Berkeley, I once had found a copy of the catalog for his 1971 exhibition at the Humanities Research Center (now the Harry Ransom Center) in Austin, Texas. Connolly, a writer and critic, had assembled the works for the exhibition himself, based on his 1965 work *The Modern Movement: One Hundred Key Books from England, France, and America, 1880–1950.* The book listed and described the one hundred books authored by writers from these countries that, in Connolly's opinion, had most influenced the movement to Modernism in literary thought. The catalog had a sky-blue cover, and the descriptions that accompanied the pictures of the works on display provided educational synopses of the astonishing items he had included. The catalog was not expensive, but it had rightly become a small collector's item in its own right. Most of the items displayed in the exhibition had come, impressively, from the vast inventories of the Humanities Research Center's own collections. The exhibition contained important examples of books—first editions, association copies with important inscriptions, and manuscripts, letters, and drawings related to these key books. When I bought the catalog, I had a fleeting thought that perhaps one day I, too, could collect the titles of the Modern Movement list. Others had done it before me, although the Ransom Center held the Golden Horde of anything to do with Modernism and Connolly.

Reading through the catalog about the treasures that Connolly had chosen for the exhibition (he and Mary Hirth, the editor, had written the descriptions), I began to get a glimmer of the importance of Modernism in literary thought. Until that time, I had not associated the works that so attracted me with the convulsive period when literary thought changed so conclusively from the strictly narrative to the more interpretative.

Ralph, who had some idea of what I owned, having sold me so many titles, was looking over the itemized list of my small collection as he spoke:

"You've got some of the titles already—Wilfred Owen's *Poems*, Sitwell's *Collected Poems*, and *The Mother*. You know that both of those are on the Connolly list, don't you—even though she's so much out of favor now as a poet. Let's see. Dylan Thomas—*Deaths and Entrances* . . . Forster's *Passage to India*. It seems that you've made a start with the Connolly list. I see that you even have a copy of Eliot's *Ash Wednesday*."

But I wasn't ready for Connolly yet. Although I was at a dead end with my motley collection of fine print, World War I poetry, and prose titles, the Connolly list seemed daunting. I was earning more money than I had ever earned before, but I still wasn't in a financial position to afford many of the titles on the Connolly list, and I had no idea how to begin to collect any of the French titles. I knew no dealers in French literature, and certainly, important French books were not what most rare book dealers in the United States had on their shelves.

Then there was the unspoken fact that I found the suggestion of creating a collection of Connolly titles intellectually intimidating. Since I was not a literary scholar, it seemed to me that assembling such a collection would require a degree of literary sophistication that I just did not possess. I always felt that any book dealer in Modern literature knew so much more than I did on the subject that I held back. It may seem surprising that, having such confidence in my professional life, and being prepared to take the significant risks necessary for a venture capital investment, I had so little confidence in my judgment about book collecting. It took a major purchase of one of the key Connolly titles to set me on my way.

Ulysses

I did not expect, when I woke up on the day I committed to collecting the books of the Connolly Modern Movement list, that before the afternoon was over I would purchase a first edition of James Joyce's key book, *Ulysses*. Not only a first edition, but one of the 150 numbered copies printed on special verge d'Arches paper. At that point in my career, after those heady first years in the finance industry, nothing was going right anymore. And so, particularly that day, I did what I usually did when things didn't go well—I turned to the world of books and authors and book dealers.

How had things gone so wrong? Partly, it was a result of my exceptional naïveté. In the four years I had been in the world of finance, the market indices had gone from strength to strength, mostly driven by technology. I had been warned by some of the more experienced of the stockbrokers at Hambrecht & Quist that sooner or later, there would be a downward correction in the market, but not having experience, I didn't understand what that meant. I remember one of the retail brokers telling me, "A market correction is when a high-flying stock you own goes down in value by 90 percent, and when you think the market has stabilized, that stock goes down another 90 percent." I couldn't begin to process that sort of information.

My timing on entry to the financial system in the United States could not have been better, even though it had been completely unplanned. Around the time I joined the world of finance, the monetization of public markets from the first wave of technology was just beginning to rouse Wall Street from its post-1970s slump, and it proceeded to propel it ever upward. By virtue of my position at Hambrecht & Quist, I was right in the middle of where everything was happening. To put this into some perspective—the day I began to work at Hambrecht & Quist, the Dow Jones Industrial Average stood at around 880, although by the end of the trading day, it had sunk to 820. Uncannily, that was the low point: from then on, with some corrections, the Dow continued to advance throughout my tenure at H&Q, so that by the time I left the firm in mid-1983 it stood at around 1,200 on an absolute basis—a nearly 50 percent rise. The change in the NASDAQ Composite Index—the over-the-counter market for stocks—was even more spectacular in that four-year period. On an absolute basis the index rose from 150 to 330 during the period of my tenure at Hambrecht & Quist. Most of that rise could be attributed to the market success of the many initial public offerings (IPOs) of emerging technology companies taking place over those years.

I was working too hard to observe how politically charged and how misogynistic the Wall Street environment really was. I should have paid more attention, but since the markets were doing so well, I didn't really need to. Fortunes were being made every day, so everybody was happy. At that time, I was blithely unaware of how women were faring more generally in the world of finance, and I continued to believe in the assumptions I had brought with me to America—mainly, that hard work brings its own rewards no matter who you are. And in fact, I was rewarded: at the end of 1981, I became the first woman to become a partner in Hambrecht & Quist. I was so happy about it that I overlooked some obvious signs of patronage. For example, the firm's annual cocktail party for new partners was always held at the venerable Pacific Union Club, which at that time did not admit women, even as guests. After some pressure from George Quist, the club agreed to allow me to attend, but I had to enter through the staff entrance at the back of the club. The women at Hambrecht & Quist were horrified.

"You can't go to that party!" declared more than one of the professional women.

"Well," I said, "I grew up under the apartheid system in South Africa. This gives me a chance to see what it was really like." Nothing was going to keep me from celebrating my moment of triumph.

At the partners' lunch, Bill Timken, the head of retail brokerage, jumped to his feet:

"Here's to Annette, our first female partner," he said. "Next year, we can have the lunch at her house and she can cook." Everyone laughed at that except me. Another of the firm's partners, Bill Edwards, who was sitting on my left, turned to me and said, audibly enough for all to hear, "Or maybe she can go on a business trip so we can go back to the Bohemian Club for our usual lunch."

It was an awkward meal.

I had been made a partner for a good reason, so I did not need to apologize. I had earned my seat at that table, because health-care investing was finally becoming of interest to financiers; owing to my hard work, Hambrecht & Quist was becoming known as a "go-to" investment bank if you had a health-care deal to discuss. As the following year proceeded, my area became exponentially busier, so, after three years at the firm, I felt confident enough to ask if the firm could hire another analyst to work with me to take on part of the increasing workload. With the new science of biotechnology emerging so rapidly, Wall Street and the venture capital world were being flooded with investment opportunities in the health-care sciences—my area. Proposals flew in the door every day—to back new companies or to underwrite IPOs of emerging businesses that proposed new technologies and ideas that could change the world. Although it was a small company, Hambrecht & Quist was now at the center of it all. We were becoming busier and busier, and it was hard to keep up. Ultimately, we hired a successful analyst, a woman, from a successful boutique brokerage firm. The partners seemed proud that the firm now had not one, but two women as partners, and all appeared to be going well. But it wasn't.

After only six months at Hambrecht & Quist, my new partner had a breakdown. I now saw the other side of what it was like for women in the cut-and-thrust world of finance in those days, when they had to fend for themselves to make headway in the profession. After Liz (not her real name) was taken ill, there was little sympathy for her among the partners, and I was blamed for bringing her to the firm in the first place. We both became radioactive; while Liz was on leave, I took over her workload in addition to my own, with no support from the firm to help me with the additional workload. Nobody reached out to help us cope, yet both of us needed a lot of support, though obviously in different ways. Naturally enough, as a result of plodding through each day in these surroundings, I became disheartened, and so began to look around for a more sympathetic environment in which to work. There seemed little alternative: I could hardly believe that, instead of helping me, my colleagues actually blamed me for having advocated so strongly for Liz to join the firm. Even today, it is deeply shocking to me. I had no support at all. I felt abandoned and alone, and as a result I jumped aboard the first ship that came along and offered me a berth. This was the investment-banking firm of L. F. Rothschild, Unterberg, Towbin, one of four small firms—known in those days as the Four Horsemen—that had in effect created the business for IPOs of emerging high-technology firms. In addition to Hambrecht & Quist and L. F. Rothschild, the other two firms were Montgomery Securities and a firm called Robertson, Colman & Stephens. Except for L. F. Rothschild, whose headquarters were in New York, the other three firms were located in San Francisco.

I've often asked myself why I didn't take a break from finance and move into another line of business. The answer is simple: I wanted badly to be a venture capital professional. I had been in the financial world long enough to know that you couldn't leave it and expect to return later, especially if you were female. At that time, the financial business was like an all-male club that only begrudgingly took in a few female members; if a woman managed to open that door even a crack, she had to put her toe into the doorway, squeeze through, and stay there. Pursuing the world of finance in the 1980s as a woman was like trying to summit Mount Everest without oxygen: your male colleagues have oxygen tanks, but you have to make it without assistance. At first, things may go easily, but as you attempt to ascend those treacherous slopes without a breathing apparatus, you have to work exponentially harder to make progress. The fact that I had become the first woman partner at Hambrecht & Quist was, for me, the peak of my career up to that point, but it was not my personal summit. Venture capital was the peak I was aiming for.

My interview for a position at L. F. Rothschild was held over lunch on a Concorde flight from Paris to New York City. I was returning from a European road show for a company IPO. It is a testament to the hubris of that first technology boom that even I, a relatively junior partner, could jump onto a Concorde flight with ease and the cost of the flight would be charged to IPO expenses. Tom Unterberg, one of the managing partners of Rothschild, Unterberg, Towbin, was also on the flight, and I made sure I was seated next to him, which enabled me to promote myself as a potential hire while the plane flew over the Atlantic. I had nothing to lose: I was so unhappy at Hambrecht & Quist that I was looking for any escape hatch I could find. I remember, as I talked with him, being transfixed by the way the peas rolled off Tommy Unterberg's knife and dribbled down his tie onto his lap, as, seemingly unaware of the fact, he ate his lunch of steak and vegetables. Concorde meals were glamorous, even though the seats were as uncomfortable as economy seats are today. The sales pitch was successful, and I was offered a position, even though I knew that in making this move, I was taking a step backward. From being a relatively new but full partner in a firm where I had established a successful department, I was going to become a mere junior partner. But unlike most Wall Street firms of that era, L. F. Rothschild had several women partners and the environment was egalitarian.

The firm had been patched together from a 1977 merger between the old-line trading firm of L. F. Rothschild and the small investment banking firm of C. E. Unterberg, Towbin. When I joined the company, it had started the steep slide in business that would lead within a very few years to the business collapsing, though I didn't know it at the time. I did not understand, when I made my move to Rothschild, that the financial indices were beginning to crack, in no small measure because not all of the emerging companies that had floated IPOs on Wall Street were stable. Unfortunately, L. F. Rothschild had underwritten more than its fair share of unsuccessful businesses. In this deteriorating environment, the last thing the corporate finance partners in the New York office wanted was to deal with a new partner claiming a share of the rapidly diminishing spoils.

The rules by which the people clustered at the shore of the money river live and catch fish are unwritten. By and large, the world of finance is a bloodless environment where the weakest are edged out with little consideration. Being on the riverbank is at once thrilling and terrifying, but the spirit of competition and the greed often rule out any real possibility of collegiality: in the end, the rewards are purely financial. When things do not go well, as they were no longer going well in the business of L. F. Rothschild, the daily routines turn into jockeying for survival. Ultimately, there are no allegiances—nor could there be in such a competitive environment. The endless quest for money is all. I never met an altruistic investment banker; the term itself is an oxymoron.

At the end of 1983, the bull market finally started to hiccup, and it was clear that a retreat was imminent. In fact, the impending retreat actually turned into the market crash of 1984, which took the NASDAQ all the way back to the 150 level where it had started in the late 1970s, at the time I joined Hambrecht & Quist. Sensing the end of easy money, the members of the banking team at L. F. Rothschild started acting like hungry, angry sharks, fighting over every bit of business that came into the corporate finance group. I didn't see all of this, as it largely took place in the New York office, but it became clear why nobody in the group had welcomed the addition of a new junior partner in the San Francisco office: the days of easy profits had come to an end. Not only that, but just as new business was declining, class-action lawsuits against the firm were increasing. Simply put, although my new partners were keen to show their animosity, it had nothing to do with me personally; it was just that the business was imploding. Too late, I realized that I had jumped out of the frying pan of Hambrecht & Quist straight into the blazing fire that was rapidly engulfing the remnants of business at L. F. Rothschild.

In addition to everything else that had happened in 1983, within a very few months after my arrival at L. F. Rothschild, I was diagnosed, at the young age of thirty-six, with breast cancer. I elected minimal surgery followed by a six-week course of radiation therapy. Naturally, I took time off work for treatment—as much for my psyche as for the disease itself. Radiation therapy, while not itself very debilitating, was terrifying. Every time I entered the radiation therapy suite, I waited my turn among ambulatory patients like myself together with those less fortunate who, lying pale and still on gurneys, were clearly close to death. I was still a young, single woman when this catastrophe struck, and I had never had a serious illness or been close to death before. For the first time, I contemplated whether I might not survive; perhaps I would soon become one of those comatose forms lying under a thin blanket, waiting for treatment.

When I returned to work after Christmas that year, my colleagues were not sympathetic. The partner in the next office could be heard muttering that his mother had not needed time off when she had been treated for breast cancer. I gritted my teeth and soldiered on, but I hated their callous treatment; nor did they much care for me in return. At this point, I was taking up space. The markets tottered and plunged and the stream of lawsuits against L. F. Rothschild grew into a small river.

Since the days of ECCO Consulting, book collecting had taken a backseat as my career burgeoned. In the years at Hambrecht & Quist, collecting had become more of a quiet hobby: my collection grew, but randomly. I couldn't by any stretch of the imagination call myself a serious collector. But now, with my morale at an all-time low, alone and afraid after the cancer treatment, and hating each new day that I had to work in an unsympathetic environment, amid colleagues who were unfriendly, at best, and distasteful, at worst, I turned again to serious book collecting.

I bought my copy of *Ulysses* on a spring day in 1984. The day I bought it had turned out to be more demoralizing than usual, for no particular reason other than the unpleasant atmosphere of the L. F. Rothschild office, which bore in on me more heavily than on other days. Instead of eating at my desk, which had long been my habit, I left the premises and walked from my office on the Embarcadero in San Francisco all the way to Union Square. Probably unconsciously, I chose to go in that direction because the world of books and book dealers beckoned as a refuge of sorts. I wanted to escape the contemplation of what seemed to be the ruins of my career. In those days, book dealers could still afford to do business on the upper floors of the buildings clustered around Union Square, which was San Francisco's central shopping district. I began to browse. I went from bookstore to bookstore, and once again, found myself immersed in the world of old books that smelled of slightly foxed paper and ancient leather. John Crichton had mostly eighteenth-century literature and fine bindings, as did the Holmes bookstore. Transition Books—hidden away near the tunnel linking Stockton Street with Union Square, was more eclectic. There I could find names that I knew and cherished. Forgetting L. F. Rothschild, I immersed myself in a search of the titles of early twentieth-century literature. Nothing resonated. And then, from behind the counter, a copy of *Ulysses*—a first edition—appeared in the hands of the owner of the bookshop, Rick Praeger. I took a sharp breath and gingerly reached out to take it.

Ulysses is one of the great underread texts of the twentieth century; despite that, it is routinely placed in the top percentile of important literature of the era, and it's one of the great collectible items of Modernism. At auction, a good example of the rarest copies of that edition—one of the one hundred signed books of the 1922 first edition printed in Paris by Shakespeare and Company, could command up to and beyond several hundred thousand dollars, depending on condition. A personally inscribed copy of the first edition—for example, a copy with a written inscription from James Joyce to a close friend—could increase the value immeasurably, depending, of course, on the closeness of the association between Joyce and the dedicatee. The book is what is known in the rare book business as a high spot, and, like a number of these high spots of literature, it is most definitely not an easy read. I confess that I have struggled to finish reading *Ulysses* myself.

The story of how the book came to be published is better known than the text. Ezra Pound was an early champion of Joyce and gave *Ulysses* its first publication in his journal, *The Little Review*, as a serial. But since the work was widely denounced as obscene, *The Little Review* editors were prosecuted, and perhaps consequently, Joyce was unable to secure a publisher. Finally, Sylvia Beach, the American owner of the bookstore Shakespeare and Company, situated on the Left Bank in Paris, undertook to publish the work, and the now coveted first limited edition appeared in 1922. The Shakespeare and Company edition is large and unwieldy, with blue wrappers and no hard cover. There was definite intent in its design. Joyce specified that the cover be the color of the Greek flag and, in addition, he was canny in his choice of paper. He specified that the first edition must consist of three different books with different trim sizes and paper quality, and this innovation gave the first edition, from the outset, the gift of collectibility. As Faye Hammill and Mark Hussey have described in their book *Modernism's Print Cultures*, Joyce's personal involvement in selecting the Aegean blue of the cover and designing the appearance of the books elevated its status as a work of art. In their words, it "provided an opportunity for speculators in the collectors' market."

This first edition consisted of one thousand copies, of which one hundred were signed copies on verge d'Arches paper. An additional 150 unsigned copies were on verge d'Arches paper as well, and my copy was number 178 of the series numbered from 101 to 250. The other 750 unsigned copies were on paper of lesser quality. Copies of the first edition had been sold by subscription, and of course the book became a sensation. Those large, fat, first edition copies, with their dull blue plain paper wrappers, are pinnacles of Modernist collecting. The scarcity of the book owes to its notoriety. Copies of the first edition sent to the United States from France by mail were seized by the US Post Office and burned, which was the fate of the book in other parts of the English-speaking world as well. Customs officials took delight in confiscating any copies that someone tried to bring into the United States.

Personally, I suspect this large differential in perceived value, and the significance of the first edition of *Ulysses* in the first place, are constructs of the modern book dealer as much as of the literary value of the work itself. Just as the dealer in art creates a market and a currency for Modern paintings and sculpture, so the book dealer, in his or her small world, creates and nurtures the market for the sale of certain key Modern first editions. The one hundred limited, signed copies of *Ulysses* are currency in the book dealer's world, even more so if they are inscribed copies with a fine association. The rest of the first edition, such as my copy, are merely fine and rare books. They are of considerable value, yes, but cannot be compared to those rare one hundred signed copies.

Another reason these first edition copies of *Ulysses* have become an informal gold standard of valuation in Modernist collecting is that they can't be easily faked, owing to their unorthodox first publisher and her handmade paper. The fact is, however, that whether you have read the book or not, no collection of Modern literature is complete without a copy of *Ulysses*.

The copy I bought that day wasn't the best copy on the market. It was a second-tier copy, belonging to the category of the 150 unsigned books printed on verge d'Arches paper, but still, the indicated price was certainly not a bargain. As I took the book from Mr. Praeger's hands, I felt its bulk and its weight, and as I examined it, it was clear there had been some repairs to the spine. The bookplate of the first owner, Oliver Brett, the 3rd Viscount Esher, had been pasted into the book, and it was still there. One wonders why Oliver Brett decided to subscribe to the first edition of such a controversial book. In some ways, the ex libris made the book more interesting, since the Viscounts Esher have on the whole a distinguished history. Despite these mild flaws, and even knowing there were far better copies of the first edition available from time to time, I bought it. It cost more than I reasonably could afford to pay, a whopping $7,500, but once I set my mind on purchasing the book, I was bound to buy it.

It's surprising to think that my collection of Modern Movement titles owed so much to my unhappiness at L. F. Rothschild. Although I didn't realize it at the time, that copy of *Ulysses* was the turning point that set me finally and ineluctably on the journey to collecting representative editions and related material centered on Connolly's Modern Movement list. Although I had bought the book without really intending to build such a collection, there was no doubt that if I wanted to become a serious collector, this was the direction in which I needed to go. That copy of *Ulysses* was the catalyst for my decision to commit to collecting the Modern Movement titles, with Connolly's list serving as the guidebook. And as with the purchase of "A Song for Simeon" those many years ago, the significant purchase price of the copy of *Ulysses* had more than a little to do with the decision. Although it was a stretch for me, I could just afford it, but I had never really bought anything in that sort of price category before. At that time, all I had in my limited collection of the Connolly series were the titles that Ralph Sipper had noted. As I wrote the check to pay for that copy of *Ulysses*, collecting the titles of the Connolly Modern Movement list seemed alluring, but it also still seemed daunting. So why did I purchase it? If I'm truthful, the answer relates more to my frame of mind that day than to any high-minded intent to focus my collection. I bought the book in a spirit of *épater les bourgeois*; buying such a key title made me feel that my life and values were somehow independent of the soulless world of finance and investment banking I encountered in my day-to-day life. I wanted to feel that, unlike my colleagues who were focused principally on the usual sorts of material things that money could buy—houses and boats and cars and bad modern paintings—somehow, my values were more aesthetic, more intellectual, and more refined. It was a sort of moral self-delusion. However, despite the fact that it was an impulse purchase made for all the wrong reasons, in terms of kick-starting me on the way to collecting the one hundred key books of Connolly's list, buying that copy of *Ulysses* turned out to be the ideal first significant purchase to encourage me to move my collection forward and confirm a satisfying focus for the collection at last.

None of my colleagues even noticed that I returned to the office with the large, fat copy of *Ulysses*, which I placed on my desk in a prominent position. I took the book out of the box that a previous owner had made for it and placed it very obviously, front and center, on my desk. I was ready to explain the item to any colleague who might actually inquire about it. Nobody did. I left it on my desk for a week before I took it home and put it with the rest of my collection. Once I had taken the book home and saw how it dominated the shelf where the rest of my still-tiny collection sat so placidly, I felt a surge of excitement: I had moved into a different category of collecting. It wasn't just the fact that the book took up so much space on the shelf, although my entire collection of World War I poetry occupied probably half the shelf space that *Ulysses* now did, especially owing to its custom-made half morocco case. As I looked at the collection in its entirety on that shelf, the passion for collecting came flooding back to me, but this time, I was certain that building a serious collection of Modern Movement literature was exactly what I now wanted to achieve.

Despite my intentions, I bought nothing for my collection in the following year, 1985. After I acquired this key copy, collecting once again had to take a backseat for a while, since I had finally accepted the extent to which I didn't belong at L. F. Rothschild. In the summer of that year, I left the firm and the world of investment banking, but I left without having a serious plan about what to do next. Leaving L. F. Rothschild had been one thing; finding a new career was another matter altogether. As long as I was professionally and financially vulnerable, I couldn't relax and focus on collecting. As it turned out, it was fortunate that I left, because the firm collapsed for good less than two years later. Sometimes, it's good to be naive enough not to know what you don't know.

The Importance of Cyril Connolly's Modern Movement List

Cyril Connolly was a contemporary of the writers emerging in literary London in the 1930s—he was friends with Evelyn Waugh, Anthony Powell, George Orwell, Harold Acton, and Stephen Spender, among many others. Although he was also a writer, he never achieved success comparable to that of such of his friends as George Orwell or Evelyn Waugh, though he did emerge as a literary critic and journalist of note. He was also, for most of his adult life, an avid collector of first edition books and autograph pamphlets of writers in English and French. Of most relevance to me was that in 1965, the firm of Andre Deutsch published Connolly's book *The Modern Movement: One Hundred Key Books from England, France and America, 1880–1950*, which presented his opinions as a literary critic on the most important books of Modernist writing of that era. Connolly assembled the list chronologically according to the years in which the works were published, acknowledging that he had not included books written in languages other than English or French, since he did not wish to rely on translations. Perhaps Connolly just did not feel as confident about his opinions beyond the worlds of English and French literature, but on that count, not much more is known. Barbara Skelton, Connolly's second wife, once cattily suggested that some of the literary influences for his list of one hundred books were questionable—that some of the entries he incorporated merely reflected whatever his current love interest happened to be reading, which book he would include and serve up as a choice based on his own opinion.

Literary Modernism was a movement of the late nineteenth and early twentieth centuries that occurred in parallel with the cataclysmic changes happening at that time in philosophical thought, largely as a reaction to the memory of the charnel houses filled with the bones of the millions of the dead, slaughtered in the wars of the late nineteenth and early twentieth centuries. This new way of thinking—introspective, analytical, mythical, and mystical—rejected Enlightenment thinking and demolished the certainty behind the tenets of religious belief. Literary Modernism had various branches, although the symbolist movement, which started in Paris in the late nineteenth century, led by Stéphane Mallarmé and Paul Verlaine, as well as the short-lived imagist movement, begun in 1913 by Ezra Pound, with his challenge to poets everywhere to "Make It New," were the earliest forms of this new literary genre. After imagism, Pound, together with Wyndham Lewis, began the literary vorticist movement, of which the only example found in the Connolly list is Lewis's little-read novel *Tarr*. However, the list included several examples of surrealism, the term coined by Guillaume Apollinaire, who is often called the forefather of the movement, along with Arthur Rimbaud, whose *Un Saison en Enfer* figures prominently on the Connolly list. Probably the key work of surrealism to be found on the Connolly list, however, is the most important of the surrealist works of André Breton—the book, almost incomprehensible to a lay reader, *Nadja*.

The full list of Connolly titles, in the order in which they appear in the catalog of the famous 1971 exhibition at the Humanities Research Center at the University of Texas in Austin, is included for reference in the appendix to this book. In that exhibition, as in Connolly's book, the list actually presented more than one hundred titles. Connolly's logic is unclear, but he in more than one case included two examples of an author's work to illustrate a particular point about a choice. Actually, I believe that he just couldn't make up his mind on those occasions and squeezed two books under one heading. I used that catalog as my guidebook over the years when I collected the works of the Connolly list, which is the reason I use this ordering of the works, rather than a purely chronological order, for Connolly's one hundred Modern books.

I don't think Connolly set out his list of key books with a goal to be perceived as a dogmatic pedagogue; rather, he was seeking to create a dialogue. However, the list is far from a complete analysis of Modernist literature—it's a list of works in English and French that he saw as important to the Modernist movement. As noted earlier, he did not attempt to address the rise of Modernism in other languages, and he even apologized for the lack of a wider reach in his selection.

Even though I was enthusiastic about collecting books relating to what I understood at that time about literary Modernism, I wasn't quite sure at the outset what the word really meant with respect to literature. In 1934, Ezra Pound had written an essay where he attempted to define Modernism, urging his fellow writers to "Make It New," as he had urged them many years previously when defining the short-lived imagist movement in poetry. I knew that in English literature, the most famous example of literary Modernism was perhaps James Joyce's *Ulysses*, which is an exhaustive description of twenty-four hours in the life of the Dubliner Leopold Bloom as told through the internal monologues of the protagonists, which include Bloom, his wife, Molly, and Stephen Dedalus. Of course, I now had a prime example of *Ulysses*, but I couldn't take too much satisfaction in that. It dominated the bookshelf where my small collection was housed, reminding me that I was a long, long way from having a collection of Modern Movement titles on that bookshelf.

One problem that I had not addressed with my decision to collect first editions and rare or inscribed copies of the one hundred titles of the Connolly list was that there were many titles on the list with which I had no familiarity at all. Once I moved beyond the familiar names of Waugh, Orwell, Henry James, Ford Madox Ford, and other English writers, I came up against names of French and American writers I knew little to nothing about. Huysmans was new to me—and I had not encountered Jarry, or, surprisingly, the works of the Americans Edmund Wilson, Wallace Stevens, and William Carlos Williams. Less surprising was the fact that most of the names of the French writers of the Modern Movement, save Proust, Apollinaire, and Mallarmé, were not familiar to me either. Verlaine, whose poetry I admired, was unaccountably excluded from the Connolly list.

And there was another potential hurdle to overcome, which was my fear that all the best examples of Modern Movement books had already been acquired by libraries or private collectors. Even with regard to what might still come to market, I was concerned that, with my still limited means, I would not be able to compete against these institutions and private collectors in order to purchase important rare books. Beyond the obvious libraries, such as the British Library or the Bibliothèque Nationale in Paris, there were major libraries with seemingly bottomless means that were acquiring not only important examples of published works, but authors' archives, letters, and manuscripts. One library that was repeatedly referenced was the Humanities Research Center at the University of Texas in Austin, which had supported that very exhibition of Modernist titles which I now desired to collect. In the late 1950s, under the guidance of Harry Ransom, an inspired scholar who later became chancellor of the University of Texas system, that library had begun to acquire archives and works of twentieth-century English and American literature at a time when these had not yet become collectible. As a result, the library was able to establish itself as the leader in this emerging field. For me, the Ransom Center symbolized the potential hopelessness of my task: I had a limited budget and no visibility.

I felt that I would have to content myself with leftovers. Still, I was keen to begin the quest and to persevere. Embarking on the exercise was like beginning a treasure hunt—and a challenging one at that. Despite the overwhelming presence of libraries like the Ransom Center, the British Library, and the Bibliothèque Nationale, as well as wealthy private collectors, could I collect fine examples—first editions, association copies, and related material—of the one hundred important works by late nineteenth- and early twentieth-century authors that Cyril Connolly had selected for his list? Another problem for me was that I had no idea, starting out, how I would manage to collect the French authors cited by Connolly. I knew no French dealers, and had no real idea how to make contact with reputable dealers in France. French dealers in rare books and manuscripts did not generally come to the United States to exhibit at book fairs, and I knew at that time no other way to meet new dealers. All things considered, I had taken on a big assignment.

In addition to the copy of *Ulysses*, by the time I started I had assembled only a very few items of works by authors who appeared on that list. Nothing I already owned was a perfect copy, and I certainly had no association or other signed copies. The titles Ralph Sipper had previously noted that I owned, none of which were in fine condition, were slightly battered copies, including first editions of Forster's *A Passage to India*; the posthumously published *Poems* of Wilfred Owen; *Deaths and Entrances*, a slight book of poetry by Dylan Thomas; T. S. Eliot's *Ash Wednesday*; and two volumes of Edith Sitwell's poetry: *The Mother* and *Collected Poems*. I had seven examples of books that were on the list—but I actually had one hundred and one books to go.

Sergeant Pilot Campbell White. New Plymouth, New Zealand, 1940.

Waiting to scramble. RAF Squadron 258. Kenley, Surrey, 1941.

Granny Pratt was a gifted gardener, creating a memorable garden in her new home in Blenheim in New Zealand's South Island.

Northern Rhodesia (now Zambia) and our house in Chingola, home to the Nchanga copper mines. The garden abounded in bright tropical flowers.

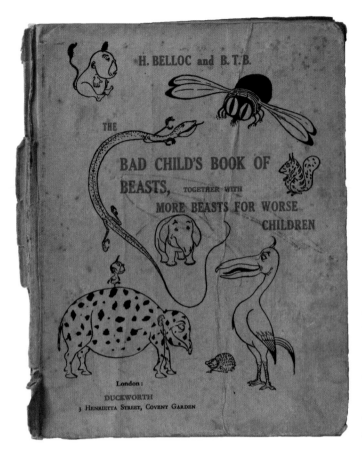

Belloc's heavy-handed Edwardian humor was not really appropriate reading material for a four-year-old. (Photographs by Reenie Raschke unless otherwise noted.)

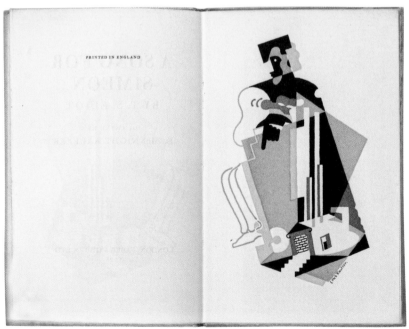

This limited, signed edition of T. S. Eliot's "A Song for Simeon" (1928) was the purchase that started a lifetime of book collecting. (Drawing by E. McKnight Kauffer. © Simon Rendall.)

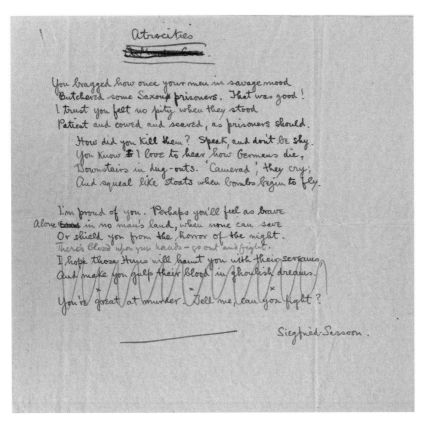

The hand of the wartime censor meant that the original version, probably written by Siegfried Sassoon at Craiglockhart Hospital in 1917, remained unknown for many years. (© Siegfried Sassoon by kind permission of the Estate of George Sassoon.)

Corrected galley proofs of Connolly's *The Modern Movement*, bought from Rick Gekoski in 1988. (Photograph courtesy Sotheby's.)

Alpha and Omega. The catalog from the 1971 exhibition at the Humanities Research Center at the University of Texas at Austin, curated by Connolly, of his *One Hundred Modern Books* and the Sotheby's catalog for the sale of my collection of Connolly's Modern Movement list, June 7, 2007.

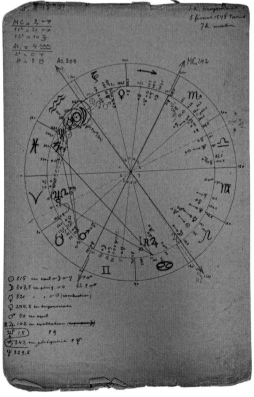

André Breton's horoscope of Joris-Karl Huysmans—one of a series cast of contemporaries and symbolist and surrealist writers. Breton embraced astrology and magic arts; it was a core belief of the surrealists that, through astrology, knowledge of self and knowledge of the world can be united. (© 2019 Artists Rights Society [ARS], New York/ADAGP, Paris.)

An original poster for Paul Verlaine's first published collection of verse, *Poèmes saturniens* (1866), by Jules Barthélemy Péaron (1867). Inscribed to Anatole France.

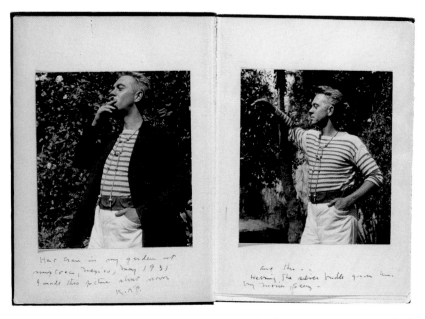

I always regretted selling this copy of Hart Crane's *The Bridge* (1930), owing to the deeply personalized content. The photographs of Crane were taken by Katherine Anne Porter at her house in Mixcoac, Mexico, in May of 1931. (Reprinted with permission of The Permissions Company, LLC, on behalf of The Katherine Anne Porter Literary Trust, www.permissionscompany.com. Photograph courtesy Sotheby's.)

Antoine de Saint-Exupéry's plane was downed in the Libyan desert in 1935 during his failed attempt to beat the Paris-to-Saigon speed record. The dedicatee of the inscription "En souvenir d'un soir de désespoir" is his sister, Gabrielle d'Agay. An inspiration for *Le Petit Prince*?

La Chanson du mal-aimé (1903, 1945). Privately printed with watercolor by Marie Laurencin, former lover of Apollinaire, presented in a *Livre d'Artiste* binding done by Rose Adler, also rumored lover of Laurencin. The many associations of this book are the reason it is an important part of my collection. (Rose Adler binding © 2019 Artists Rights Society [ARS], New York/ADAGP, Paris; Marie Laurencin watercolor, © Fondation Foujita/Artists Rights Society [ARS], New York/ADAGP, Paris 2019. Photographs courtesy Sotheby's.)

E. M. Forster in India, playing a game called *jubbu* in the palace courtyard, during the time of his service as secretary (1912–1913) to Tukojirao III, the Maharaja of Dewas State. The second photograph dates from his second visit in 1921. (Photographs courtesy Sotheby's.)

And Pan through anguished pipes doth blow
His sudden heart in one wild stream,
Fond and tremulous and low;
For springs he cannot know again,
For springs before the world grew old,
For blond-limbed dancers lemon-clad
From vales and hill-tops fiery cold —
A world fantastical and sad.

William Faulkner's drawing of a nymph accompanied by a short, unpublished verse dating from 1919–1920, sent to Mrs. Estelle Franklin, née Oldham, who later became his wife. (© Copyright 2019, Faulkner Literary Rights, LLC. All rights reserved. Used with permission, The Literary Estate of William Faulkner, Lee Caplin, Executor. Photograph courtesy of Sotheby's, Inc. © 2013.)

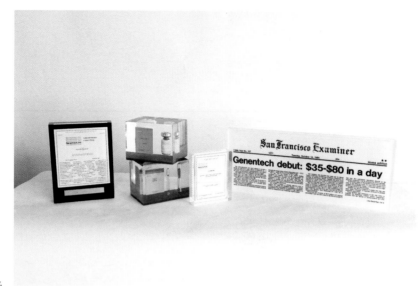

Genentech was the first of the biotechnology startups to go public in 1981, creating a whole new biopharma industry.

Over thirty years, we raised and managed five investment funds for MedVenture Associates, to make seed capital investments in biomedical startup companies.

MedVenture Associates invested in the first venture capital round of TheraSense, whose technology enabled development of the first off-fingertip blood glucose monitor and, later, the first continuous blood glucose measurement monitor.

Beginning the
Connolly Collection

Before I could begin to collect in earnest, I needed a new job. Although thankful to have left L. F. Rothschild behind me, I was now in professional limbo. What to do? One way or the other, the time had come to find a way to achieve my long-held ambition of becoming a venture capital investor. To have one's own venture fund seemed a route to professional independence, and after my departure from L. F. Rothschild, this became an immediate goal.

Thanks to those years at Hambrecht & Quist, I finally had decent experience in finance and investing, and a profile of sorts in Silicon Valley. Taking all of this into account, I decided first of all to try my luck in a few interviews with key venture capital firms, which were far fewer both in number and size in the 1980s than they are today. Back then, a so-called megafund could be of the order of $100 million; in today's world, you couldn't call anything less than $1 billion a megafund. In the late 1970s, Hambrecht & Quist, with $7 million in available investment capital, had one of the biggest venture funds on the West Coast of the United States. Joining one of these funds could have been a simpler route than going it alone, as I eventually did, but in the end none of the big venture firms were interested in bringing me on board in anything other than an associate role, which I thought to be a step downward. So I reverted to what had always been Plan A and took the plunge, beginning a fundraising process to create a venture investment fund of my own. My goal was to raise $12 million for a small fund that would make what are called seed capital investments, which are the very first investments made by outside investors in start-up or very early-stage biomedical companies. I called the business MedVenture Associates, which sounded as if there were many of us, when in fact I was the sole general partner.

I was painfully aware that, in addition to the drawback of being female, in going it alone I had yet another liability to overcome in order to be accepted in the venture capital community, and that was my recent therapy for cancer. I was only two years past the treatment, and people are very aware that the potential for recurrence is very real for some years after therapy. I had to acknowledge the issue for diligence purposes, and I knew it would deter some potential clients: even so, I felt the bigger drawback was certainly being female, and more than that, attempting to raise investment capital without oversight of senior male partners. Venture capital investing was then, and to some extent is still today, a closed shop. There are no rules relating to how venture partnerships should behave, but at that time the partners of these funds were almost overwhelmingly male. They moved in a world where deals were discussed over long lunches in such San Francisco clubs as the Bohemian Club or the Pacific Union Club, whose membership was confined to men. Still, there was nothing to be lost by trying to gain admittance to that rarefied world.

Owing to the emergence of biotechnology and the rapid advances in biomedical technology in the 1980s, investor interest in those sectors of the life sciences industry at that time was enormous. Indeed, it was similar to the social media investing frenzy that has taken place in the early years of the twenty-first century. I was one of the few young professionals with deep knowledge of what the early work in life sciences meant for the future of health care and disease management, and I had as well a good understanding of what was happening in medical technology and diagnostics.

Yet raising a small venture fund was not going to be simple. All I really had to work with to locate investor prospects at the beginning of my fundraising process was a list of my former clients from my days at Hambrecht & Quist. Most of these people were professionals at large financial institutions, but some of them were wealthy individuals and contacts at family money management offices. There were a few corporations on the list as well. My approach was not sophisticated. I arranged various forms of this list around the floor of my living room and began each day by calling some of the names on the list, a task I fondly nicknamed "dialing for dollars." I knew the odds were stacked against success, but I was optimistic and persistent. I couldn't become a venture capital investor without first having a venture capital fund to invest.

When I started the fundraising exercise, I had no administrative help, and there were few practical tools at my disposal to help with the task at hand. In the 1980s, our tools of communication were the telephone, the US Post Office, and Federal Express. There was no Internet, so there was no social media, and there was no email, no Skype, and no video conferencing. There were no cellphones, of course, so no text-messaging, either. Faxes were considered the best mode of rapid transmission for documents, but we were barely beyond the years when faxes had to be printed out on long rolls of paper. All personal computers had limited benefits in those days, having limited memory and being cumbersome to use. Microsoft Word applications were still in their infancy; Word for Windows had only just become available for PC, but it was not a stable program and the system was likely to crash. In fact, use of personal computers was just emerging from an installed base mainly confined to computer geeks, although MS-DOS enabled limited office applications. In 1984, I had bought a Macintosh computer to help with report writing, but it had sat in its box unopened for a long time, until finally, I sold it, because it seemed like it would be too complicated to learn how to operate. So, with none of today's modern office tools available to help me to prepare the investment prospectus, I had to resort to using an IBM Selectric typewriter to write the document, even though I couldn't touch-type. The prospectuses were printed for me by a local print shop.

Each morning, I would sit on the living-room floor with a mug of coffee, and my cat for company, shuffling papers before starting the day's allotment of that seemingly endless series of telephone calls. Occasionally, sensing potential investment interest, I would sprint upstairs to my small study and create a letter, which I typed up on the same IBM Selectric that I had used to write the investment prospectus for the fund, and which I would send out as a cover letter for a copy of the investment prospectus, of which I had printed far more copies than I ever needed; those extras lay in boxes that were strewn about the study. Day after day, I sat on the living-room floor, surrounded by paper, phoning and phoning, trying to get past secretaries and assistants in order to make my pitch. When I sensed real interest, I would try to arrange a meeting, and if I was successful on that score, I would jump on a plane to head to wherever the potential investor might be located in order to make my pitch in person. In this way, the summer of 1985 passed into autumn. Investment commitments were not flowing in, but I persevered.

Despite the slow progress of fundraising, good things were happening in my personal life. The best and happiest outcome from my short tenure at L. F. Rothschild had been that I met my future husband, Ruediger (Ruedi) Naumann-Etienne, who was a partner in a turnaround team that Hambrecht & Quist had hastily assembled to save Diasonics—the same Diasonics that had been a pioneer in those early years of growth in the ultrasound diagnostic business, and the same Diasonics for which I had consulted and in which I had invested. Diasonics had ultimately gone public in 1983 at a $1 billion valuation, which was an astronomical valuation in those days, but by the following year, owing to gross mismanagement, the company was nearly bankrupt. Although the initial public offering had been one of the largest of the early 1980s, Al Waxman and his team had become caught up in the same hubris as L. F. Rothschild. In the search for ever-increasing growth, they had cut corners and as a result, nearly bankrupted the company. Lawsuits came pouring in. Even I was deposed by counsel.

"We note that you sold half of your Diasonics stock," said one of the lawyers, disapprovingly.

"Well," I answered from the depths of my inexperience, "Probably if I had known then what I know now, I would have sold all of it."

Fortunately, all the lawyers in the room laughed.

One thing that drew Ruedi and me ineluctably together was a discovery of a mutual love of and regard for books and writers. Ruedi, being German, knew Mitteleuropean literature and poetry in the same way that I knew the works of English writers, through constant reading and insatiable curiosity. Like me, Ruedi would read one work that would lead him to another, and another, and so on. When I told him about the Connolly list and my intention to collect prime examples of all the works on it, he was intrigued. Our friend Elisabeth Siekhaus, a professor of German literature at Mills College, the oldest women's college on the West Coast, prepared a list of Mitteleuropaeische works for him as a companion, of sorts, to the Connolly list. Her list of thirty writers who could be considered the most important Modernists of Central European countries in the early twentieth century—such as Georg Trakl, Rainer Maria Rilke, Franz Kafka, and Thomas Mann— was intriguing, but they were outside my prospective field. Ruedi put the list away until a number of years later, when he, too, began collecting, but his collecting interests remained confined to Central European literature and fine print, which fortunately never coincided with my own interests. I like to think that my collecting passion started Ruedi on the road to his own collection, but that's debatable. However, since Ruedi's collecting interests stayed focused on works of different Central European writers, it was just as well that Connolly's list had concentrated only on English, French, and American works of literary Modernism.

Like me, Ruedi had come to the United States from abroad—in his case, initially from Berlin, to study at Georgia Tech on a Fulbright Scholarship. He later obtained a PhD in international finance from the University of Michigan. I was enormously impressed by his erudition. Ruedi knew about things I was only beginning to learn about—the world of opera, for example. On one of our first dates, we went to the movie *Amadeus*, a fictionalized story about the supposed rivalry between Mozart and the composer Salieri. Ruedi was familiar with every Mozart aria and opera referenced in the film. The friends I usually hung out with didn't know such things.

Ruedi had what I considered to be a very romantic and glamorous background. Whereas I was a New Zealander descended from British Colonial stock, Ruedi's family had occupied high positions in Leipzig in Germany before World War II, and the family's history there traced back for generations. His parents had escaped the city just before the Russians took control in July 1945, thanks to a timely warning his mother received from a relative, who happened to be the Swedish consul in Leipzig at the time. Ruedi's two older brothers were four years old and six months old when the family walked out of Leipzig to the west, and other than a bicycle, his parents had no means of transportation. The family ended up in a refugee camp in the district of Oedelsheim, near Hanover. They were not the only ones: several million Germans from the eastern part of Germany headed west after the war, creating a refugee crisis in the impoverished western part of the country. It was an untenable situation for a small family, trapped between resentful landowners in the west and the floods of refugees pouring in from the east. The Marshall Plan had not yet been created, and Germany's future looked grim.

Ruedi's mother had a goat, which she kept to provide milk for the children, and this she grazed at the grass verges of the roads, which angered the local farmers and landowners, who were themselves struggling to make ends meet. Stones were even thrown at the little family.

There seemed to be no future in Germany, and now they had a third son, Ruediger, who was born in the refugee camp, followed by the birth of a daughter, Sabine, a year later. By then, with four children to feed, it seemed that living in Germany had become impossible, so Ruedi's parents decided to emigrate to Argentina, where a branch of the family had been established many years previously. So Ruedi grew up in Argentina, but returned to Berlin to study, and that led in time to the Fulbright Scholarship, which took him to the United States. I thought Ruedi's background far more interesting than my own, but there was a similarity in our stories that connected us. We were both immigrants who had come to America to seek our fortunes. Sometimes, we would even hold silly contests between ourselves to decide which of us had been most impoverished upon our arrival in the United States.

Ruedi and I married in that autumn of 1985, in the middle of my fundraising quest. Fortunately, the fund was showing signs of coming together by late autumn; indeed, by February of the following year, MedVenture Associates was formally in business. I had reached my goal to raise an investment fund of $12 million, which was respectable for the times. All was right with the world again: the fund provided money to invest in emerging health-care technologies on behalf of my investors, and it also gave me a livelihood, so I could safely begin the task of collecting books once more. What I had realized over time was that serious collecting required not only focus, love of the collectible items, and sufficient available funds, but also enough stability in one's life to make it an integral part of one's routine. Real collecting is not for dilettantes. It is a demanding pursuit, but now that I had personal and professional stability, assembling a real collection could commence in earnest. I was ready to address the problem of how best to locate and acquire prime examples of the many titles on the Connolly list that I did not yet own. I was determined to do two things—to make a success of my venture capital work, and to complete my self-assigned task of assembling a representative collection of the Modern Movement books.

At first, I was so anxious to get started that I didn't concentrate on the condition of the books as much as I should have; nor had I learned to have the patience to wait until a great copy of a work came my way. Prime association copies of major books, where an author signs or dedicates a work to another author, were beyond my budget. But my early collecting of such works was also hindered initially by my natural caution against spending what seemed like—to me, at any rate—vast sums of money on books. How much could I—should I—spend? In venture capital investing, every decision is, to some extent, a roll of the dice, but those decisions are also based on financial analysis and the potential for investment return. Buying books and manuscripts was different because I wasn't looking for profit. On the contrary, I had chosen to build this collection simply because it was the ultimate expression of my passion for books and for the written word.

Although I bought a number of books that were on the Connolly list in that first year, because of my concern about overspending none of them were significant copies, with one exception: D. H. Lawrence's *Lady Chatterley's Lover*, which, in its original box and in fine condition, cost $1,800. None of my other acquisitions that year cost anywhere close to four figures. Nevertheless, by the end of the year I had added six titles to those which I already owned. These were:

Dylan Thomas	*Twenty-Five Poems*
George Orwell	*Nineteen Eighty-Four*
W. B. Yeats	*The Winding Stair*
Stephen Spender	*Ruins and Visions*
James Joyce	*Finnegans Wake*
D. H. Lawrence	*Lady Chatterley's Lover*

Despite the relatively slow start, I found immense satisfaction in the task set by my collecting commitment. The time spent with book dealers and at book fairs was always rewarding, a respite from my professional life. I found that although building a good book collection and engaging in venture capital investing had some things in common—the need to focus, to have funds available for investment, to be ready to invest at all—it was there that the comparison stopped. The world of finance, and its subset, venture capital, is ruthless, with success depending on having an edge. The world of book collecting is more refined, and it proceeds slowly, even ruminatively, among a group of people—whether collectors or dealers—who value the merit of the written word above all.

Venture Capital Investing

When I started out in venture capital, my edge was the fact that I had broad knowledge of the health-care field—particularly biotechnology, medical device technology, and health-care services—the sort of knowledge that professionals in Silicon Valley and elsewhere were only slowly starting to realize they had to acquire. Thanks to all the years I'd spent analyzing health-care companies, markets, and technology in the United States, and being steeped in the trends and emerging technologies of the medical sciences, I also had an enviable list of contacts.

Venture capital investing is a challenging but rewarding profession, both intellectually and financially. Listening to a pitch from an entrepreneur, and making estimates of both the value of the technology and the caliber of the entrepreneur, are visceral skills—that is, partly intuitive—although some investors make investment decisions only from calculations they can make on the strength of answers to stock lists of questions, which are then laid out in spreadsheets of diligence items, where the answers can be checked off and filled in one by one. As I began what ultimately turned out to be my thirty-year-long career in the business, I soon found that to me, the key diligence question to ask and to answer was a simple one, which I had learned back in my early days with British Oxygen, during a visit to Professor Peter Wells, head of medical physics at the Bristol General Hospital. He was an early pioneer in the world of ultrasound technology and was a learned, humane, and very sensible man, so I asked his opinion on what he thought made a good investment proposal in the health-care field.

He took this question very seriously and pondered the matter carefully before answering. "Well," he mused, "I suspect that anything that adds to the improvement in the quality of human health care should ultimately provide a good investment opportunity." It was as good a judgment yardstick as any, and as it turned out, it served me well for the thirty years of my venture capital career.

I like to think that the investments of my first fund made a difference in health-care management and the treatment of disease, although when I proudly opened the first office of MedVenture Associates on Pier 33 in San Francisco in the spring of 1986, I had no idea that this business would occupy me for the rest of my career. The office was unfortunately situated above an Australian barbeque restaurant, but otherwise it was an ideal location, at least I thought so. In the bay beyond the big windows, the ships glided silently by. In those days, there was more navy shipping, rather than the big cruise ships that are now so ubiquitous; occasionally, I would look up and see the menacing turret of a nuclear submarine coming to port. But always the ferries churned busily to and fro from Marin County on the opposite shore and the birds swooped across and above the waves. Occasionally, a seal would alight on the pier and recline on a bollard or engage in an afternoon's fishing. The office was cheerful in all sorts of weather, its high windows framing the dramatic view.

The first years of my new career in venture capital were little short of idyllic. Despite the chauvinism of the business as a whole, I found a small circle of like-minded young colleagues, and we worked hard to make a name for ourselves. My fund invested in technologies across all the many sectors of the health-care industry. It made investments in companies creating products in such diverse areas as biotechnology, implantable defibrillation, ultrasound imaging, home health care, and percutaneously managed therapies for treating arterial and vascular diseases. It was a period when miniaturization of electronics combined with the development of new materials to enable the creation of many exciting new diagnostic and therapeutic tools.

I was not by nature or background a likely candidate for the venture capital business. In those days, a typical venture capital investor would be an MBA graduate from an Ivy League school, who was most likely to be a privileged white male. In addition, and by and large, venture professionals are extremely competitive and dry individuals who are interested above all in making money. I wasn't as interested in the financial rewards as I was competitive. I was determined to show that I could succeed in this chauvinistic—sometimes even misogynistic—world. The venture world has changed, but not by a whole lot, since those early days. There were—and are—no rules except those born of the desire to fish directly in that river of money. The way venture funds were set up inspired a spirit of aspirational greed, and the business became ever more competitive in my investing years.

Institutional investors are typically the source of money for a fund, which means that each and every person in the community who draws money from a pension is, without knowing it, somehow part of the chain of money that leads to a direct venture capital investment. The professionals of a fund receive not only a management fee, typically a percentage of committed funds, but also up to 50 percent of fund profits, depending on how successful they have been in past funds. Whereas successful investing—in other words, strong investment returns—is key to the formula dictating the percentage of profits a fund can command for the fund principals, management fees for many years were set at a percentage—usually 2 to 3 percent—of committed capital. I believe that the management fee formula contributed significantly to the later epidemic of inflation in the size of venture funds, causing the sums invested in venture-capital-backed companies to increase exponentially over the years, with more and more capital entering the business. Larger funds meant larger management fees, and over time this placed control of the investment business in the hands of several giant funds at the expense of small seed capital funds—such as the MedVenture Associates group. However, all of that was in the future.

In hindsight, I can see that the late 1980s and early 1990s were a golden age for seed capital investing in medical device technology and life sciences, so once again, I was in the right place at the right time. But I know that the largest personal rewards I received from my venture investing career were not financial, but psychological. What was most satisfying was seeing the products made by MedVenture Associates' successful portfolio companies advance patient care and management in small and sometimes even large ways. For instance, the familiar blue butterfly on the box of Abbott's Freestyle blood glucose monitoring kit always catches my eye whenever I stand in line at my local pharmacy, because I know that MedVenture Associates was the first venture capital investor in the company TheraSense, Inc., which developed it. TheraSense was later sold to Abbott Laboratories for over $1 billion, following a successful period as a stand-alone public company.

Within the broad field of health care, MedVenture's investments were diverse. We created companies that improved patient care in a variety of fields, including diabetes management, cardiovascular disease therapy, medical imaging, neurology, and treatment of spinal disorders. Just as with Freestyle's blue butterfly logo, whenever I see a hospital or clinic using a product that came from an investment made by MedVenture Associates, I look back and think that it was all worthwhile. Professor Peter Wells's counsel all those years ago did not always turn out to be prophetic, but there were enough successes that I owe his memory a debt of gratitude.

Yet the business was still very difficult for a woman in those days. We had to battle for every deal that came along, and I know that among some of my male colleagues, I developed a reputation for being "difficult" and "tough" to deal with. But they were not walking in my shoes. In the beginning, MedVenture Associates was appreciated as a source of diligence knowledge, but not taken seriously as a true investment partner. It seemed that women could supply market knowledge, but did not have the gravitas to be investment peers and serve on boards of directors alongside male colleagues. Although this attitude softened as time went on, and particularly, as MedVenture Associates achieved investment success, in the beginning I found that I had to struggle to achieve peer recognition. Several times I introduced investments to colleagues in which I later had to fight to be an investor myself.

The founding of a biotechnology company that became one of the seed capital investments made by MedVenture Associates in 1988 was a good example of the investing environment in those days, although there are many others that could serve equally well to illustrate the problems. The company started out as merely a biotechnology concept dreamed up by the oncologist who saw me through that first bout of breast cancer. He was an expert in the field of active carbohydrates, and he suspected that altering the sugar molecules that typically sit at the terminal branches of long chains of DNA could potentially lead to pharmaceutical innovations, just as modifying the chains of amino acids that make up DNA structure was leading to the development of new biopharmaceutical compounds. He and I had many conversations about active carbohydrates, particularly during my checkups with him, which usually focused more on that discussion than on the status of my health. Intrigued, I decided to introduce the concept to a senior investor, one of the founding partners in a significant Silicon Valley venture fund that also had a small investment in MedVenture Associates. This man has since sadly died, but in his time he was a powerful figure in Silicon Valley, and having his support would mean that we could easily put together a deal to fund this nascent venture. Because of the investment into MedVenture Associates, I believed that, despite his high standing in Silicon Valley, he and I were colleagues of a sort.

My relationship with that firm made what happened next particularly hard to understand.

I convened a meeting in my office on the pier late one afternoon to introduce my oncologist, who by now had become a personal friend, and his investment thesis to several investors, including my putative colleague. I remember that meeting well, even down to how, as we sat at a tiny round conference table in my offices, the light reflecting from the water of the San Francisco Bay streamed through the windows as the sun set over the Golden Gate Bridge, which was clearly visible from the large windows. It was summer, and for once I felt I was being taken seriously, so I was happy; I thought we were on the brink of creating something important. My colleague was a man of few words, and those words were often spoken in such a soft voice that one had to strain to hear them. But it was clear that he was interested; before we closed our meeting, we all agreed that this new company should be funded.

Following the meeting, I heard nothing for a week or two, but soon after that I discovered that much had been happening. In fact, my colleague had immediately taken ownership of the investment concept: he had agreed to fund it with a partner in another leading Silicon Valley firm, which also had a long and successful track record in funding successful emerging life sciences companies. None of these professionals had "remembered" to let me know—I had to find out on my own that an investment was coming together. There are no friendships in the venture investing world, and certainly, women were not taken seriously at that time, but this was not even fair play. Of course, I protested loudly, being "difficult," until finally MedVenture was allocated a share of the investment. To this day, I believe that the other investors in that company, if they ever think about it, have no idea that this particular company was initially created by MedVenture Associates. Some years later, it also became a public company, from which MedVenture Associates received a good investment return, but it was not as successful an investment as many in my first portfolio.

There are so many examples that I could cite, but this is a story about books, and the point of that account is merely to illustrate why my alternative life in the world of books was so important to my personal universe. Fortunately, nobody I knew in Silicon Valley had any interest in rare books and manuscripts; most of them read little beyond technical and financial periodicals and newspapers. In any case, book collecting is a solitary pastime. It does not have the glamour or the sophistication of the big art world; we collectors and bibliophiles go about our business hidden away like moles. Our closest associations are with our dealers. There is an impediment to communication in the book world in that there are so many subsets of book collecting that the act of collecting per se does not automatically lead to rapport with others or the meeting of minds. Just as I might not be particularly interested in hearing a lecture on the collecting of incunabula, so other collectors might have little interest in literary Modernism. I never encountered another Connolly collector like myself during all my years of chasing down those one hundred titles, although I heard of various Connolly collections that had been assembled and dispersed over time.

Still, the refuge that the world of books and book collecting provided could not compensate for the stress of the daily struggle to remain competitive as a venture capital investor, and I began to question whether I was truly cut out to be in the field. Fortunately, this period of self-doubt occurred around the time I met a collector who influenced me deeply. Indeed, she made such an indelible impression on me that, even today, I remain in awe of her achievements, both in business and in the world of book collecting. Along with her husband, Sandy Lerner had founded Cisco Systems, arguably one of the top technology businesses in the world today. With her flair, her insouciance, and her take-no-prisoners confidence, Sandy filled me with admiration. It is to her that I owe my persistence. Despite having to push each day against so many closed doors, I followed her example and never gave in or gave up along the way.

John Crichton of Brick Row Bookshop introduced me to Sandy so many years ago that I can't remember exactly when it was; he was helping her to build a collection of books written by eighteenth-century women writers in original editions. Sandy had enormous wealth at her disposal as a result of selling her Cisco holdings when the company went public. She sold everything on the IPO, which was unusual, but it was said that the decision largely resulted from a disagreement with her key investors that had resulted in her leaving the company. It was another example of how venture capital was not friendly to women entrepreneurs and managers back then.

One day in the late 1990s, when the first dot-com bubble was roaring ahead, I had lunch with Sandy at the Village Pub in Woodside, a prime hangout for financial professionals.

"You know," said Sandy conversationally, as we munched on our salads, "if I had held onto my Cisco holdings, they'd be worth $4 billion in today's market."

"Sandy," I replied, "that's a problem that I simply cannot identify with."

Sandy was probably the most successful female entrepreneur of her generation. By that time, she had started another business, an online cosmetics company called Urban Decay, which is now owned by the cosmetics giant L'Oréal. The lipsticks and creams had names and colors like "Acid Rain" and "Sludge." The genius of Urban Decay was not only its product appeal—because of the goth craze among young people at that time—but also Sandy's canny marketing instinct, which led her to take the sales side of the business online in those early years of Internet commerce.

When we got together for these rare lunches, Sandy and I had fun playing with words—words that defined how differently professional men and women were regarded at that time. For instance, where a man might be described as "forceful," a woman would usually be dismissed as "pushy." Describing a man as "assertive" did not carry the negative connotation that it immediately gave to a female professional. I remember many curious heads turning in our direction as we laughed over our wordplay game. We once had a long list of these adjectives, but I forget most of them now.

That day, Sandy had also caused a small sensation among the dusty financiers in the Village Pub, entering dressed in leather from head to toe, with flowing, hennaed hair and gothic Urban Decay make-up. How I admired her: she had no fear of anyone and went her own way regardless of what people would think. I needed to do just that. Sandy set the bar for women entrepreneurs such as myself. Today, her book collection is housed at Chawton Manor, in Hampshire in England, the former home of Jane Austen's brother Edward. Sandy in fact bought the historic home and turned it into the headquarters of a foundation created to support the study of the role of women in eighteenth-century literature. To my regret, I have lost touch with her, although I do know that she moved to a farm in Virginia where she raises horses, chickens, and all manner of organic products. I have always remembered that she provided inspiration for me at a time when that was important.

Books, Book Dealers, and Literary Associations

Despite my misgivings about the difficulty of assembling a meaningful collection of Modern Movement titles, once I had committed to this direction I plunged in, beginning the task of building on those few volumes I already possessed. My investing career and the acquisition of the Connolly titles moved ahead in parallel over the ensuing years. Although initially I concentrated on the names I knew, without considering where the search would take me, it soon became clear that this was not going to be a collection built by serendipity and browsing bookshops. The first Connolly titles I acquired had all come from dealers—not only Ralph Sipper, but also David Mayou in London, Tom Goldwasser in Berkeley, and Robert Link in Oakland—but they were not prime examples, and now I was becoming more ambitious. Paging covetously through the catalog of the Ransom Center exhibition, I saw that, if I wanted to assemble a meaningful collection of Connolly Modern Movement titles, I would have to invest in it more heavily. It wouldn't be enough just to have shabby copies of first editions. And so I began to shed my earlier caution in search of better books.

The fine examples, association copies, and signed first editions of the works I now sought took me to a higher level of collecting, much to the dealers' delight. I continued to add to my burgeoning collection of Ariel poems, but even these, it seemed, didn't turn up by chance anymore. Even with that part of the collection, I was relying more heavily on rare book dealers to find perfect copies of the ones I didn't yet possess. It took another significant purchase for me finally to overcome my reluctance to spend on the collection and invest in it in a meaningful way.

Some of the items on the Connolly list had extra personal significance for me, so I was anxious to acquire the best examples of them that I could find and afford. One book that was high on my "want" list was a good copy of Robert Graves's *Good-Bye to All That*, one of my favorite books. I owned a good copy in a nice dust jacket, which I had bought from David Mayou in London, but it was not a significant copy of the book. David, working from his home, made his living by stealth acquisitions and subsequent sales of overlooked items. The book was in good condition, but I felt no personal connection to it.

It was Ralph Sipper who came up with the definitive copy of *Good-Bye to All That* for my collection. I still remember acquiring the book, because it was a large purchase for me at the time, certainly the highest price I had yet paid for a book. I had gone to Santa Barbara mainly to look through the shelves of Maurice Neville's library, since rumor had it that he was on the verge of selling up at auction and retiring from the book trade. Of course, no visit to Santa Barbara could be complete without spending some time with Joseph the Provider.

"Do you have any new Connolly titles for me to look at?" I asked Ralph.

"Well, yes, I have something that just came to me," he said. "It's a rather special item, so it's very expensive."

He handed me an object in a folding case; I opened the case expectantly. It was a proof copy—Robert Graves's proof copy—of *Good-Bye to All That*. The book contained penciled corrections and additions written in Graves's own hand. It was the definitive copy of the work that still remained in private hands, as far as I could tell. The price of the book was an astronomical $12,500, but those pages—I couldn't stop looking at them. They were full of penciled comments and small text changes. It was a pivotal copy of the work: the final proof, corrected by Graves, before the book went off to be printed. The pages were well thumbed, indicating a book that had been read and reread as it was corrected. I went away to sleep on it. I thought about that book the whole night and the next day; having made up my mind, I returned and bought it. Although it was a colossal price, I determined to pay it because the book related so well to my first passion, World War I poetry. I never regretted the purchase for one instant in the following years, and it encouraged me to increase my level of collecting: I wanted to find truly excellent examples of the works on Connolly's list.

Yet I was still so ignorant! My decision to collect the Modern Movement titles had been made without really considering how broadly Connolly had cast his selection, and I certainly had no inkling that, later on, I would ultimately find his list of titles limiting. All of that was in front of me. I really knew very little about literary Modernism; in fact, I had based my whole decision to collect rare examples of the one hundred books on the fact that Connolly's list included works that appealed to me—authors such as Evelyn Waugh and George Orwell, poets such as T. S. Eliot, and, of course, in America, the two key names on the list, F. Scott Fitzgerald and Ernest Hemingway. Fortunately, the same stubbornness that kept me going in the venture capital world also kept me committed to the project. I wanted to assemble a meaningful collection of the works on the list, and once I had collected more than a few titles, I knew that was what I should be doing. It felt just right.

As my small collection grew, I tried to learn what I could about the books on the list. I read, I listened, I attended book fairs, and I read hundreds of catalogs that arrived in the mail. Those catalogs were tributes to a dealer's knowledge of his or her subject, but they also made a statement about the dealer's prosperity or lack thereof. Some of the catalogs were on glossy paper and contained many carefully photographed pictures; others were merely typed lists on stapled-together sheets of paper. Later, as I found myself on the mailing lists of some of the French and Swiss dealers, I would periodically receive their heavy catalogs printed on expensive paper and bound between hard covers.

I also started reading about Cyril Connolly the man. I think the best and most entertaining of the descriptions of Connolly are to be found in the memoirs of his second wife, the diarist and socialite Barbara Skelton. Reading her accounts of Connolly's personal life with interest and amusement, I decided his chief attraction must have been that he was wonderful company, because physically he was not a handsome man. He was chubby and round faced, with a bad complexion. There had to be a seductive side to his character that made him so wonderfully interesting, I decided, because otherwise it was difficult to understand how someone so congenitally unfaithful, so lazy and unkempt, and so physically unattractive could have been so successful with women. Obviously, he had extraordinary charisma.

I was now collecting voraciously, mostly out of interest, but also because it became important to me to create a solid core of material to justify the collection. I acquired some books simply because they were on the list; these otherwise had no real meaning for me, but I bought them dutifully and placed them on the shelf without ever looking at them again. I found much of the work of Henry James—and, dare I say it, Virginia Woolf—stuffy, and the poetry of Wallace Stevens I deemed impenetrable. This is my failing, not theirs. Although I recognized that

William Carlos Williams's *Paterson* was a masterpiece, I wasn't interested in studying it. I was strongly influenced by the poetry of his fellow Americans Ezra Pound and T. S. Eliot, who had both worked in England, and against their poetry Williams's seemed to be a purely American rebuttal. Still, Williams's works were part of the list, so I had to acquire them.

On the other hand, I treasured books I found that had personal meaning for me, and especially those with inscriptions that led to association with other authors or notable people. These volumes I took out from their cases or folders time and again to look with reverence at them or the signatures. Later, as my collecting proceeded, there were other related documents—typically letters, photographs, or contemporaneous drawings.

There was no shortage of dealers in Modern English and American literature lining up to help me on my journey with the Connolly collection. Ralph Sipper, Robert Link, and Tom Goldwasser in the United States, and in England, the dealers Rick Gekoski, David Mayou, and Paul Rassam, in particular turned up more interesting items than most, but of course, all of them were very familiar with the Connolly list and they knew where to look for its key titles. These were still the days before computers became ubiquitous, and the Internet, which later made such searches easier, remained chiefly a tool for researchers. The commercial World Wide Web had not yet come into being. If I were to start the same search today, I would probably be able to assemble prime examples by myself over time, but it wouldn't be as much fun. I enjoyed my London lunches with Paul Rassam, my visits to Rick Gekoski's North London treasure cave, and my hours with Tom Goldwasser, who was surely the most knowledgeable autodidact ever to become a rare book dealer. Visiting Ralph Sipper at Joseph the Provider or Maurice Neville at Casa Ramirez was always an excuse to spend a weekend in Santa Barbara. Tom Goldwasser was a friend of long standing from his days at Serendipity, but he became very influential in my search, as did Ralph Sipper and Rick Gekoski. Although Ralph eventually faded from my life, both Tom and Rick have remained friends. I quickly found myself on the mailing lists of so many book dealers that I lost count, but I always read every catalog that came my way. I became an expert in the rapid scanning of catalogs for items that related to my collection, and even read through catalogs of dealers presenting unrelated items, because sometimes a dealer in one specialty happened to have something of interest to another.

Some books came up quite by chance. For instance, Paul Rassam managed to find interesting key works, and for many years we would lunch together every time I was in London—he always had something of interest to show me. Although rare books seldom are found in old bookshops, Paul had once been lucky: in a West Country bookshop, he found a first American edition of Joseph Conrad's *Youth*, with an inscription to Hereford Hope; he produced this volume triumphantly at one of these lunches. Hereford and Conrad Hope were the sons of Joseph Conrad's friend G. F. W. Hope, who had served as the model for the captain in *Heart of Darkness*. G. F. W. Hope's yacht, the *Nellie*, was a model for the yawl *Nellie* referenced at the beginning of the book, so it was a terrific association. That sort of serendipitous find in a bookshop is what every collector or dealer dreams of, but it seldom happens in real life. Like most book dealers, Paul had his private sources, but dealers guard those sources jealously, so I never had access to any sale by a private owner myself.

It was a good thing I scrutinized every catalog that came my way, because sometimes a key work would be hidden in an otherwise unrelated catalog. For instance, the Oregon-based dealer Phillip Pirages produced beautiful catalogs of fine print, which I admired even though I had little interest in the works he sold. I met Phillip at a book fair in Marin County when he was just starting out, and he put me on his mailing list. Later, by chance, he was offered a perfect copy in its original wrapping of D. H. Lawrence's *succès de scandale*, *Lady Chatterley's Lover*, in the 1928 signed limited edition printed in Florence. The rarity of the item and the excellence of its condition had an interesting history that directly resulted from the scandal relating to the book's publication. Because it had been deemed obscene, and D. H. Lawrence was castigated as a writer of perverted fiction and censored, a number of the books had been seized upon entry to the United States and put into storage. Ultimately, they were forgotten, so that when they finally were rediscovered and reemerged, they were in a condition almost as perfect as the day they had been printed. I bought this book, of course. It was the only purchase I made in 1986 that exceeded $1,000.

Some of the dealers I worked with became real friends over time. In fact, book dealers and collectors have a symbiotic relationship; they are drawn together by a strange mutual passion for the written word, first editions, and manuscripts in a way that really doesn't translate into general conversation or small talk, or even into conversation with other collectors. The only time collectors can really have a good conversation about their collecting obsessions is with their rare book dealers, because most collecting activities are not congruent. I wouldn't want to spend an evening hearing about collecting incunabula, for instance. In any case, even if there had been another Connolly collector around in my time, it would have been difficult to be collegial, since we would have been competing. And I would not have been introduced. Just as dealers guard the sources of material on offer, they are usually reluctant to divulge client lists, unless the collecting spheres are different. There were collectors around who specialized in the work of perhaps one or more of the key writers of the Modernist period, but even they were off-limits for introductions as far as the dealers and auctioneers were concerned. For instance, I knew about, but never met, the collector Stanley Seeger, who seemed to have an unlimited budget. He bought almost everything written by and about Joseph Conrad that came to the market over a period of many years. In that sense, I was a competitor, but I did not have unlimited funds as he did, so I could only hope I would be offered the Connolly titles *The Secret Agent* and *Youth* despite his presence in the market. Many years later, after Seeger's death, his Conrad collection was sold in two successive sales, held in 2013 and 2014 at Sotheby's. I bought heavily in both of these sales, and was glad that I could purchase free of the confines of the Connolly list by then, because I acquired some important letters, manuscripts, and inscribed books.

Book dealers are in an unusual position with regard to their clients. On the one hand, book dealers like engaging in literary conversations with clients—how else to display their knowledge and insight?—but the harsh reality is that clients are their source of income. As a result, one needs to be confident about the relationship with a dealer, and feel certain that the price of a purchase is fair. Because the dealer is certainly offering the item to more than one prospective buyer, there has to be a sense of trust between dealer and client, a certainty that one is not being used as a tool to leverage the price of a transaction, as has happened to me in the past. When a dealer tells you an item is rare— that in all of their years of book dealing, they "have never come across an item quite like it"—you have to be able to believe they mean what they say, and further, that the price quoted is commensurate with the rarity and quality of the item. In those early years of collecting, when my knowledge of rare books was quite insubstantial, I needed to be able rely on the expertise of dealers. More importantly, I had to be able to trust that what they told me was true. It's a commercial transaction, but there has to be integrity on the part of the dealer.

It can take time for a relationship to evolve, to move from the strictly transactional to a more personal level. When I met Rick Gekoski, for example, in the early years of my Connolly list search, he ran his business from his home in North London. Peter Selley of Sotheby's, who has now been a friend of mine for years, was at that time working for him. Rick was then and is now larger than life, both physically and intellectually. Initially, I found him intimidating, because I felt he thought of me as an amateur with little knowledge—assumptions that were, at that time, quite close to the truth. His prices were always very high, and he was not ashamed of that. He would feign astonishment if I declined a purchase, and because he spoke loudly and with authority in his mid-Atlantic accent, I felt uncomfortable discussing prices with him. It was "take it or leave it," and more often than not, I left the proposed purchase on the table. Nevertheless, as my records show, I was for many years a faithful customer, particularly because Rick's knowledge of the era of Modernism was unparalleled, as befits someone who has written, taught, and lectured in the field, and besides all that, has been a successful dealer of rare books for at least as long as I have been collecting. From Rick I bought works by Graham Greene, in particular. I envied the fact that he had visited Greene and acquired rights to sell his library, which he sold in lots and through auctions for many years. It would have been almost impossible for a single collector to buy directly from Graham Greene. The dealer always has the contact with the owner of the library or collection, or, except in very rare cases, with the author.

In general, I preferred the milder style of Peter Selley, and I tried to work with Peter whenever I visited Rick's establishment. Peter was every bit as knowledgeable as Rick, but somehow he didn't make me feel like as much of an amateur. Peter ultimately left Rick for the book department at Sotheby's in Bond Street, which may be part of the reason for my attachment to Sotheby's auctions over those of the other auction houses. I wonder if I would have been such a keen customer of Rick's if not for Peter's quiet authority. I bought a key work from Gekoski Rare Books in those first years—the corrected proofs of *The Modern Movement: One Hundred Key Books from England, France, and America, 1880–1950*. This set of proofs became one of the cornerstone pieces of my collection.

Tom Goldwasser was a friend of mine from my long-ago Berkeley days of the late 1970s. His quiet demeanor concealed a ferocious intelligence and an unrivaled knowledge of English, French, and American literature. I had met Tom at the beginning of my Berkeley days, because he worked at the famous West Coast bookshop Serendipity Books, which was owned and run by the eccentric Peter Howard. The shop was a mess—books piled high on the floor, stacked on ever-multiplying shelves, spilling out of cabinets. The back rooms were just as bad, and I think I remember that for some time, there was an antique car housed at the very back of the shop.

It was impossible to find anything at Serendipity, so you just rummaged around and hoped for the best. Fortunately, Tom knew his way around the items of interest, and most of the really collectible things were kept separately from those crowding the shelves in the general disarray that was the main store. Peter could not help himself—he bought indiscriminately—at estate sales, at auctions, from other dealers—and although catalogs periodically appeared from Serendipity, you had to see the premises to understand what a miracle it was for that catalog to have been prepared in the first place.

Tom was a friend of Barry Humphries and knew him well. Barry, an Australian comedian best known for his creation of the character known as Dame Edna, a sort of comedic pantomime dame, was and remains a passionate book collector, and he was one of Tom's clients. In 1989, Tom sold me Barry's copy of Evelyn Waugh's *Black Mischief*, which, while not a Connolly title, was one of twelve copies on handmade paper from a later privately published edition. The key point of interest in the book was a witty dedication to Nancy Mitford:

Waugh Emulation Prize
1932
Awarded to Miss Mitford
With the Founder's Fond Encouragement
"He for God Only; She for God in Him"

The quote from Milton probably referenced the fact that the Mitford style mimicked the more biting and witty satire of Waugh's, a fact of which Waugh was perfectly aware. On the strength of that flimsy connection, Tom introduced me to Barry, and we struck up an acquaintance of sorts. During one of Barry's visits to San Francisco in the late 1990s, I took him to Serendipity for a browse. The store was in its usual state of dismaying chaos, and as I picked my way along the aisles, dodging boxes and papers, I wondered whether there could be anything worthwhile to purchase among that astonishing clutter. And just as I thought that, suddenly, an amazing coincidence—I spied, at the top of a teetering pile of old books, a copy of one of Barry's earliest literary endeavors. It was beyond a surprising coincidence, because it was one of the Barry Mackenzie graphic novels published in Australia in 1974, in the days when Barry Mackenzie was making an early sensation in the pages of *Private Eye*, the British satirical journal founded in 1961. Barry Mackenzie was another character that Barry Humphries had created. In 1974, nobody outside a very limited circle had any idea of the existence of either *Private Eye* or Barry Mackenzie, and certainly, nobody in the United States would have been a collector of Barry Mackenzie memorabilia. Barry Humphries himself most likely hoped privately that any remaining copies of those books had long ago been pulped or shredded. Finding that graphic novel on that particular day of all days was completely unexpected, but this is why I believe that Peter Howard's cluttered and messy shop deserved its name—Serendipity.

When Peter died a few years ago, it took months for the book department at Bonham's, which had bought the rights to Serendipity's inventory, to sort through the mess. Bonham's concluded that there really was little of value left to sell on behalf of Peter's estate. Still, I bought many items from Serendipity in the period when Tom worked there. In the midst of the chaos, he worked diligently as an associate at the shop, but he also worked as an intermediary between consigner and collector, or auction house and collector, and in this way he could avoid having special items join the general uncataloged confusion that overwhelmed the bookshelves at the shop.

It was Tom who opened up to me the possibility that my Connolly collection could house more than one rare example of a key book. I already owned an extremely important first edition of Ford Madox Ford's masterpiece *The Good Soldier*, which I had purchased from Paul Rassam; it was an important copy because it had an extremely rare (though torn) copy of the dust jacket that accompanied its publication. In fact, I never did see or hear of another copy with a dust jacket in all the years that followed that purchase. After that, through Tom's association with the family of Julia Madox Loewe, Ford's daughter with the Australian artist and writer Stella Bowen, I was offered a copy of the 1927 second American edition of the book, together with the printer's dummy for the cover of that edition. Despite being only a second

American edition, this edition of the book contained a printed personal letter written to Stella as a dedication, and this dedication is the only known dedication of the book in any edition or any format. What made the copy of the book even more important was that it had also been personally inscribed by Ford, with a handwritten inscription in the book itself, which read "To my dear Stella / the Dedicator / Ford Madox Ford / 16th May, 1927." This was a very effusive dedication in light of the fact that the couple had a partial separation in 1927, followed by a permanent break in 1928. The book is not as valuable as the first edition of *The Good Soldier*, especially if the latter could ever be found again with its extremely rare dust jacket. Nevertheless, for me, that copy of the second American edition was a fascinating example of the book, since it shed light on Ford's turbulent personal life. To me, that inscription meant that he continued to love Stella, despite the interruption caused in their relationship by his constant series of affairs.

My collection of ephemera relating to authors I cherished also began with this association with the estate of Julia Madox Loewe. Through Tom Goldwasser, I later bought from the family a portrait in pastels of Ford Madox Hueffer, as the author was known as a child, wearing a little white collar over a tightly buttoned charcoal-colored jacket. The portrait has not been confirmed as the work of a major Pre-Raphaelite artist, although it could be the work of Ford Madox Brown. Most art dealers don't appear to think as highly of it as I do myself. I'm very fond of it, whoever painted it. The portrait is in Pre-Raphaelite style, and Ford Madox Ford is depicted with rosy cheeks and pale green, penetrating eyes. Although the portrait is literary ephemera, nobody who appreciates the work of Ford Madox Ford could look at the face of that child without seeing in it some of the genius of the grown man. I would have liked to meet these direct descendants of Ford Madox Ford in person, but Julia died in 1985, and by the time I bought the portrait in 1992, her son, Ford Madox Ford's grandson, was mortally ill. He died later that year. In any case, Tom zealously guarded his sources, so the possibility of any meeting was unlikely.

My copies of *The Good Soldier*, along with the portrait of the young Ford, opened up to me the possibility of collecting not only books but also items of ephemera related to the lives and works of authors who appeared on the Connolly list. By this time, in addition to reading about Cyril Connolly, I had also begun to assemble a small collection of biographies of some of the writers whose works I was collecting. Knowing more about the authors and their lives, as well as more about the life and career of Connolly himself, was a much better way to comprehend what the list of one hundred key books was all about and to improve the chances of making collecting choices that were better informed. Modernism was a concept I was beginning to understand, and moreover, I was beginning to comprehend that Modernism had sprung from a burst of creativity that had its genesis in France. Unfortunately, I had not yet begun to address the French titles on the list or to understand the selection of books on the list representing the branch of Modernism that was forged in the crucible of Paris in the late nineteenth and early twentieth centuries. The fact that there were a significant number of French titles on the list was a problem that I still wasn't sure how to address.

The French Modern Movement

DU CÔTÉ DE CHEZ SWANN

The first French poet with whom I developed a relationship was not included on the Connolly list at all. Paul Verlaine was one of the founders of the French symbolist movement, and his work had appealed to me since my schooldays, when I learned to read French poetry from a textbook titled *French Verse from Villon to Verlaine*. Of the works we studied, one poem that resonated with me through the years was Verlaine's "Chanson d'automne" ("Autumn Song").

Herschel School had not been designed to equip young ladies for a career. Although I've described the school in less than favorable terms, one redeeming feature was that it had a beautiful library, with oaken floors and a big bay window with a window seat of smooth wood. You couldn't see the school grounds or its buildings from the window, because the view was largely obscured by the leaves and branches of a giant oak tree, whose leaves tapped the mullions of the window panes when the Cape winds blew. This was my secret place. I hid away with a book in the window seat whenever I could, and during the three and a half years of my incarceration as a boarder at Herschel, I think I read steadily through most of the literature in the small library, which contained chiefly a random selection of books written in English by famous authors of the eighteenth and nineteenth centuries. I read with no fixed plan. Whatever appealed to me after browsing a few pages was the book of the moment, and if I liked an author, I'd go back for more. Names I remember from that time are Jane Austen, Charles Dickens, the Brontë sisters, Leo Tolstoy, Ivan Turgenev (which I didn't understand), Fyodor Dostoevsky, and Sholem Aleichem. Somehow, the library's collection did not have much of anything from the twentieth century. Perhaps donations had dried up a long time ago, or perhaps, since nobody ever seemed to be in the library, nobody had ever spent enough time there to notice that the collection was in urgent need of updating.

Owing largely to the lack of academic credentials among our teachers, any lessons at Herschel were dull, and I suffered particularly during our interminable French lessons. I learned little and received no pleasure from studying any of the poems in our syllabus. To make matters worse, our French teacher, Mrs. McCormick, was really not qualified to teach French to anyone, let alone lively girls of high school age. She was a former ballet dancer who had, once upon a time, been to Paris. Her spoken French was execrable. Even I could hear that her accent was terrible, but unfortunately, she was the only instructor the school could conjure up. Still today, I squirm if I am called upon to speak French; I know my spoken French is laughable and I still blame Mrs. McCormick. Fortunately, however, I retain sufficient knowledge of the language to read the ubiquitous French book-auction catalogs that come my way.

Yet, in those classes, when it came to the poetry of Verlaine, I sat up and paid attention. Mrs. McCormick herself could not ruin the music of Verlaine's famous poem "Chanson d'automne." Even at a young age, it seemed to me remarkable that a twenty-two-year-old poet could prefigure the desolation of old age in such a musical way:

> Les sanglots longs
> Des violons
>   De l'automne
> Blessent mon cœur
> D'une langueur
>   Monotone.
> Tout suffocant
> Et blême, quand
>   Sonne l'heure,
> Je me souviens
> Des jours anciens
>   Et je pleure;
> Et je m'en vais
> Au vent mauvais
>   Qui m'emporte
> Deçà, delà,
> Pareil à la
>   Feuille morte.

(The long sobs of the violins of autumn
Wound my heart with a singular languor.
Suffocating and pale, when the hour sounds
I remember days of old and I cry.
And I blow away on the strong wind
Which carries me hither and thither,
Just like a dead leaf.)
[My translation]

You don't even really have to know French to understand something about the poem. If you say the words slowly, those long, extenuated syllables immediately induce a sense of melancholy.

"Chanson d'automne" is a fine example of French symbolist poetry. We learned in class that the symbolists felt that a poem's meaning should be able to be extracted from the sounds of the words. Owing to the study of "Chanson d'automne," I became very early a fan of Verlaine and his work, and subsequently, of the school of French symbolist poetry. I could never understand why Connolly did not include Verlaine in his list of one hundred key books.

In 1896, Anatole France, once a friend of Verlaine's, wrote in the *Revue encyclopédique*:

> *C'est un poète comme il ne s'en rencontre pas un par siècle . . . Certes, il est fou. Mais prenez garde que ce pauvre insensé a créé un art nouveau et qu'il y a quelque chance qu'on dise un jour de lui ce qu'on dit aujourd'hui de François Villon, auquel il fait bien le comparer: C'était le meilleur poète de son temps.*

> He was a poet such as one meets only once a century . . . Certainly, he was mad. But take note that this poor fool created a new art and there is a chance that one will say of him one day what today one says of François Villon, to whom it is fair to compare him: He was the best poet of our time. [My translation]

This was a sincere acknowledgment from a man of letters who had fallen out with his former friend many years previously.

From the late nineteenth century onward, artistic thought and expression were being turned upside down in France. French Modernism encompassed all the arts, and the Modern Movement flourished, in Paris in particular, in the period that began at the end of the Franco-

Prussian War and continued up until the late 1920s. The movement benefited from a sort of cross-pollination of the arts, and café society was the place where visual, literary, and performing artists routinely met to socialize and exchange ideas. Pablo Picasso, Guillaume Apollinaire, and Amedeo Modigliani, among others, met routinely at Café de la Rotonde, and it was at the famous Café de Flore that the French symbolist writer Joris-Karl Huysmans, and later, Apollinaire, were regular customers. The Café de Flore can also claim to be the place where the Manifeste du Surréalisme had its gestation; Andre Bréton and Louis Aragon spent many hours there. Later, it became known as the informal headquarters of Simone de Beauvoir and Jean-Paul Sartre.

Since France was the birthplace of Modernism, a selection of key works by French Modernists was central to Connolly's list, and included such French authors as Stéphane Mallarmé and Arthur Rimbaud, the symbolist poets, as well as Apollinaire, who was perhaps the forerunner of surrealism; André Breton, the master of surrealism; and Albert Camus, who pioneered the philosophy of absurdism. The writings of the symbolists in the late nineteenth century were catalysts for the explosion of ideas in literary thought and expression that were to follow in the first half of the twentieth century. Arguably, the pivotal work of Modernism was the famous 1897 poem by Mallarmé titled *Un coup de dés jamais n'abolira le hasard* (*A Throw of the Dice Will Never Eliminate Chance*). I bought one of the fifteen proof copies of this poem for a considerable sum in 2016 at the final auction of the collection of one of the greatest French collectors of literature in modern times, Pierre Bergé. Although the final cost, including a buyer's commission, was close to six figures, I don't regret it. It anchors my collection of works of French Modernism.

I admired the level of creativity that poured from the pens of those poets and writers working in Paris in those fertile years. The French symbolists and surrealists focused on the sounds and flow of words to give meaning to a thought. Apollinaire's poetry, as collected in *Alcools* or *Calligrammes: Poèmes de la paix et de la guerre (1913–1916)* (Calligrams: Poems of Peace and War [1913–1916]), demonstrated a total break from the past, where rhyme and formal structural rules had dictated the outlines of a poem. A calligram can be described as "visual poetry," because the typographical images created by the placement of words on a page are integral to the meaning of the whole. Even earlier, the writings of Alfred Jarry and his seminal work of surrealism—the play *Ubu Roi* (Ubu the King)—influenced much of what came later, from surrealism to Dada. *Ubu Roi* was one of Connolly's earlier entries on the list. He must have enjoyed the work, because I own the draft of his translation of the play into English, which was, however, never completed and never performed in English.

Because I had begun to read so voraciously about the lives and works of the French Modernists, and what life was like in Paris at the time of the Modern Movement, I was developing opinions about some of Connolly's choices of French literature, even though I had not yet acquired any of the works that were on his list for my collection. Connolly's choice of Rimbaud over Verlaine for the list, for example, continued to be something of a mystery to me. Perhaps Connolly just preferred the vivid text of Rimbaud's poetry. However, if not for Verlaine, the collected poems of Rimbaud would never have come together in published form as the work known as *Illuminations*, which is, ironically enough, a Connolly title. Seeing to the publication of the forty-two poems of Rimbaud that are collected under that title was one of the last acts of Verlaine's life. Verlaine died, but Rimbaud lived on, having given up poetry in favor of business: he lived and worked in North Africa before dying himself of an osteosarcoma of the knee at the age of thirty-seven.

What was it, I wondered, that inspired Verlaine to leave his wife for Rimbaud, and to indulge thereafter in frankly self-destructive behavior, fueled by absinthe? Verlaine and Rimbaud tore their lives apart in alcohol and drug-inspired frenzies of artistic creativity. Yet to me, Verlaine seemed more true to his calling as an artist than Rimbaud. Like Ezra Pound, who anonymously contributed so much to improving the work of his contemporaries, such as T. S. Eliot, James Joyce, and Ernest Hemingway, Verlaine selflessly promoted and saw to the publication of *Illuminations*, despite the fact that his parting from Rimbaud was so dramatic that he served a prison term for shooting at his friend with a pistol.

But I couldn't just continue to read about these Modernist French authors and poets, although it was important to learn about them and to develop opinions about their writing. The matter of finding a way to acquire the French titles on the Connolly list was becoming a matter of some urgency. The collection of English and American titles was moving ahead, so whatever my developing personal opinions regarding Connolly's choices in French Modernism, I had to find a way to collect those titles chosen by him, but from my base in California. Fortunately, at this point, Priscilla Juvelis blew into my life.

Whether I met Priscilla through another dealer or at a book fair, I don't remember. What I do remember is that she came into my life like a whirlwind in the late 1980s. Priscilla, sensing the potential to acquire a good client, took charge of me and my French project.

"Let's get going," she told me briskly on one of our first meetings. At that point, I simply had a "want list" of the titles I needed for the collection. I was an amateur, but Priscilla was knowledgeable and well connected. Indeed, she had the confidence inherent in one born into the world of international connections. Early in our acquaintance, when I was making a trip to Paris, she arranged for me to visit an important contact of hers there who was a dealer in Old Master paintings. His gallery was unobtrusively situated on the Faubourg St. Honoré. As I tiptoed, awestruck, around the rooms of this gallery, whose walls were covered with enough ancient and priceless art to create its own museum, I developed an even deeper respect for Priscilla and her cheerful assumption that these very sophisticated Parisian gallerists would be happy to show their treasures to a young and impecunious but hopeful book collector. If it was a marketing tool of hers to convince me of her credentials, it was a very successful ploy.

Priscilla had begun her career at the feet of the famous book dealer John Fleming, later entering into partnership with him over the sale of a large collection of *Livres d'Artistes* books, which she had secured from an Argentinian collector. Perhaps some of my purchases from Priscilla came from those high shelves in his premises in New York. I only once met John Fleming, but I remember a high-ceilinged and almost gothic setting. His office, which held the collections, was a huge room, tapestry-hung, whose ceilings appeared at least thirty feet high. It looked like the nave of a cathedral. The room was filled with bookcases, and a long refectory table stood in the center. I entered and left feeling quite overwhelmed, which was probably the reaction he endeavored to elicit from a customer.

There were some significant French auctions in the late 1980s and early 1990s, but I was still too green to think about participating in them personally. The most important of these, perhaps, was the sale of the collection of the self-styled colonel Daniel Sickles, which took place at the Hôtel Drouot in Paris over a series of years beginning in the late 1980s. Colonel Sickles, who was distantly related to Major General Daniel Sickles of American Civil War fame (or infamy, depending on how you look at it), was one of the great collectors of French literature in any age. Born of an American father and a French mother in Brussels in 1900, he lived his life in France, his only indulgence being the purchase of rare nineteenth- and twentieth-century books and manuscripts.

French auctions of rare books did not daunt Priscilla. She was on first-name terms with many of the specialists who are allocated by different auction houses to give learned opinions about the works on offer at a particular sale. I was not confident enough to pick up the telephone and call a specialist; they seemed to me to inhabit a rarefied and distant world that I, with my minimal knowledge of French literature, and indeed, of the language itself, could not hope to penetrate. I was always conscious of my lack of intellectual credentials when talking with experts on works I had set my heart on acquiring. Priscilla had no such inhibitions; this was her world, and I was her client. She set to work, and I have records showing how much she found for me over a five-year period starting in 1987.

The most important of the titles that Priscilla secured for me was actually the first book that I bought through her. She purchased it through one of her specialist agents at a sale of part of Daniel Sickles's Modern Literature Collection at the Hôtel Drouot in April 1987. It was the Duchess of Clermont-Tonnerre's copy of the first volume of Proust's epic work, *À la recherche du temps perdu* (*In Search of Lost Time*), which was the most important title, *Du côté de chez Swann* (*Swann's Way*). This was a very significant acquisition, for which I paid $17,500, a higher price than I had ever paid at that point for any item in my growing collection. However, like the proof copy of *Good-Bye to All That*, it had the effect of becoming the cornerstone on which I eventually built the library of French titles included on the list of one hundred key books. It opened a door for me into the world of French Modernist literature, an area for which my fascination has only increased over the years.

The book itself was significant in many respects. Elisabeth de Gramont, Duchess of Clermont-Tonnerre, was best known as a minor writer, but, more spectacularly for those years, she was also known for her lesbian relationship with the American socialite Natalie Clifford Barney. She was a close friend of Proust's, and the book contained an affectionate dedication to her by Proust, as well as a pasted-in photograph of Proust and two important letters he wrote to her. It was a real prize.

I find it amusing to look through the invoice for that purchase, which is now more than thirty years old, because my purchasing activities are now so very different than they were at that time. The book was actually purchased for me by an agent working on Priscilla's behalf. In those days, when even telephone bidding was still not widely used, it was common for dealers to work with agents who would represent them in the auction room. The only other method was to leave a written bid with the auctioneer, but that was riskier if you really wanted to acquire an item. Colonel Sickles had bought the book directly from the estate of the duchess, so this provenance and the book's associations were impeccable. In those days, the buyer's premium at auction was about half what it is now, but I also paid a commission to Priscilla, which is common if a dealer works on one's behalf at an auction. The prices shown on the invoice for the book are calculated in francs, not euros, and in addition, in my records, there are copies of the checks I made out to various people before I could actually take possession of the book—checks for shipping, customs, insurance, taxes, and so forth. Numbers of people had their hands in that pie, and the price I paid for the book grew and grew until it finally arrived and I could put it on the shelf and know that I was on my way with the French literature I needed to acquire to complete my Connolly list.

Sadly, after five years of our association, having made a major contribution to my collecting project, Priscilla drifted out of my life just as surprisingly as she had entered it. I look at the listings of her invoices, notes, and descriptions, which stop by the early 1990s. Partly, I think that Priscilla's personal interests had continued to move further into the field of fine print, and beyond that, into women's studies, while I continued with my Modern Movement collection. Partly, as well, I had begun to discover that I could acquire titles on my own without an intermediary. Later still, I discovered the thrill of buying at auction for myself.

Friends of Cyril Connolly

SIR HAROLD ACTON

Unfortunately, life does not proceed in a linear fashion. Fate is unpredictable, and things don't always go the way you would like them to. In the end, we have little control over what happens next, even if we pretend that this is not true. So it was in my case. The first few years of my venture fund had gone smoothly, and my collection of Connolly titles was growing. Life looked rosy. But fate had some nasty surprises in store for me in 1989, my personal *Annus Horribilis*. The only good thing I can remember about that year was meeting with Sir Harold Acton at his famous villa outside Florence, La Pietra, which came about entirely owing to my burgeoning collection of Connolly's Modern Movement titles.

As every venture capital investing professional active in the 1980s and 1990s knows, one of the yardsticks by which progress of investment returns was measured during the period, as it still is today, related to the so-called J-curve effect. Particularly in that period, it was expected that, in general, losing investments in a fund would fail before the winning companies matured and were either sold or able to go public. In other words, before profitability, most funds lost money, and experienced negative returns in the early years. This is the principle that has been christened the J-curve effect. Of course, the effect of the principle has not been as evident in recent years, which have been dominated by investments in Internet startups. Developments in technology investing, particularly social media investing, enable rapid returns on successful investments by virtue of the short cycle times involved. But back then, the trajectory of MedVenture Associates followed the norm, and by the end of the 1980s, the first fund was in the red. Despite knowing that this was the norm, ever pessimistic, I felt that I had failed my investors.

I had staked my professional future on the success of MedVenture Associates, and I knew I couldn't face my investors if I actually lost the money with which they had entrusted me. It was a depressing and anxious time professionally. I remember during this period, I returned one evening from Los Angeles, where I had monitored a board meeting at a company called Total Pharmaceutical Care, a home health-care delivery business. Although this business was going well, the company was taking longer to develop than anticipated, and requiring more money than anticipated to reach profitability. For an early-stage investor, the problem with this sort of situation is that, with each unanticipated financing, the fund's ownership percentage gets diluted, so the potential return on investment becomes limited. And as if that were not enough, in addition to this crisis, I already had a failing business in the fund, a company into which I had invested more of the fund's money than I should have. This company, Health Assurance, was one of the first companies created to store autologous blood (that is, the patient's own blood) or donor-directed blood for surgery, and it had recently become the target of angry advertisements from the blood banking business, which used the Red Cross as its poster child. How could we, the advertisements demanded, sell blood, the substance of life, for profit? Never mind that this was the patients' own blood, and that the patients themselves were happy to pay for processing and storage so they could receive their own blood back in a surgical intervention rather than an infusion of donor blood. The source of the supply on which the Red Cross and the blood banking industry depended in those years was chiefly donor blood; they had yet to gear up for the world of donor-directed and autologous blood.

Health Assurance later had to declare bankruptcy and my fund lost a lot of money. At the height of the AIDS crisis, and with learned papers coming out every day about the superiority of autologous blood for surgery patients, the investors in Health Assurance thought the company was providing a needed service. What we didn't know was that we were threatening the monopoly of the blood banking business, which set out to decimate Health Assurance by means of angry advertisements and newspaper articles. Interestingly, Health Assurance did contribute to improvement in health-care management: today, it's routine for a patient to receive autologous or donor-directed blood if needed during surgery. In a strange twist of fate, we were one of the reasons the slow-moving blood banking business learned that it had to modify its policies to allow for autologous blood collection and storage. Nevertheless, the failure of Health Assurance was a blow. As a result of that investment I developed the personal thesis that diligence on an investment, while necessary, is unreliable. You can know 98 percent of the information you need, but the 2 percent of information you lack could account for 100 percent of the weighting about the importance of that information to the diligence process.

But to return to where I was in the narrative: on the plane back to the Bay Area after the meeting with Total Pharmaceutical Care, I sat with Gordon Russell, one of the partners in Sequoia Capital, which was then, as it is now, one of the top five venture funds of Silicon Valley. Downhearted about how things were going, I spent the flight telling Gordon how badly I was doing.

"What are you planning to do?" Gordon asked as the plane began its descent into San Francisco. "Can you close the fund and declare a loss?"

"Why would I do that?" I responded. "I'm invested in several businesses that will be going public within a couple of years, so I think we'll end up with a good profit overall."

Gordon looked at me in surprise. "Well," he said, "why have you just spent this entire flight talking as if you are going out of business?"

But that's how I spent my entire career in venture capital—with a knot in my stomach and fearing the worst. I never celebrated my successes half as much as I worried on sleepless nights about everything that could go wrong. And things were about to go awry in my personal life as well. Just over three years after I started my career in venture capital investing, I was again diagnosed with breast cancer. This time, I was sure I was going to die, because a recurrence of cancer usually presents a grim prognostic picture. I had more extensive surgery and was told that I should undergo a course of chemotherapy. After studying which course of chemotherapy would offer me the best chance of survival, I chose to complete my treatment at the Royal Marsden Hospital in London, where I could receive promising drugs that had yet to be approved in the United States. So I got on a plane and went to England, where I remained for some months. Ruedi joined me when he could, but he was still up to his ears in the Diasonics turnaround. My professional slate was clearer, since by that time, the fund was fully invested. Aside from participating in further rounds of investment into existing companies, there were no new investments to be made and therefore no new business plans to read or diligence to pursue.

Time passed slowly in London, and between treatments, I would travel if I could, mainly for distraction. For some reason, I went several times to Florence. There was something about the age of the city and its streets and pavements and buildings that inspired me. No matter if I died, I thought, I was only one tiny speck among the myriads of people who had gone before me, had lived behind these Renaissance facades, had loved and quarreled and walked these streets. I was part of a flow of history. Somehow, I took comfort from that fact.

Although my collecting had proceeded rapidly over the previous two years, I made few additions to the collection during my illness. In fact, in 1989, my most significant purchase was a prime copy of Hart Crane's famous poem *The Bridge*. Although it was only the first American edition, published in New York in 1930 by Horace Liveright (the limited first edition of 283 copies was published in Paris, also in 1930, by the Black Sun press), this book happened to have been owned by Katherine Anne Porter, and it was a significant presentation copy given to her by the author with a fond inscription. In addition, inside both the front and back covers were pasted a series of photographs, taken by Katherine Anne Porter of Hart Crane in her garden in Mixcoac, Mexico. (Mixcoac used to be a separate municipality, but today is incorporated into Mexico City.) That book was a real find, and it rapidly became one of the highlights of my collection. The only other significant acquisition that year was of an original draft of one of the poems that appeared in Apollinaire's book of collected poetry—*Alcools*, published in 1913. This was an early draft of the poem "Cortège," which had recently been sold at auction by the British Rail Pension Fund. How the British Rail Pension Fund happened to own an original draft of a major poem by Apollinaire remains a mystery. Apparently it had been hanging on the wall of someone's office for so many years that it had become invisible. The poem draft, which had been framed, hung on the wall of my own study at home over all the years I owned it. It had probably been scrawled by Apollinaire as he sat in Café de Flore, as the draft was written on the reverse of a sheet of paper advertising a literary review called *Vers et Prose*. The purchase inspired me to begin reading even more widely into the lives of Apollinaire and his compatriots, and this reading probably contributed to my later, post-Connolly interest in the personal worlds of the French Modernists, when I began to seek out original letters and manuscripts by and about the French Modernist authors of the late nineteenth and early twentieth centuries.

I also missed some important items that were offered to me in 1989, and I remember those almost as much as the ones I bought that year. Perhaps regret is also part of collecting, in that we remember certain items that we didn't buy or weren't successful in obtaining almost as much as we treasure what we find. The feeling soon passes, because fortunately, other attractive rare books—like buses—always come along. And sometimes, items that we have missed purchasing the first time around return to the market, or better yet, sometimes we find more significant examples of a work or a manuscript we have coveted after passing on the first. For many years, I regretted not purchasing an inscribed edition of perhaps the first great spy novel ever written— Joseph Conrad's masterpiece *The Secret Agent*, which was offered to me in 1989. I presumed that it went into the collection of that important American Conrad collector, Stanley Seeger. However, many years later, when the Seeger collection was sold following his death, I was able to buy so many better examples of Conrad's work—manuscripts, letters, and drafts of important works—that the regret faded entirely away. In those sales of the Seeger collections, there was so much of interest that I didn't even look at the inscribed copies of *The Secret Agent* that were in the catalogs; nor did I spend time thinking about buying back my previously owned copy of *Youth*, which I had bought from Paul Rassam so many years ago, and which Seeger must have bought from my sale of 2007. Focus—and patience—bring rewards to a collector in the long run.

Along with reading and collecting, I had developed a habit of seeking connections that might lead me to people who had known people who had known Connolly authors. For instance, I felt that I had a very peripheral connection to Evelyn Waugh through his youngest son, Septimus, because a colleague at British Oxygen who had been at school with him had, many years previously, facilitated his acquisition of a treasured marijuana plant of mine when I left for the United States. (At least, I thought he had done this. It later turned out that Septimus Waugh had no recollection of receiving the plant, although he told me in an email that he wished he had—the donation would have been enthusiastically received at that time.)

The sad fact was that the possibilities for such meetings had become rare; that generation of Connolly writers had almost disappeared in England by the late 1980s. In Florence, however, I knew that Harold Acton, the famous aesthete and writer, was still alive and living in his Palladian villa, La Pietra. Since I traveled to Florence several times that year between treatments, I decided to try to meet him. But how could this be accomplished? Tom Goldwasser held the key, because he had a valuable customer, Neil Ritchie, an elderly Englishman who lived outside Florence, who knew Acton. Inquiries were made, and Tom offered to introduce me to Neil.

Neil Ritchie was in fact Harold Acton's bibliographer, and he lived in Lucolena in Chianti with a buxom Irish widow named Philomena. I went to visit them in Lucolena, but the day did not start in a promising way. The hotel provided me with an enormous white limousine, which embarrassed me terribly, but it was the only form of transportation available to take me to the villa. What Neil must have thought on this, our first meeting, as the limousine tried to maneuver down his narrow driveway, I cannot imagine. I looked like a chemotherapy patient, even though I tried to disguise it with makeup. Nevertheless, we enjoyed a long and lazy lunch in the sunshine. Philomena bustled around while Neil and I talked, and as I prepared to leave, he offered to introduce me to Harold Acton.

"Call him directly," he advised, giving me the phone number. "If his butler answers, try to speak French. You may get past the butler if you speak French."

It was a little surreal, but I took it all in stride. In retrospect, I think my system was probably toxic from all the chemotherapy agents swirling around my bloodstream. Whatever the cause, I didn't think twice about the prospect of actually telephoning Sir Harold Acton himself. Also, as so often with my endeavors, I had nothing to lose by trying! There's something to be said for just taking action without thinking about it too much: if I had reflected on it first, maybe I wouldn't have had the courage to call. But call I did. I practiced the right words in French, picked up the phone, and yes—the butler answered and put me straight through to Harold Acton himself. Perhaps my French was so garbled that he felt it best to pass me on, but whatever the case, the call was successful, and Harold Acton invited me to tea at La Pietra. Neil was enormously impressed.

"You have to take him something," he told me, suggesting a book he knew would be acceptable. "Can I also take a book to be signed?" I asked. Neil sighed.

"It's not advisable," he said. "But do it if you think that you must."

I arrived in a taxi, having learned from the limousine experience. When we turned into the long drive of La Pietra and drove between the rows of manicured yew trees, Harold Acton was waiting at the door.

Perhaps I should have ordered a limousine, I thought to myself, seeing my host waiting at the door to receive me. Just not that long white one. The taxi was fairly battered. Sir Harold led me into a long room facing the garden. It was dim and dusty, with rows of scarlet chairs stacked up against one wall. I took a seat near a table that, I noted, was crammed with photographs of Acton with various members of the English Royal Family. I was impressed, but I suppose that back then, we Colonials were always impressed by talk of Royalty.

Harold Acton noticed me eyeing the photographs and sat back in his chair with a half-smile.

"Ah, dear Margaret," he murmured, "dear Margaret. She was here only last week."

But I wasn't interested in anecdotes about the Royal Family. Harold Acton had been part of the generation of writers, critics, and aesthetes who composed the overlapping circles in which Cyril Connolly had moved. Like Connolly, Acton had been at Eton College, along with such notable later figures as the writers Eric Blair (George Orwell), Anthony Powell, Henry Yorke (Henry Green), Robert Byron (the travel writer), and Ian Fleming. At Oxford, he became close friends with, among others, Evelyn Waugh, whose writing he greatly influenced, and Waugh had based a number of his characters on him, most notably Anthony Blanche in *Brideshead Revisited*. Acton had declared himself an aesthete at Oxford, and in later life he wrote two volumes of memoirs—*Memoirs of an Aesthete* (1948) and *More Memoirs of an Aesthete* (1970). I was looking forward to hearing some good literary gossip relating to the authors whose works I was collecting.

The visit did not disappoint, although I felt that Harold Acton was rather bored by my questions. I'm sure he spent more time than he really cared to in discussions about the writers and notables of his generation with teams of visiting matrons from the United States. He had made himself and his garden available to such groups, and no doubt they took full advantage of his time. Nevertheless, he was polite and courtly, and of course he provided me, as he probably had many others on dozens of occasions, with light gossip about his friends and acquaintances of past times—particularly Evelyn Waugh, Cyril Connolly, and contributors to *Horizon*, a magazine Connolly had founded. Although Acton had never contributed to *Horizon*, he knew most of those who had. I found that he didn't want to be drawn into discussion about his early life in China after his graduation from Oxford, and in fact, the only part of our conversation which seemed to animate him was when we turned to Graham Greene, who was living then on the Côte d'Azur with Yvette Cloetta. For some reason, the fact that Greene was living with a woman who was not his wife aroused considerable venom in that elderly aesthete.

I rather wonder what Harold Acton thought of me. Much as I had dressed carefully and put on makeup, I was obviously ill. I had lost a lot of weight, and my outfit, which was all that I had brought with me for dinners in the hotel, was a badly fitting and dated red and black suit from a Jean Muir collection. Acton was polite enough to pretend not to notice. We drank tea and ate small and rather dry scones, and as the visit drew to a conclusion, he went to the door leading to the garden and said, somewhat ruefully, "I'd show you the garden, but my legs are very bad today."

Of course, notwithstanding Neil's advice to the contrary, I had taken a book along with me to be signed, in addition to the book I had brought, on Neil's advice, as a gift to him. The gift was an illustrated tome on Italian gardens, which he received politely, although he probably had dozens of books just like it in his personal library. My book was an enormous volume by Acton called *The Villas of Tuscany*. As I left, I screwed up my courage and asked him to inscribe it. I still have the book, in which he wrote:

In memory of a happy visit to La Pietra in September, 1989. With warm regards and hopes to meet again. Cordially, Harold Acton.

So polite. Over his lifetime in Italy, he must have signed dozens of such books for visiting members of English and American garden clubs. Of course, I never saw him again. Nevertheless, for me at that point in my life and my collecting, it was a literary high point.

Literary High Spots, *The Great Gatsby*, and the Modern Book as Currency

The technical definition of a high spot of Modern literature is that it is a first edition of a key book written by a significant author, usually in English or French, which is in perfect or near perfect condition. Which books count as these "high spots" of Modernist literature? Generally, the titles are predictable—works that probably were studied in high schools across English-speaking countries, certainly in my generation. The names are household names—Fitzgerald, Hemingway, Joyce, Faulkner, Proust—and the books that have been made into movies are often of greatest interest. Perhaps the interest in exactly these authors results from the people behind the new fortunes—wealth created late in the twentieth century and the early part of the twenty-first— beginning to look for intellectual validation. And after Modern art, what could be more chic than a first edition of *The Great Gatsby* placed casually in the library of one of the new hedge fund or tech billion- aires? The trade in these perfect copies, the high spots of literature, has become as outsized in its own way as the overheated art market, and there is no sign of a retreat.

One of the most instrumental of the dealers involved with the cre- ation of this branch of rare book collecting was a canny dealer from the Midwest, Jeffrey Marks. Jeffrey specialized in high points of Ameri- can Modern literature and was very successful in creating a high-priced trade in such items. His focus was on the trade in perfect and inscribed copies of works by Ernest Hemingway, William Faulkner, and F. Scott Fitzgerald. I never knew what sources Jeffrey relied on to acquire what he offered for sale. Usually, the source of major titles are sellers of sig- nificant collections, but sometimes dealers have access to sources that come directly or by descent through an author. Like Rick Gekoski, Jeffrey Marks clearly had impeccable sources of material, because the items he had for sale were mostly in exquisite condition, or as good as could be found, while others he had on offer had extraordinary associations—inscribed copies to the dedicatee of an important first edition, for example.

I had frequently met up with Jeffrey at book fairs, but initially, I didn't buy from him. His prices always seemed too high. Sadly for me, it is this same way of thinking that has led me over the years to refrain from buying high-priced, high-flying stocks. In both cases, I miss the fact that high-priced items are that way for a reason, and whether they are high points of literature or significant emerging companies, often the price can only go higher, at least for a time.

I wasn't buying much of significance in the period immediately following the personal trauma of having to undergo that second round of cancer therapy. I felt that I should let my career lie fallow, at least until the proverbial post-therapy five years had passed and an "all clear" could be issued. However, things were improving with the fortunes of MedVenture Associates. Having completed the investment cycle in the fourth year of the fund and weathered the dreaded J-curve, the fund was starting to yield dividends. The promising businesses in which I had invested were now bringing products to market, and the fund was entering a new stage: the harvesting, as it was known in the profession, of the successful investments. Over the 1990s, some of our companies were successfully sold, and several of the businesses in which I had invested carried out successful IPOs.

The most significant of the IPOs was for a company called Ventritex, which had successfully developed, clinically tested, and launched to the market an implantable defibrillator, the second of its kind, but the first that was fully programmable. MedVenture Associates invested in Ventritex from the seed capital round; the investment had been one of my first after raising the money to found MedVenture Associates. I had followed the pacemaker industry as an analyst at Hambrecht & Quist, so I was armed with good knowledge about the management of cardiac arrhythmia. It seemed obvious to me that the development of an implantable defibrillator was likely to be a next step in the emerging field of minimally invasive coronary diagnostics and therapy. The successful completion of the clinical trials of the Ventritex defibrillator allowed the company to carry out an IPO in the middle of 1991 in order to commercialize the technology. Investors snapped up the stock on the IPO, which meant a large profit for all of the investors, not least for the investors in my fund.

On the day when the offering went effective on the NASDAQ exchange, I was far from California. Ruedi and I had joined my parents in Italy for a private celebration of their golden wedding anniversary, and we had rented a little house with the charming name of Il Pozzino—the meaning of which is unclear, but it is probably "little well." The house was near the tiny village of San Casciano, about a thirty-minute drive from Florence. When a colleague—a fellow investor—called to tell me the good news about the successful IPO, the phone line was impossibly bad and there was a summer thunderstorm overhead, so I could barely make out what he was telling me. However, I did manage to understand, despite the crackling on the phone line, that things had gone very well for the offering. In fact, once I did the arithmetic, I saw that my investors would realize a good profit—not only from that investment, but from their investment in the fund overall. I went to bed that night feeling relieved. My investors were going to be happy and I was happy. In particular, it meant that over the next few years, I could concentrate on my book collecting without worrying about letting my investors down. I also took satisfaction from the fact that, in addition to making money for my investors, I had promoted a company whose product was going to make a difference to the lives of many thousands of cardiac patients. Without the commitment of MedVenture Associates to invest in the Ventritex technology, the company would not have been funded, since my colleagues were initially skeptical that such a therapy could successfully be developed. In this respect, MedVenture's investment was the all-important catalyst that brought the deal together.

Over time, other companies from that first fund made a profit for our investors as well. For example, Total Pharmaceutical Care, that same health-care services company over which I had agonized on that short plane ride with Gordon Russell, carried out a successful IPO, too, and the profits rewarded investors several times over. Glycomed, a biotechnology business, became a public company, and two other businesses—Acoustic Imaging, an ultrasound imaging company, and Simborg Systems, an early hospital management software database system—were both successfully sold. There were others, but this is not a comprehensive list of corporate successes for that first fund; the point is that, in the end, the fund did so well, returning to the investors nearly three times their committed capital, that I was able to continue with a second MedVenture Associates investment fund. Despite my fears about being sidelined from the venture community owing to my history of cancer, I was able to raise that second fund in the mid-1990s, and it was more than twice the size of the first.

And there was a renewed focus on my collecting activities. In addition to perusing dealer and auction catalogs, I began once again to attend book fairs, where I immediately noticed a subtle shift in the trade of Modern first editions: an emerging market for literary high spots. At one book fair, I observed, over the few days of the fair, a copy of Faulkner's *The Marble Faun* trading hands among dealers several times over, until finally it was offered to collectors at close to twice the price at which it had started. Maybe the dealers had always done that, and I just hadn't noticed, or perhaps I hadn't had enough money to participate in that game—because it was a game, and artificial. But it became part of the Modern rare book business, and it went on for a number of years. At some point, after the Internet made it possible to review comparable prices of rare books on offer—and the power of the auction houses grew—this practice of selling and reselling key books of Modernist literature ceased, or at least it was no longer openly carried on at book fairs. I can only assume that it happened in the beginning because different dealers, having different collectors as clients, knew what their clients might be prepared to pay for a title—or perhaps they were just gambling on what those clients might pay. At any rate, after I had observed that first instance of price escalation taking place, it seemed to me as if every time I went to a book fair, there were one or two significant Modernist items on display for sale, which moved from booth to booth as the fair progressed, and were offered at ever-increasing prices. And while the rest of the book trade trundled on in its stately way, these high-spot titles were becoming something else—currency. Almost like hot stocks, their prices went up and up and up. Jeffrey Marks was a master at maneuvering the market for high spots of Modern Movement literature, but to some extent, I think he really believed the books he sold were undervalued, and he wanted to bring that part of the market up to a level that, in his opinion, was the correct value range for perfect examples of the books.

The condition of a Modernist rare book is the principal criterion by which value is set. It's artificial, and manufactured largely by dealers, but book dealers of Modern first editions are hard pressed to create value in the copies they sell, and so they have come up with the formula of the perfect copy as the yardstick for value measurement. Dealers could just as easily have come up with association being the criteria for value—and it is true that important inscriptions add value to otherwise dull copies. But in the main, it's condition, and especially the condition of a dust jacket, that is the fundamental principle driving the value of a high spot of Modernist literature. The better the dust jacket, the higher the price. One reason for the relative scarcity of perfect dust jackets is that the books printed in the middle years of the twentieth century were not valued for their dust jackets; purchasers of such books usually discarded the dust jacket, however beautiful and contemporary the art, because they wanted to show rows of perfect book spines on their bookshelves. *Autres temps, autres mœurs!*

The dust jacket has now become a form of currency in the business of high spots. For example, while browsing an online auction catalog for a sale of rare books recently, I noticed a copy of F. Scott Fitzgerald's *Tender Is the Night* estimated for sale in a range of $300 to $400. It was described as "fine, with no dust jacket. Pages uncut." Right after this was listed another copy of the same book, registered for sale at an estimated $10,000 to $12,000, despite the condition not being similarly described as "fine." The difference was that the second book had a dust jacket. I looked at the facing page of the item description. Of course, there was a picture of the familiar yellow and blue dust jacket of *Tender Is the Night*. I sighed. It wasn't even a very good dust jacket—the edges were frayed, and the backing looked as if it had been repaired. What is the justification, except scarcity, for a book with a dust jacket to sell for so much more than the same book without a jacket? I would not have been surprised if that dust jacket had been swapped from a lesser copy to cover a very clean copy of the book in order to create a pristine work. What is the fascination with dust jackets, anyway? I am almost certain that some important books have been married by a dealer to a fine or near-fine dust jacket from a different copy of the work in question in order to increase the value of the whole item. Is this fraud? Or is it merely compilation of a work of art? What it really turns out to be, in my view, is a manufactured market—the Modern book as currency. It makes me wonder if, in today's world of sophisticated desktop publishing, a clever counterfeiter could actually someday manufacture some of these fine, perfectly preserved dust jackets.

That's not to say that some dust jackets, from the 1920s and 1930s in particular, are not works of art in themselves. The dust jacket of the 1925 first edition of *The Great Gatsby* is an arresting work by the Spanish artist Francis Cugat. The picture on the front of the jacket depicts two huge, disembodied eyes floating in an evening sky of deepest blue, a color suggestive of a clear evening at the moment when the marine of the evening sky is changing to the navy blue of the reflected night. The eyes stare out of the picture toward the viewer, anonymous, melancholy, floating above a brightly lit carnival scene, which shines brightly, almost gaudily, at the edge of a large city, presumably New York. You can see the outlines of the city showing dimly in the background. A rosebud mouth, also disembodied, makes a triangle in this night sky. A large, green tear speeds to earth below like a fluorescent torpedo, and there is the merest hint of a turban encasing the head. That dust jacket from the first edition of *The Great Gatsby* is a thing of great beauty, one of the finest of the Jazz Age publications. Perhaps this is the reason that a fine first edition copy in dust jacket of the book is one of the most expensive works of Modernist literature that you can buy.

Connolly had included two of F. Scott Fitzgerald's works on his list—*The Great Gatsby* and *Tender Is the Night*. I had bought a copy of the latter from Joseph the Provider in my first years of serious collecting; it wasn't a major copy, but it had a good dust jacket and had been signed by Fitzgerald. Somehow, *Tender Is the Night*, Fitzgerald's next novel after *The Great Gatsby*, had escaped the extreme price escalation in the market for literary high spots that *Gatsby* was experiencing. Despite my reservations about the high-spot movement, however, my collection needed a significant example of *The Great Gatsby*, so I finally gave in and bought a top copy of the book from Jeffrey Marks. It was in almost perfect condition, with a very fine, original dust jacket. Once again, I reached beyond my budget and increased the level at which I was funding my collection. I paid $25,000—which was worth far more in 1991 than it is today. The purchase caused me a number of sleepless nights, worrying about what a fool I had been to pay so much for a copy that didn't even have an inscribed dedication. But there are collectors to whom condition matters so much that price is irrelevant, and certainly, *The Great Gatsby* is one of the top five or ten works of Modern American fiction. The truth of that statement came when I finally sold my Connolly collection; the copy of *Gatsby* reached many times the price I had paid for it in 1991.

Having to give in to the prices demanded for high-spot movement books only because they were part of the Connolly list created a slight feeling of reservation about my decision to collect the Connolly Modern Movement list. Now that I was collecting so seriously, I found that the further I proceeded, the more I felt at odds with what is perceived in the world of Modern literature collecting as desirable. Which is more valuable—a signed association copy or a perfect copy of a distinguished book? It was a matter of internal debate for me whenever I encountered a significant work in my field of collecting. Of course, having a perfect copy that includes a dedication, or even just an author's signature, is the best solution, but it isn't often that such works can be found.

It is certainly true that if you are looking to make a profit from collecting books and high spots of literature, condition is the key factor in determining value, particularly for a scarce item. I can't say I entirely regret the price increases for fine copies with dust jackets, since I benefited from that trend myself at times. But making money from collecting is certainly not the norm: generally speaking, nobody in his or her right mind would begin a collection of Modern first editions with a profit motive in mind. Nor are valuable books useful as decorative items or even as reading copies: you can't hang books on your walls for all to enjoy as you can a painting, and if a book is really fragile, you certainly don't want to crack its spine or—God forbid—inadvertently tear a page. So why are the prices so high, and why do this at all? Why collect literature if the books are only going to sit under lock and key in special cases and cupboards? For years after I began seriously collecting the Modern Movement list, I sometimes thought of my collection as a personal folly. It was a money sink, like ownership of a boat, or belonging to a golf club.

As the collection continued to grow, I began to find ownership of these fine books, these examples of some of the high spots of Modernism in perfect condition, to be ultimately not rewarding. I felt that the books were inert, with no associated history. They didn't speak to me. Inscribed copies of high spots of literature, particularly inscribed copies with literary or personal associations, were inherently of much higher interest to me personally. Maurice Neville, the Santa Barbara book dealer, famously said about a copy of *Tender Is the Night* with an important inscription that owning a key book with an author's inscription is the next best thing to being able to reach out and touch the writer. He was quoted in an interview with the *Los Angeles Times* in 1987:

"I would rather have a later printing with a great inscription than a first printing that says 'Best wishes, Scott Fitzgerald.' I'd rather have a fifth printing that maybe he spilled a drink on, that had a long, humorous inscription." Pause. "I actually do have a later printing of 'Tender Is the Night' with a long inscription to Zelda's psychiatrist, talking about

Zelda's case and the travails of the last years and sort of apologizing for the book, which is typical Fitzgerald." He pauses. "The inscription is the next best thing to sort of touching the man."

I developed a similar feeling about key inscriptions, and in my case, this is demonstrated by my feelings about the copies of *The Great Gatsby* that I have owned. At one point I had two of them: the perfect copy Jeffrey Marks had sold me, and an inscribed copy. Today, I possess only the inscribed copy. This book has a rather ragged dust jacket, but the inscription inside is an important one. It reads:

For Walter Bruington from an unknown admirer
F. Scott Fitzgerald
Autumn, 1940

The dedication is written in an unsteady hand. The writing scrawls across the inside cover page, ink scratching and blotting from the pen. The author's failing health, his mental state and sense of despair, and his capitulation to alcohol are all implied by those brief lines and the shaky handwriting. To me, the dedication and the scrawled handwriting say more about the final disintegration of this man, who in his time had been one of the most celebrated writers of his generation, than you could learn from reading a dozen biographies. Bruington may well be the last dedicatee for any copy Fitzgerald signed of any of his books, as he died only months after that of a massive heart attack.

Bruington, the recipient, was F. Scott Fitzgerald's lawyer, and by 1940 Fitzgerald was broke and owed Bruington a lot of money. My guess is that Bruington was shrewd enough to accept a number of inscribed copies of various works by his famous client, and that they had been taken from Fitzgerald's personal bookshelves in partial payment for what he was owed. I don't know how many books Fitzgerald inscribed for Bruington, because by that time, Fitzgerald wasn't even wealthy enough to have a library of his own. I once saw a similarly inscribed copy of *Tender Is the Night* in the online catalog of a small auction house, but by the time I noticed it, the book had already been sold. Through the auction house, I tracked down the purchaser and attempted to buy the copy, but this was a purchaser who knew the importance of the inscription. He offered it to me, but at a significant multiple of the price that he had paid, so I did not buy the book. Bruington was probably aware of the potential value of the signed copies, because fine and inscribed copies of Modernist works had already become very collectible by that time. They had been sought after since the first publication of *Ulysses* in the specially designed limited edition. Bruington doubtless knew that some admirer of Fitzgerald's writing would be prepared to pay for ownership of the signed books at a later stage, yet I could be wrong about his motivation. Since he was also a friend of Fitzgerald's, it is possible that he just wanted the signed books for his own library.

To me, this copy of *Gatsby* is a much more interesting example of the book than one that is merely in fine condition; that melancholy inscription to Fitzgerald's lawyer is a piece of history, and it encapsulates one of the final scenes in the author's life. And since this book and its dust jacket are not in perfect condition, I don't have to be concerned about keeping the book in a pristine state to preserve its value. I can open it and look at the inscription and think about Fitzgerald's life as it must have been at that time without worrying about disturbing the less-than-perfect dust jacket or whether the spine is too fragile and could crack. For me, this makes it an entirely more interesting and more approachable copy of the book, although it's certainly not a reading copy. The state of the inscription confirms what biographers know of Fitzgerald's history at that time, and the copy is still a fine example of a first edition of one of the key books of the Modern Movement.

Buying at Auction

As the last decade of the twentieth century rolled on, I continued to refine my collecting focus. Unlike the late 1980s, when I had been in such a hurry to add titles to my collection—mostly first editions of books that were on the Connolly list—now I was beginning to seek out special copies of books. First and limited editions were not sufficient. I wanted to spread my net wider, especially because by this time, I possessed adequate examples of more than half the titles on the Connolly list. In addition to continuing to collect pristine, but anonymous, first edition copies of books on the list, I began to look for signed, inscribed, and dedicated books as well as rare editions of these titles. Of most importance, I started looking for manuscript material. This part of the search began timidly enough, but in the end it has become the real focus of my collecting activities.

Like many inexperienced collectors, I had initially relied entirely on purchasing from book dealers. Even when I did buy at auction, I usually asked dealers to bid on my behalf or to leave a bid for me with a specialist. Because of this, I probably missed some of the more important of the European book auctions of the last years of the twentieth century.

Knowing this fact, by the middle of the 1990s I had become disenchanted with working with dealers and specialists at auction, particularly since my knowledge had increased to the point that I was no longer relying on being offered Connolly titles by dealers. More and more, I was finding things of interest to me in auction catalogs, and asking the dealers and specialists merely to bid for me on items that I had already selected as being of interest.

In many respects, working with a dealer or specialist at auction was just an expensive way to leave a fixed price, or so-called left bid, because you had to assign limits to what the dealer or specialist could bid, just as, in leaving a bid directly, you had to set limits for the auctioneer. Over time, I had found that if I really wanted to ensure the purchase of something important, leaving bids with a dealer was not a much more successful strategy than placing a left bid with the auction house.

So I took the plunge and let it be known among my regular dealers that I was going to start bidding for myself at auction. The prospect of doing so was daunting. In the 1990s, if you couldn't participate personally in the saleroom during an auction, the only way to bid live was through a telephone bid. Since I was still living and working in California, and most of the auctions were held in London, Paris, or New York, I had to learn the art of telephone bidding. It is definitely an art that has to be learned; I made many mistakes before I finally grasped the technique of how to be successful bidding on my own behalf. At first, I found that the anonymity of the telephone encounter was difficult, but every telephone bid proceeds the same way: as your item is about to come up, you receive a call from a soft-spoken agent of the auction house whose specific role is to report the latest bid standing with the auctioneer and, when your item actually comes up, to inquire, after every bid, whether you want to bid or not. It all goes very quickly, and you have little time to consider what to do before either bidding or losing the item. As someone who likes to consider and ponder and to ask opinions of others around me before making a decision, I found those first telephone encounters somewhat unsettling.

In fact, the anonymous voices on the telephone mirror the style of the leading auction houses: when the artifice of presentation is stripped away, they are really just sophisticated financial machines dedicated to the selling of art, jewelry, and collectibles of all manner and description to a wealthy and cosmopolitan audience. My first experience of telephone bidding unsettled me because I felt that the unseen person on the telephone knew how naive I really was; I remember well that the first time I entered the sacred portals of Sotheby's, I also felt as if I was an imposter. There was so much money in that rarefied air, with its quietly exotic employees gliding across thick carpets, and sleek receptionists condescending politely, but with little enthusiasm, when asked to call the person in the book department whom I had come to see—in my case, usually Peter Selley, who by that time had left Rick Gekoski for Sotheby's. Although I grew accustomed to the atmosphere over time, I never felt like I was part of the scene. The receptionists, for instance, always seemed like members of the *jeunesse dorée*—young people working for amusement for a while before returning to stately homes or heading for cruises on yachts in the Mediterranean. They were all beautifully dressed and perfectly groomed.

The foyer at Sotheby's in Bond Street was always busy, especially if an auction was underway. If there was a Russian sale, the air would be thick with conversation in Russian and other Slavic languages—those were the years when Russian oligarchs were busy assembling collections of Russian art and artifacts to fill their new palaces on the Riviera or in London, or their expensive penthouses in New York City. The men were burly, and the woman exquisite, with perfect complexions and figures. These were the new Russians of high society.

If there were no interesting people to watch while I was waiting for the book department representative, I would view the screens showing the progress of live auctions, or else displaying pictures of choice items to be presented at upcoming sales. Although the art auctions were held in the evenings, many of the viewings for sales of art were held in the daytime, so when I happened to be at Sotheby's I had ample opportunity to observe the passing show. Waiting in that foyer was like being on the set of a movie, and just as in the movie business, the same symmetry applied behind the scenes. From being backstage at times at Sotheby's and other auction houses, I can confidently attest that the back rooms of these auction houses resemble how I imagine the backstage area of a movie set appears. The auction house foyers, cafés, and showrooms are dedicated to an atmosphere of quiet sophistication, in order to help wealthy people spend their fortunes on expensive collectibles of all kinds, while the back office quarters are as cramped and higgledy-piggledy as the front showrooms are aesthetic and cleverly decorated.

The first time I bid at auction on my own behalf was at Sotheby's. It was an important sale, during which I made one of my first large purchases of a work written by one of the English authors on the Connolly list. This was an annotated typescript copy of Evelyn Waugh's key book of the Modern Movement—*Decline and Fall*. The great collector and bibliophile Anthony Hobson, who at one time had been the director of the book department at Sotheby's, auctioned off the most significant part of his magnificent collection at Sotheby's in London in 1996. There was so much of interest for me in the catalog that I felt I couldn't possibly consign responsibility to a dealer to bid on my behalf. For the first time, I had to think strategically: if some item of interest went up too far in price, I wanted to progress to some other item on my "want list." Since I was becoming more expert on what I wanted to buy, the main objection to buying through a dealer was, as I have mentioned, that, just as with a left bid, one had to decide beforehand exactly what one was prepared to pay, without knowing the extent of the competition and what might actually happen on the auction floor. For this reason, I was becoming less inclined to pay a dealer's commission. I couldn't see the point anymore of paying that commission on top of taxes and the buyer's premium charged by the auction house. There was also the remote possibility that asking a dealer to bid on one's behalf could create a conflict of interest, because dealers are not always disinterested third parties. Dealers sometimes buy on behalf of multiple clients, or they may have a client in mind for a particular item. On other occasions, they are merely buying attractive items for their own inventories. In any and all of these cases, asking a dealer to bid on one's behalf is almost like showing one's hand prematurely in a bridge game.

As it happened, I was feeling more confident about the auction process by then, so I registered to bid by telephone at the auction, which was held at Sotheby's Bond Street salerooms. Strangely enough, my biggest concern about telephone bidding was not the fact that I was a novice; it was that those dealers who were used to purchasing on my behalf at auction might take umbrage. In particular, I had bought an increasing number of fine items with Tom Goldwasser as my intermediary, and I didn't want to offend him. I remember that I wrote to Peter Selley at Sotheby's, expressing my concern that taking the auction reins into my own hands could cause dealers to give me a cold shoulder. He just laughed, and of course, he was right to laugh, because my concerns proved completely unfounded. Dealers are in the business of selling rare books and manuscripts, and I was a good client in those years.

One must be committed to the auction process to engage in telephone bidding, especially when participating in an auction from another time zone. Living in California meant that I had to be prepared to bid by telephone at all sorts of odd hours. If an auction is in London, it can begin as early as 10 a.m. in London, so that you will be called effectively in the middle of the night in order to participate in the sale. Imagine how it goes. Your telephone rings in the early hours of the morning, when the sale is still several items ahead of where your own want list begins, and a disembodied, refined voice politely introduces itself and inquires if you are ready to bid. As you struggle to become *compos mentis*, you listen to the auctioneer selling off the items that come a few numbers ahead of your first item, while you feverishly page through the catalog that you have marked up with your notes. After a time, as a result of making a few mistakes along the way, I learned that it was best to set an alarm clock ahead of the estimated time if the auction was an early morning one, and to make a cup of strong coffee before that phone call arrived.

Fortunately for me, although the Hobson sale started in the morning, I happened to be visiting my father, who then lived in Bath, in England, so there was no problem with different time zones. My parents had finally decided to retire to England when my father left the mining business, and they had been living in the Georgian city of Bath for over ten years. New Zealand was not then, as it is now, a destination, and after a lifetime of traveling, New Zealand had seemed to my parents to be just too far away from the mainstream as a place for retirement, particularly since I was living in California and my sister was a professor of psychiatry at the University of Cape Town Medical School. She was the only member of our family who had always remained in Cape Town and made South Africa her home.

Unfortunately, my father was now alone in Bath, after the death of my mother early in 1996, so in the summer of that year, I was traveling more frequently to England, as my father was not coping well. I tried to visit him as much as my work demands would allow, and one visit coincided with the date of the Hobson sale. The prospect of my first telephone bidding was something to look forward to, although, when I first heard that distant, polite voice at the other end of the telephone inquiring if I was ready to bid, I nearly panicked. Perhaps I was not as experienced as I thought. Still, I had my list ready, and waited for the first item to be announced.

There was so much of interest that I could have, would have, bought in that sale if funds had been available. The item I was determined to acquire was the *Decline and Fall* typescript, which came up near the end of the sale, while the first item of interest to me was a splendid copy of W. H. Auden's first book of poetry, *Poems*. That first edition was limited to at most forty-five existing copies, but this copy also contained dedications from the author and corrections in Auden's own hand. In the end, I managed to acquire both of these items, but the catalog from that sale, which I have kept, shows how many missed opportunities there were for me in the Hobson sale, among which was significant correspondence relating to and from Robert Graves.

I was a nervous wreck. The bidding started. Should I go in at first or wait? At every pause, the polite voice asked me quietly, "Do you want to bid?"

Restrained panic ensued. Did I want to bid or not? Would this affect the amount I had available for the next item? Would the polite voice think less of me if I declined to pursue the item? Almost immediately, the Auden went above my limit, but I decided to continue anyway and achieved the purchase with little difficulty, although at a substantially higher price than I would have expected to pay.

When the sale reached the desired Waugh manuscript, I really had to concentrate, because it was not as simple as the purchase of Auden's *Poems*. Now, I entered my first bidding war. Bid followed bid—it was excruciating. Should I go on, or should I stop? How far above my limit was I? Oh God—what was this going to cost with the buyer's premium? Let's see—add 20 percent—no 25 percent. Damn—the other bidder just bid again. Well, so much for them! I wanted the typescript, so I continued to stay with the bidding process and finally achieved the purchase, but at over four times the estimated price listed in the catalog. Yet, in the end, it didn't matter. That purchase of the *Decline and Fall* manuscript was significant for me because it was an important but hard-won acquisition. I left the Hobson sale feeling confident and successful about bidding on my own, although the confidence was probably misplaced. In the Hobson sale, I had overpaid. But despite spending close to $50,000—a record for me for any auction or purchase—the value of what I bought held up over time.

If I had left a bid, I know I would have lost both items, and this illustrates the real difference between participating live in an auction or leaving a bid. There are things you don't know ahead of time that only come into play when the bidding starts. Most particularly, you don't know what the extent of the competition will be for your desired item, or what you really might be prepared to pay. In a live auction, you have to decide on the spur of the moment just how much you want that item and what you are prepared to pay, as opposed to the amount you might have designated in a left bid. Maybe what you will pay when confronted with the possibility of losing a coveted book or manuscript is more than what you would have estimated in a written bid. In participating in a live auction, you learn just how much you really want that item. It's a fact that although I have gone above my own estimated limit time and again at auction, I have only once had an instance of buyer's remorse, even though I have overpaid more times than I should have. (This is the difference between collecting for the love of it and collecting for investment potential.)

Bidding is competitive, and I was working in a competitive business at a time when money was freely available. It was now the late 1990s, and the first dot-com boom was well underway. Everyone was competing for those dot-com deals. I took the same competitive spirit that served me well in venture capital into purchasing activities for my collecting, and as I look at the records of my collection, I realize that, by and large, I paid more than I had expected to pay for nearly everything I bought at auction after that first Hobson sale. Unlike my earlier, more stately pace of progress in assembling my collection, like every investor or entrepreneur in the dot-com world, I was now, in my world of collecting, in a hurry to get where I was going. My list was just over halfway complete, but since I was earning good money, what better way to spend it than to buy at auction and hurry to complete my collection of books on the Connolly list? Of course, I still bought from various dealers, but I had fallen under the spell of the auction hammer. How the auctioneers must have loved me in those years.

Terre des hommes

ANTOINE DE SAINT-EXUPÉRY

Anyone who has ever had to clear out a family home after a death knows what a heartbreaking and backbreaking chore it is. My parents finally retired to the Georgian city of Bath in the mid-1980s, as mentioned earlier, but they would only live there together for twelve years. In 1996, several years after my own therapy for breast cancer, my mother died of the same disease. The following year, my father experienced a debilitating stroke, and afterward, he could never cope on his own. It was tragic that, after finally and belatedly closing that loop between the colonies and England and restoring their mythical ties to a homeland, my parents had so little time together to enjoy it. They were not yet very elderly, but the stresses they had endured in their lives, which spanned the Depression and World War II, had no doubt taken a toll. Still, during that time they had together in Bath, they created a cozy home for themselves. It was in a flat covering two floors of a house in Lansdown Place East, abutting Lansdown Crescent, one of the famous neoclassical crescents built in the city during the late eighteenth century.

After the stroke, my father was semi-paralyzed and mostly bedridden, so I had selected a nursing home for him in the countryside near Bath. Since it was clear he was never coming home again, it had fallen to me to go through everything and clear out the flat. With her demanding schedule as a professor of psychiatry at the University of Cape Town, my sister had little leave; I had a more flexible schedule, so I went to Bath to carry out the arduous chore of sifting through a lifetime of memories and dismantling the home. There was a lot to be done. Things naturally accumulate in a home over time, and there were family items and memorabilia going back several generations. I wanted to be as efficient as possible, since my own time was limited; I was anxious not to be away from my office for a long period of time.

My business was going well. After raising that second venture fund, I had brought in a young partner, and together we were investing the new fund and finding many exciting opportunities.

Although Ruedi was as busy as ever, he had made time to come along with me, but there was not much he could do. He couldn't pick and choose what to keep and what to save among the memorabilia of a family's life. It was an enormous task, and I needed to be as organized as possible to get everything done as quickly as I could. I created four categories for the project, and would allocate each item to its prospective destination as swiftly as possible. There was one category for things that were going to be tossed; another for items going to the Sue Ryder charity shop, a cancer charity that had been dear to my mother. A third was for items that a friend would take to the local car boot sale, a flea market of sorts; and finally, and of most significance, there were the things I wanted to keep. The final category included not only the obvious items—furniture and antiques and china—but also items of more personal value, those family memories that were contained in photographs, letters, papers, and books. And there were many books, lots of them old, but none of them valuable.

Since Ruedi had little to do, he immersed himself in looking over some of the family memorabilia, and, to my annoyance, sat comfortably while I worked, but somewhat in my way. He took a post at the foot of the stairway, leaning against the newel post, while he looked through photos and documents, sometimes chuckling over old pictures or smacking the dust off ancient family medals, the better to scrutinize them. I huffed and puffed, skirting around him on my frequent trips up and down the stairs. I wanted him to get more involved, but at the same time I realized this was really my task and mine alone.

After a time, I noticed that Ruedi was poring over pages and pages of scribblings in a series of old school notebooks, but I was too intent on the task at hand to stop and look over his shoulder, to see what was so engrossing him. Finally, he raised his head.

"Stop a minute and come and see what I've found! You have to look at these!"

Suppressing a sigh of irritation, I went to sit beside him at the foot of the stair. I was on autopilot, intent on moving full speed ahead, and didn't want to be interrupted.

"Just look at this," he exclaimed, as he turned the fragile pages of a closely written school exercise book he was holding. There were in fact eight other such books on his lap. I leaned across and looked at the open pages and saw that not only the pages in that book, but indeed, every page of each book was filled with line after line of neat script, accompanied in some instances by little drawings and diagrams. What was remarkable was that there was little crossing out and rewriting. The cramped handwriting marched on and on, filling page after page, one exercise book picking up where the former left off, until the story came to an end in the ninth book.

What had caught Ruedi's attention were the diagrams in the first of the notebooks. There were parabolas and trajectories, sketches of propellers, and tiny maps. As I picked up the books and leafed through them, I understood with a shock of recognition that these notebooks contained my father's memoirs. Until that moment, I had had no idea that he had ever written anything like this. My parents had never talked of the past, and my early memories are of silences; my parents' generation did not look back. But now here it all was. Everything I had ever wanted to know about their history in lines of neat, tiny script, completely filling those nine exercise books. The diagrams and maps in the early notebooks accompanied a narrative of his experiences as a young fighter pilot in World War II, experiences about which I knew nothing. I remember catching my breath; if Ruedi had not picked up these notebooks, if he had not become so intrigued by the little diagrams that he began to read the accompanying prose, a priceless family record would have been lost. In addition, I would never have learned what I now know about what happened to my parents in that grim time—and it all fitted together with my father's devotion to the works of Antoine de Saint-Exupéry.

The dark cloud of memories from World War II hung heavy over children of my generation. Most of us had parents who had participated in the conflict in one way or another. Many young men and women had not returned from the war, and those who did had seen and experienced things they could never bring themselves to discuss. My sister and I were not the only children to be brought up in a household heavy with silences, punctuated by whispers or sudden outbursts. In hindsight, I can see that many of our fathers were suffering to one degree or another from what today is well known as posttraumatic stress disorder (PTSD), and it is now treated as such. Back in those days, especially among Colonials, this was more directly referred to as "keeping a stiff upper lip."

When I was a child, there was a copy of Saint-Exupéry's 1939 memoir, *Wind, Sand and Stars*, in my father's bookcase, next to the chair where he sat every evening after dinner. This was true wherever we happened to be living around the world. In this book (titled *Terre des hommes*, "Land of men," in the original, but given the more poetic English title in its translation by Louis Galantière), Saint-Exupéry wrote about flying the mail routes above the deserts of North Africa and the South American Andes. He had first recounted stories of flying the French mail over the deserts of North Africa in his first book, *Courrier sud* (*Southern Mail*, 1929), while his most famous book after *Le Petit Prince* (*The Little Prince*)—*Vol de nuit*, (*Night Flight*), published in 1931, is a thoughtful fiction, largely based on his experiences flying the mail over the Patagonian desert. (*Vol de nuit* is Number 68 in the catalog listing of Connolly's 1971 exhibition, which is the order given in the appendix.) Although I eyed *Wind, Sand and Stars* from time to time, owing to its exotic title, I never took it from the shelf, because, by and large, the books in that case were of little interest to me. Winston Churchill's history of World War II was too daunting, and although I took a stab at my great grandfather's copy of Greek myths and legends, I preferred to occupy myself with books of my own choosing, which were in my own bookcase next to my bed. Still, I can place exactly the position of that book in the bookcase, and I remember the color and style of its dust jacket very clearly in my mind's eye. I wonder why I never picked it up. After all, an author familiar to me—the author of *Le Petit Prince*—had written it. I do remember being told that it was about flying and that I'd find it boring.

The climax of the narrative in *Terre des hommes* concerns events surrounding Saint-Exupéry's airplane crash in the desert in 1935, when he and his navigator, André Prévot, nearly lost their lives to dehydration. They were ultimately saved by a passing Bedouin, who was able to provide them with a native desert remedy that enabled rapid rehydration. This true story from Saint-Exupéry's life also served as the genesis of the story of *Le Petit Prince*, which was only published in 1943. Nominally a children's story, *Le Petit Prince* is scarcely that. It's also a work of philosophy, using poetic allegory to ponder major themes of love, loss, and the follies of mankind. Like all the best children's stories, it can be read on two levels—the superficial narrative of the Little Prince who fell to earth and met a stranded pilot in the desert, or a philosophical meditation on the vagaries of human behavior and the ultimate loneliness inherent in being human. As in all of Saint-Exupéry's writing, there are autobiographical threads that weave throughout the story, so the works blend seamlessly into one another. In fact, when I finally read *Wind, Sand and Stars*, I was surprised that my father had not encouraged me to read it. He knew I loved *Le Petit Prince*, and he also knew I was a voracious reader. *Terre des hommes* is a lyrical and poetic book: Saint-Exupéry has an uncanny knack of being able to describe exactly why a pilot flies. He is constantly filled with awe by the world he sees from above, and he is in love with the adventure of flying as it was in the days when he was a pilot carrying the French mails across the deserts of northern Africa and navigating the corridors of the Andes ranges in Patagonia. His experiences as a mail pilot took place at a time when commercial aviation was just being established, in the decade before the world needed pilots to carry out the business of war.

The narrative of my father's experiences in World War II, written in that tiny, cramped script in the notebooks, turned out to be almost as dramatic as anything described by Saint-Exupéry. He enlisted in the Royal New Zealand Air Force pilot training program in 1939, after war was declared on Germany, and was sent to England, where, in 1940, he trained to fly Spitfires and Hurricanes. His squadron, RAF Squadron 258, was based for a time in Surrey, from which posting I have a photograph. It shows a group of young men, dressed in full flight gear, waiting to scramble. They are sitting around a pot-bellied stove, and there is a happy dog in the middle of the picture, warming itself at the stove. The photograph is unbearably sad to contemplate. Few of these young men survived the war; even the dog, posing happily for the camera, didn't know anything except that it was happy to be with these young men, safe for a moment in the hut, sitting around that pot-bellied stove. Although these young men of his squadron appear hopelessly young, it's also true that, despite—or perhaps because of—the dangers facing them every day in the skies, they look—if I can describe it this way— impossibly glamorous. The photograph could be inserted among any of the contemporaneous photographs of Saint-Exupéry and his colleagues, because the emotional impact is the same.

After the air war in England was over, and the Battle of Britain won, my father's squadron was ordered to the Indian Ocean by sea, through Suez. But in Gibraltar, there was a sudden change of plan, since the giant aircraft carrier HMS *Ark Royal*, which was supposed to be their transport, had been sunk by an enemy torpedo late in 1941. The young pilots were then shipped instead to Takoradi in the Gold Coast (now Ghana) in West Africa, where they were transported by Dakota airplanes across Africa—stopping to refuel at places with exotic names such as Accra, Lagos, and the Sudan. They slept under mosquito nets under the stars until they could rejoin the rest of the squadron in Aden. This experience parallels the territory of Saint-Exupéry, and the presence of *Wind, Sand and Stars* on that bookshelf starts to make sense. Of all these things I knew nothing as a child.

The rest of the story is as dramatic as anything ever written by Saint-Exupéry. The young pilots flew across the deserts of Africa, and after meeting in Aden, they embarked with their Hurricanes in the hold on another transport, heading for Singapore. But the timing of those in the War Department who had sent them to Singapore could not have been worse, because the Japanese were sweeping down through the Malaysian Peninsula, intent on taking Singapore. Scarcely had the squadron arrived than the pilots were told to unpack their Hurricanes and prepare to leave immediately, which they did. As they flew south, over the Straits of Malacca, my father's plane was shot down in Sumatra; he wrote in the memoir about lying in the wreckage of his plane in a tree, pretending to be dead, while Japanese Zero pilots circled overhead. After dark, he descended from the tree and found his way to a river, where kindly Indonesians paddled him downriver to a Dutch oil outpost; there, he found that the Dutch employees who remained onsite were burning all their records and preparing to flee. They took my father with them, and thus he arrived in Colombo, Ceylon, in time to be told to "get a plane and prepare for combat." The Battle of Colombo, which turned the tide in the Allies' favor in the Pacific War, was brutal, and the death toll very high. In the memoirs is a cryptic entry—"I attended funerals for three days after the battle." After that, there was a spell on Norfolk Island, and finally, with the Americans in Guadalcanal and Bougainville. And all this happened before my father was twenty-five years old. He was just nineteen when he enlisted.

I read most of this narrative sitting on those stairs in the Bath flat, and the story made an indelible impact. I believe now that my father read Saint-Exupéry to remember things that he himself, in hindsight, could not articulate. From that point on, I continued to read Saint-Exupéry in order to understand things that otherwise had no words for expression, because the experience of reading my father's narrative was shocking. I had not known the things the notebooks recorded, but I felt immediately certain that if I had known them, it would have made a difference to my young life. It's clear that we never really know other people, even when we live alongside them. How my father must have suffered, so much so that he could never give words to what he had seen and done in those terrible years. I tried to imagine how it must have felt to be a young pilot in the midst of an air battle, watching one's friends get shot down while trying to stay alive, and still do one's job. My father survived the war, but the remainder of his life must have been like living in a shadowland.

All of this is what makes reading the work of Saint-Exupéry such an intensely personal experience for me. Saint-Exupéry was not only a pioneer aviator, but also a gifted writer, so that he was able effortlessly to capture the world of adventure and the romance of the pioneering days of aviation in the late 1920s and the 1930s, when it was still an adventurous and glamorous occupation. For me, to read Saint-Exupéry's descriptions of the joy of being alone in a cockpit, buffeted by the wind, heading for the sunrise or the sunset just across the horizon, is to gain a visceral understanding of the reasons that so many young men flocked to enlist as trainee pilots once World War II had been declared.

I had read all of Saint-Exupéry's flying books—not only *Terre des hommes* but also *Vol de nuit* and *Courrier sud*. I had read some of his writing more than once, and although I loved his work, I now understood that his deceptively simple writing gave voice to those things that I think that my father understood only too well. I had always wondered privately about the fact that the copy of *Wind, Sand and Stars* in the bookshelf was so well thumbed. In hindsight, it's obvious that, since *Terre des hommes* is the most autobiographical of Saint-Exupéry's books, the lyrical descriptions of flying must have been close to my father's heart. He could read the words of a master writer who could understand both the joy and the terror of flying in those far-off days.

For his list, Connolly had chosen *Vol de nuit*, from 1931. To me, this was not an obvious choice. Perhaps Connolly chose it because it was Saint-Exupéry's first inspired writing in novel form that nevertheless found its inspiration from his experience as a pilot, navigator, and explorer. The plot of *Vol de nuit* creates from the narrative a philosophical conundrum—Which matters more, an individual life or carrying out duty on behalf of a whole? In the novel, the pilot, Fabien, dies in a storm while carrying the Patagonian mail. He has taken off on the instructions of the station manager, Rivière, who believes the delivery of the night mail is almost a sacred trust. Saint-Exupéry is constantly questioning the meaning of duty, what is owed to friendship, and our place in the world. Connolly could just as easily have chosen another of Saint-Exupéry's works. *Le Petit Prince* may be the most philosophically profound of all his writings, but perhaps Connolly considered this to be merely children's entertainment. Connolly's choice of *Vol de nuit* later became another of my points of contention with the whole Connolly list, once I had begun to question some of the choices he made.

In later years, particularly when I was no longer focused on the Connolly list as a locus for my collecting interests, I tried to find more items that related to Saint-Exupéry and his love of flight, but not necessarily just wonderful copies of his books. Now that I felt my father's personal experience was so bound up with that of Saint-Exupéry's, I wanted to acquire such other material that I could find that related to him and his life, that I could afford—letters, manuscripts and even drawings. Drawings by Saint-Exupéry, particularly of the Little Prince, are the most collectible of Saint Exupéry ephemera, and although many collectors seek items relating only to *Le Petit Prince*, all Saint-Exupéry material is desirable. Owing to its collectibilty, I decided that I needed to focus and to concentrate my efforts on acquiring material concerning the writings of Saint-Exupéry, since, in addition to being of most interest to me personally, for some reason these books and manuscripts were less pricey. Very recently, I was successful at the auctions for the vast collection of the now defunct Société Aristophil (of which more in a later chapter). From the most recent of these Aristophil auctions, which took place in June 2018 at Hôtel Drouot, under the auspices of the auction house Artcurial, I acquired proof copies and other material related to the books *Pilote de guerre* (which translates as "War pilot," although the book was published in English as *Flight to Arras*), *Vol de nuit*, and *Terre des hommes*.

Despite the acquisition of such important material, one of the prizes among the works of the author in my present Saint-Exupéry collection remains a copy of *Terre des hommes* that, though battered, has a personal inscription and drawing dedicated to General René Bouscat. Saint-Exupéry met this famous Algiers-based French general in Rabat, the capital of Morocco, probably following his return to active enlisted status (Saint-Exupéry enlisted in the FAFL, or Forces Aériennes Françaises Libres [Free French Air Forces] in 1943, at the relatively advanced age for a war pilot of forty-three). Bouscat had been charged by General Charles de Gaulle with the mission of merging the FAFL with the former Armée de l'Air (French Air Force), which was under the command of de Gaulle and General Henri Giraud. Following the merger of the two forces, Bouscat was placed in charge of the French Air Force. The inscription is dated February 1944, which was only a few months before Saint-Exupéry's death. It is now certain that his plane crashed near Toulon, in July 1944, but this was only confirmed in 1998 after many years of speculation, when a fisherman found a bracelet in the waters that carried the name of both Saint-Exupéry and his wife, Consuelo.

Perhaps the most important of my small but meaningful collection of items related to the life and work of Antoine de Saint-Exupéry can be found among a series of photographs I acquired at an auction at Sotheby's in Paris in 2013. The particular photograph of importance in this group is an inscribed original photograph of Saint-Exupéry's plane after the crash in the desert in 1935, that same crash that led to the anxious few days hoping for rescue, which were the genesis of the inspiration for the book *Le Petit Prince*. The anonymous inscription reads "En souvenir d'un soir de désespoir, Antoine" ("In memory of an evening of despair, Antoine"). There's no denying that it's an evocative photograph. When you look at the picture of that downed plane in the surrounding barren, desert landscape, you can almost see the Little Prince peering from behind the ruined wing of the plane.

The Turn of the Century and the First Dot-Com Bubble

By the dawn of the twenty-first century, I had raised and was investing a third fund for MedVenture Associates. The firm was now an established entity in the competitive world of Silicon Valley in our small niche of investment finance, as the first two funds had proved very profitable for our investors. Just as the second fund was larger than the first, so the third was larger than the second, reaching nearly $100 million. I fervently believed that success had come and would continue in the future because the funds "invested in people with good ideas." In other words, we invested in people, and while our mission was to be the first investor in a new concept, and to take a significant ownership position early on in the process of creating a business, first and foremost we wanted to be in investment partnership with the top entrepreneurs in our field. The strategy seemed to be working—I had invested in such diverse but ultimately successful endeavors as the first company to develop an artificial cervical disc, and the first company to use radio-frequency energy in minimally invasive surgery to treat a torn meniscus in the knee.

I had hired a young partner over the course of the second fund, George Choi. Now, with the third and much larger fund and a sea change in the investment horizon, George and I decided we needed to bring in new people. The first dot-com bubble was in full swing, and Silicon Valley was humming. Every health-care investor in the Valley, including me, was trying to work out how the Internet could affect and improve health-care delivery.

Investment proposals were flowing in the door by the hundreds. At that point, at the height of that first dot-com bubble, we were particularly overwhelmed with ideas for use of the Internet for delivery of health-care information and services. During the late 1990s, countless new companies were financed whose mission statement was to provide online commerce, education, or services in the health-care field. Medical device investors had to become dot-com specialists in a hurry. Personally, I was initially skeptical that young technology entrepreneurs with no knowledge of the complex field of health-care management could compete against the established payment and management networks of the giant health-care providers, and yet, for MedVenture Associates to remain at the cutting edge, I had to dive headfirst into this new dot-com world. There were large numbers of online health-care companies being created in the years leading up to the year 2000, and our investors wanted the firm to be part of this new and exciting field. Initially, owing to the general frenzy that surrounded dot-com investing, the speed at which things were moving, and the general excitement about this emerging investment field, all of us initially made a lot of money on paper for our investors. In the end, however, few of us cashed out for those investors, because when that first dot-com bubble burst, the decline in the value of technology stocks in general was sudden, sharp, and catastrophic, and that of the health-care dot-com companies was even more striking. The end of the first technology explosion came as suddenly as it had begun—fiercely and dramatically. In fact, the dot-com bubble didn't really burst; like a hydra, Internet technology has many heads. So while Google and Yahoo were the vanguard of that first bubble, nobody then anticipated social media and the fact that the next wave of online technology would create more wealth in an even younger population than the first wave did in the late 1990s.

In the end, Internet technology did affect and improve health-care delivery. But as I had conjectured from the outset, the online health-care world was mostly developed by institutional health-care providers. Most of the online startup companies struggled to create meaningful business enterprises in the huge, unwieldy, and nonhomogeneous area of health-care information. Today, it's taken for granted that the large health-care providers, including various branches of state and federal government, have put the administration of their businesses online. No small outside company was ever going to be able to compete with that.

For those of us who worked as medical technology investors, there was a small silver lining in all of this, because for a while after the crash, the old style of investing came back into favor. Medical technology

investing still had a few years to go before we became totally super-
annuated by the next great wave of investment into online technology. Fortunately, there were still many significant opportunities that
remained for investors in the old-school field of medical technology
after the implosion of the dot-com bubble. Other new fields of investment were opening up, and I discovered opportunities in the emerging business for aesthetic medical practice. In particular, the third fund
invested in the seed capital round of the first company to work inde-
pendently in the aesthetic field. Cutera was an aesthetic laser company
founded by a group of engineers out of the industrial laser company
Coherent, Inc. The company struggled initially to find venture capital funding, because none of my colleagues were interested in creating a company devoted to the removal of tattoos, spider veins, and un-
wanted facial hair. As a result, MedVenture Associates initially funded
the business as the sole venture investor. Over time, the business took
off, and in the end Cutera became one of the most successful IPOs in
the portfolio of that third fund, owing to our large ownership position
in the company.

The first technology boom and bust changed the face of Silicon Valley forever. One notable result was that Hollywood and legendary investors from other fields were desperately trying to work out how to
join the exclusive group of newly minted multimillionaires who were
emerging, seemingly on a daily basis, from Silicon Valley. There were
many parties, and it was at one of these, as I was standing beside a
swimming pool in an elegant Atherton back garden, teetering precar-
iously on a pair of very high-heeled shoes, that it became clear to me
that I was not really part of this emerging new scene. Atherton is the
town in Silicon Valley where money glints discreetly, rather like the little diamonds of light that were glancing off the shiny blue water of the
pool that day. The crowd was large and growing with every minute, it
seemed. Although it was the middle of the afternoon, I had a cocktail in
my hand, as did everyone else. It was the sort of party that epitomized
that first Internet boom. Despite the warm buzz in my head from that
unaccustomed midafternoon cocktail, I felt like a dinosaur among the
horde of young tech barons, who were whooping it up to the sound of
a Jamaican reggae band. Two drink stations created the cocktails that
fueled the increasing intensity of the noise, while the crowd grew in
size from moment to moment. It became increasingly difficult even to
move around.

The event was a charity auction, sponsored in part by NetJets, and its owner, the legendary investor Warren Buffett, was somewhere in the crowd. Hollywood royalty were also around. Goldie Hawn and Ben Affleck were early investors in the Internet and had come to donate dinners and events with each of them for the charity, and Arnold Schwarzenegger, who was still governor of California at that point, had donated one of his Hummers. Dana Carvey, the comedian, was the auctioneer.

"Do you want to meet Warren Buffett?" Our host, Silicon Valley godfather Ron Conway, had materialized out of the crowd.

"Yes please," replied Ruedi, before I could even think to reply. Ruedi was a huge fan of Warren Buffett. Ron took my elbow and steered me along the poolside tiles until—a few meters away—there was Warren Buffett himself. He wasn't as tall as I had expected.

"I owned your stock once," said my husband, awkwardly, "but I sold it to buy a house." Warren Buffett looked over in my direction.

"And I bet the little woman was happy about that," he said.

There's absolutely nothing you can say in response at moments like that, but I was used to it. Ron, however, was more than a little surprised by the remark.

"U-m-m-m—Warren, I must tell you that Annette is in the venture capital profession," he tried to point out, but he was not going to get through the Warren Buffett filter, although it was good of him to try. "She's raised several investment funds and they have been big successes."

It didn't matter. Warren Buffett was indifferent as to whether I was a professional woman or a snowball. In his world, I think women were firmly in the backseat. He was locked into a world of the 1950s where professional women had little place. But I was impervious to this sort of chauvinism by now, and besides, being in the company of all of this new Hollywood glamour in our otherwise staid and conservative world was an interesting diversion.

Those years of the dot-com boom were important for my collection, because the fact that I was now earning more significant money than ever before translated into being able to purchase more and better books. That was really all it ever was about for me. My career had come about more or less by accident, and although time had shown that I was a good venture capital investor, what I really yearned to achieve was respectability among those who lived in the world of books and literature. My collection of the one hundred Modern books was racing ahead, because I could now afford those titles to which, in earlier times,

I had merely aspired. Unlike many of my contemporaries, I didn't want a yacht or a plane or a big house—I just wanted to buy books. It was a heady time, and I was able to acquire some important titles.

Thanks to Priscilla Juvelis's help, I had been successful in obtain-
ing a number of the French titles on the Connolly list in addition to that fantastically inscribed copy of *Swann's Way* from the library of the Duchess of Clermont-Tonnerre. I now owned copies of Apollinaire's *Calligrammes* and *Alcools*, both Connolly titles, as well as Camus's *L'étranger* (*The Stranger*) and *La peste* (*The Plague*). These were books that I immediately cherished. Of less interest to me were the works I acquired merely because of their presence on the Connolly list, such as books by Henri de Montherlant and Henri Michaux.

Now that the search was narrowing, I was eager to complete the list of French titles. I also wanted to improve the quality of some of the items I had purchased through Priscilla. However, I still had not found the courage to participate on my own at auctions of French literature. It was not only the language barrier that concerned me: I felt that my lack of serious knowledge about French Modernism would be received with condescension at best, or cynicism at worst, if I registered to bid for myself at one of the large French auction houses. Finally, it was the result of losing some important items at an auction of the estate of André Breton that made me realize I needed to be present at significant auctions in France on my own behalf.

The auction house of Calmels-Cohen, now no longer in existence, sold the estate of André Breton in 2003. It was a huge auction. Breton's entire estate had lain undisturbed in the nearly forty years from the time of his death until his daughter agreed to sell. There were many important books and manuscripts in the series of catalogs that documented the items that were to be sold, which also included paintings, sculpture, and Breton's private papers. I studied the catalogs assiduously, sorting out what I hoped to buy, and gave the list to a dealer friend who was active in the French sales, so that he could forward bids on my behalf. Among the items in the catalog, alongside many important association works, was a series of horoscopes Breton had cast for friends and for his own interest. He had also cast the posthumous horoscopes of some of the key authors and poets of the French Modern Movement, such as Rimbaud, Mallarmé, and Huysmans. My dealer friend sent a fax with his and my fixed bids listed for the auctioneer, and I waited impatiently to hear the results of the auction. Finally, having heard nothing from him, I called.

"What's the news?" I asked. "How did I do?"

"Not well," he told me, somewhat evasively. "You got the Breton horoscope of Huysmans." I had wanted this item because of the significance of the association that this horoscope created between those important representatives of different schools within Modernism—Breton and Huysmans.

"What else?" I asked. "Surely, there were other items?"

It turned out there had been a problem with the transmission of the fax, which had not completely arrived. Most of my left bids had been written out on a sheet of paper that, the dealer told me, he had found stuck in his fax machine the next day. Thus, most of my bids were never entered for the sale: all I acquired from that historic sale was the single horoscope. The Huysmans horoscope was a good purchase, but it was not the best of the horoscopes that came up for sale at that auction. I was not happy, to say the least. However, the error had one salutary effect—it confirmed for me that I would have to begin to participate in French book and manuscript auctions on my own behalf.

French Bibliomania and the Rise and Fall of the Société Aristophil

The French are natural bibliophiles and derive much pleasure from displaying their literary treasures at auction. Willa Silverman, a professor of Jewish and French studies at Penn State University, wrote a book on the subject, *The New Bibliopolis*, where she described the rise of an upper-bourgeois bohemian class in late nineteenth-century France that had an intense interest in bibliophilic activity, which in turn came to define French culture at the turn of the century. This interest in books has continued to the present day. The Association Internationale de Bibliophile (International Association of Bibliophiles, or AIB), the most exclusive of the bibliophile societies, is headquartered at the Bibliothèque Nationale in Paris and carries out all its proceedings in French. Many years previously, Neil Ritchie had arranged for me to be invited to join the AIB, but I resigned membership after a few years. The members of the AIB concentrated mostly on collecting incunabula, and rather looked down on collectors of any literature of note written after the turn of the eighteenth century, so that I never ceased being an outsider. People like me, who merely collected works of Modernist literature, were considered *arrivistes*, despite the fact that the noted collector of Modernist writing—Anthony Hobson—been very involved with the society during his lifetime.

The extent of French bibliophilia is evident in any major bespoke sale, an example being that of the collection of Pierre Bergé, which came to market in several sales between 2015 and 2018. Over the years, together with his partner Yves St. Laurent, Pierre Bergé assembled important collections of art, furniture, rugs, and tapestries as well as an important book and manuscript collection, the first part of which came to auction in 2015. The publicity surrounding the three sales provided an interesting snapshot into French collecting. In Bergé's case, the sale projected his image in the public eye as an intellectual and aesthete in a way that the sale of his other collections of important objets d'art had not done. Before each sale, Sotheby's and the house of Pierre Bergé et Associés undertook a worldwide tour with some of the most important items in the sale. The presale publicity also included video clips, available online, which showed Bergé in serious literary conversation with such intellectuals as Jean-Yves Tadié, the specialist on Marcel Proust, and the French author Charles Dantzig. Despite, or even because of, the cost of the presale publicity, the sale was probably not profitable for the auction houses, but since one of the houses involved in the sales was owned by Bergé himself, that probably was not one of his concerns. The catalogs for each sale were large books, printed on exquisite paper, intended to be collectors' items in their own right. In a nation where a philosopher such as Bernard-Henri Lévy can have the status of a rock star, Bergé was probably content with the outcome.

I hadn't intended to buy anything in the Bergé sales because I considered them overhyped. However, the third auction contained one of the fifteen corrected manuscripts of one of the cornerstones of Modernist poetry, Mallarmé's famous 1897 symbolist poem *Un coup de dés jamais n'abolira le Hasard (A Throw of the Dice Will Never Eliminate Chance)*. I registered to bid, proceeded to bid online—which is a wonderful development of recent years in the auction business—and acquired the item. This time I did not overpay. It was quite a difference from the experience of bidding in the first French auction in which I participated by telephone!

That French auction had been held in May 2003 at the Hotel George V in Paris. Here was one of the few occasions when the refined worlds of books and manuscripts collided with my business life. Since the auction began at 7 p.m. in Paris, that meant it was only 10 a.m. in California, so I decided to monitor the sale and bid in the auction from my office. By that time, MedVenture Associates had moved to new premises in Emeryville, California, a small, active city that sits at the apex of a triangle bounded by Berkeley and Oakland in the East Bay, just across the Bay Bridge from San Francisco. Owing to the dotcom and biotechnology booms, it had developed rapidly from the late 1980s to become a hub of the new technology economy, thanks also in part to an enlightened city government that took advantage of the anti-development policies of the city governments of its neighboring towns. Both the life sciences industry and the new information technology cultures flourished within Emeryville's borders. Although previously known primarily for its abandoned railway lines, surrounded by rotting warehouses and ancient office buildings, the small town became in the 1990s an example of modern design and town planning because it had by then remodeled its wasted spaces, making them into high-density housing and office premises. I had yearned to have our offices in that location, but unfortunately, until the dot-com bust temporarily threatened to return Emeryville to its previous isolation, we couldn't afford the rents charged by the Emeryville landlords. All of that changed as the technology markets crumbled in the earliest years of the new century, and I was able to establish our offices in a brand-new office building, with large windows looking directly west across to the bay, with the Golden Gate Bridge just visible in the distance on a clear day. The train lines that still ran from the Port of Oakland passed almost directly opposite our windows, so we had views of freight and passenger trains, industry, freeways, and finally, the water. We had a corner suite with a small patio, which I filled with tall pots full of plants that could resist the dry sea winds. There never was and never will be such a hospitable environment from which to conduct business. I looked forward to work every day of the nearly fourteen years that MedVenture Associates inhabited that space.

I was in the new offices on the morning of the auction, where I settled myself at my desk, swiveled the chair to face the western sea view, and awaited the first call from the auctioneers. The auction was being held to sell the famous collection of the Monégasque collector François Ragazzoni, whose large collection of French titles sold over three successive days at the French auction house of Tajan. The Modernist items that interested me were to be sold on only one of those three days, but the extensive catalog contained many delicious, expensive, and highly desirable items. I was going to have to make many choices and decisions about what to pursue and what to let go to another bidder, but despite my initial anxiety about the sale, in the end I acquired most of the lots in which I was interested. On the other hand, it wasn't quite as simple as that, and the auction was a significant learning experience for me, because I was definitely unsuccessful in controlling my budget. I got carried away by auction fever and overpaid for nearly every item I acquired. Not only that, but the appearance of some of the items when I finally received them did not match my interpretation of the catalog descriptions. Perhaps I had failed to take into account the nuances of the French language in reading the descriptions? I took it all to be part of the learning process, but it was a harsh first lesson. Even today, none of the items I purchased in that first Ragazzoni sale have regained in value anything close to what I paid for them that day.

The item in the sale that I was most eager to buy was one of twenty copies of Louis-Ferdinand Céline's famous book *Voyage au bout de la nuit* (*Journey to the End of the Night*). It was a Connolly title that I already possessed, but I had only a trade copy; this copy was exceedingly rare. It had been dedicated to a Monsieur Raymond Saucier and was presented in a *Livre d'Artiste* binding. Unfortunately, I entered a bidding war and paid over twice what the book had earned at its previous auction. Sadly, the book, when I finally took possession of it, was not in the sort of condition that justified the price—the inscription had been nearly washed out by a later owner, perhaps someone who resented Céline's embrace of the fascist movement in the 1930s. I later wondered if, by chance, the counterbidder for the Céline book had been a representative of the infamous Société Aristophil.

I had not yet heard of the Société Aristophil by that time, or else I might have been more judicious in my approach to the French auction market for rare books and manuscripts. The Société Aristophil met its end after the unraveling of a major scandal that would be difficult to imagine occurring in any country that was not as devoted to the book and to literature. Founded in 1990 by a minor dealer, Gerard Lhéritier, the mission of Aristophil was simple, and it preyed on the French love of books, manuscripts, and history. Aristophil bought rare books and documents and sold shares in what was bought—sometimes creating a value many times the actual worth of the item itself. The best known of these schemes was its purchase in 2002 of documents and correspondence that had passed between Albert Einstein and his friend Dr. Michele Besso, concerning the theory of general relativity. Lhéritier bought this important exchange of letters at a New York auction at Christie's for $556,000. Aristophil then sold shares in the manuscripts to a group of investors, who paid, in the end, a total of $12 million for the documents. In addition to selling shares in each item purchased, Lhéritier promised investors an annual 8 percent return on their investment, providing they did not expect to withdraw money in the following five years.

To further legitimize the Aristophil venture, Lhéritier created the Musée des Lettres et Manuscrits at a good address on the Boulevard St. Germain, to which investors could come to view the collection, including items in which they had fractional ownership. You can imagine a devoted grandfather taking a grandson to look at Breton's original

Manifeste du Surréalisme (*Surrealist Manifesto*), or Charles de Gaulle's wartime papers, proudly imparting the news to his grandson that the family actually owned a share in these important documents. The French dealer Frédéric Castaing encapsulated the bibliophilia of the French when he said, in an interview with BBC News reporter Hugh Schofield in March 2016, that true collectors "aren't that interested in the pecuniary value of a document. They love the touch of it, the sense of communing with a personage who is normally shut up in an encyclopedia." What he said, in fact, is no different from Maurice Neville's comment many years previously about the inscription in a copy of Fitzgerald's *Tender Is the Night* that he owned at that time. Perhaps this feeling of wishing to commune with the literary personage is something that I have in common with many bibliophiles.

Over the years, Aristophil's operation went from strength to strength. By the time the regulators swooped in and shuttered the business in 2014, a total of 18,000 hapless people had invested a total sum estimated to range between 300 million to 700 million euros—the actual amount was difficult to quantify amid all the inflated valuations of the documents that had been purchased. It was the literary equivalent of the Madoff financial scandal, and as long as Aristophil was in business, it meant that at auction, if Aristophil wanted an item, Lhéritier or one of his people would just continue bidding until the item was theirs. If they overpaid, they simply sold more shares in the item to drive up their profits. It was foolish to even think of bidding for an item in which Aristophil had an interest, but I did not know about its activities until the scandal came to a head. The firm had a particular interest in some of the same writers I was trying to collect, including Apollinaire and Saint-Exupéry. No wonder the works I bought over those years were so expensive.

The atmosphere in the room in any sale of French literature is always electric, at least in my experience. Nothing in the book auction world comes close to the thrill of being present in person at a major literary auction in Paris. Despite the demise of the Société Aristophil, dealers and collectors are still not afraid to bid items up to levels far above the estimates. Indeed, estimates in catalogs for French book sales can give only a rough indication of the price that will finally be paid for any given item. Enthusiastic applause breaks out if someone has broken some previous sales record after an intense round of bidding. There's also an element of surprise post-sale, because the Bibliothèque Nationale is also active at manuscript and autograph sales, and has the right to preempt what one thought until then was a successful purchase. After a sale, the Bibliothèque Nationale might tell the auction house that it will acquire an item that has been bought in the sale; all it has to do is match the price and your acquisition is lost.

The role of an auctioneer at a literary sale in Paris is very different from that of his or her English or American counterparts. The latter are far more matter-of-fact—the French auctioneers have a more histrionic role. They are on the auctioneer's podium to cajole, to entreat, to enjoin—to work the room. Each item in the sale is first presented lovingly to the saleroom almost with regret, as if it would be a shame to sell something so rare and so beautiful; nevertheless, it must be done. In many auctions, the "expert" will give a learned opinion about the item before the bidding begins. I've been present at auctions where a veritable team of these "experts" have been seated near the auctioneer's podium and the proceedings have taken twice as long than they would in another country, owing to the time given to the experts' opinions. The auctioneer expresses astonishment at any lack of bids and will address the saleroom reproachfully, concentrating attention on any previous bidder who might have dropped out, entreating that bidder to realize what he or she is giving up, and urging a further bid. Needless to say, this entire process takes a lot of time; on average, I've noticed that whereas in a New York sale, one item will probably sell every thirty or so seconds, in Paris, you can sometimes safely quadruple that estimate. It also means that choice items generally can be sold at hammer prices far beyond the estimates shown in the sale catalog.

We collectors had been waiting for the denouement of the Société Aristophil story and it happened quite suddenly. Shortly before Christmas in 2017, I made a special trip to Paris for a singular auction, billed as the first of many, to be held at the Hôtel Drouot. The Hôtel Drouot was established in the mid-nineteenth century to provide facilities for major sales held by small, regional auction houses. It has sixteen auction halls, which are used by about seventy different small French dealers and auctioneers. The premises are bustling, crowded, modern, and utilitarian. It was not the place where I would have expected to find the first auction of the contents of the over 130,000 items of the Aristophil collection. However, upon further thought, I realized that Hôtel Drouot was the only possible venue for the sale advertised, because, in the end, the receivers had allocated the task of selling the collection to a provincial French auction house, Maison Aguttes.

The news of the sale broke in November, when Aguttes held a news conference about its plan to sell the Aristophil works held in receivership. There would be a series of three hundred auctions over the course of six years. This would have been a herculean task even if it had been undertaken by a major auction house like Christie's or Sotheby's. Expected to go under the hammer at the first auction were two items of major literary significance—the manuscript of the infamous *Les 120 Journées de Sodome* (*The 120 Days of Sodom*) of the Marquis de Sade and the manuscript of the *Manifeste du Surréalisme*, which Breton wrote in the late 1920s. In the end, the French government swooped in fortyeight hours ahead of the sale and declared that neither work should be sold at auction; instead, private funds should be found to preserve both items for French heritage. Despite the fact that neither of these works would be sold at the auction, the sale proceeded for the other items that had been listed in the catalog, which depicted any number of important drawings as well as some paintings, some items of art nouveau jewelry, and some letters, manuscripts, and first and rare editions of the work of major writers (though not all of these were French). Artifacts relating to Napoleon were also among the offerings. The fact that the auction would be held so close to Christmas, that the announcement of the sale only came out in November, and that the catalog was only available a few days ahead of the sale all contributed to a general air of confusion about the whole matter.

On the afternoon of the sale, I arrived promptly at the Hôtel Drouot, but to my dismay I found that the entrance to the room where the auction was to be held was blocked by a small crowd of people, all shouting and gesturing angrily. Many of them had press credentials, and they had been denied entrance as a result of overcrowding in the auction room. I managed to find a guard to escort me through the scrum, brandishing my entrance permit as I pushed through the milling crowd. This in itself was unusual—you don't normally need a special permit to enter an auction room. The room was full, but not with buyers, who represented at most 30 percent of those present. The rest of the space was filled mostly with press, television cameras, and onlookers. There was still a free seat in the front row, but it had a "reserved" sign on it, which I removed. When I sat down, no one challenged me. The second row was full of faces I recognized from Sotheby's and Christie's, people who had come out of curiosity to audit the proceedings. Now I was seated, and the auction was about to begin, but I was still a little baffled by it all. Even though I was nominally registered for the sale, I had no auction paddle, and so I had no idea how I would bid. Once the auction began, however, the mystery of the missing paddles was solved. In order to bid, people either waved their hands or called out their bids, because the room was too crowded for the auctioneer to see who was bidding and who was a spectator. Only if you won a bid did you receive an auction paddle! I left the auction halfway through the sale, having purchased a series of letters written by Jean Cocteau to the journalist André Parinaud—not letters of particular importance, but the price was reasonable. It felt strange to be buying items that had previously been purchased by representatives of Aristophil, people I had doubtless bid against many times over the past twenty years. While I was still in the auction room, I observed that the sale proceeded at an even slower pace than usual, owing largely to the presence of the experts, but even so, there were few surprises, and there were no records set for the prices achieved by the literature in the sale. The most significant price that had been achieved by the time I left was for an art nouveau Lalique pendant, which sold for close to 80,000 euros, over ten times the estimate given in the catalog. Few examples of the literature on offer achieved prices beyond the catalog estimates.

The administrators learned from that first chaotic sale. The next group of sales was handed over to four different auction houses to conduct seven contemporaneous sales in June 2018, and three of these were dedicated almost entirely to Modernist literature. Also held at Hôtel Drouot, this series of auctions was equally unusual, but in a different way than previously. To start with, the second series of auctions was held over a period of three days, and the sheer volume of what was on offer stretched both budgets and the ability to review the sale offerings in a timely manner. Once again, Maison Aguttes produced a catalog that included works by many Modernist writers, while another catalog produced by the auction house of Drouot Estimations, containing more extensive offerings of Modernist French authors, competed for attention. A third—and exquisite—catalog was created by the house of Artcurial; called *Histoires Postale—Héroes de l'Aviation*, it featured, to my delight, extensive examples of the Aristophil holdings of the writing and art of Antoine de Saint-Exupéry as well as related letters and other ephemera.

Once again, I made the trip to Paris to view the presale exhibition and arrange my telephone bidding for the days of the three sales. The exhibition of the treasure trove of literature and music on offer was held in a claustrophobically small room lined with densely packed glass-fronted cases of material. What was on show was magnificent!

I couldn't believe my luck: the estimates, for once, were reasonable, and there didn't seem to be too many prospective buyers browsing the Modernist items. But the atmosphere was tense, because the luckless Aristophil investors clearly continued to feel cheated by this injudicious disposal of the treasures—while I was there, security guards had to be called to take a former Aristophil investor into custody. Quite reasonably, in my view, he had mounted a platform and begun to rant loudly about Aristophil's crimes and fulminate about how Lhéritier had cheated the grandparents of France out of their savings.

The Saint-Exupéry material was significant, and I noticed that while there was interest in the drawings, nobody except me seemed to be taking much interest in the manuscripts. It was clear that the administrators had been charged with selling the Aristophil material regardless of how the prices fell, although there were reserves.

On the days of the three sales in which I was interested, I participated with difficulty by telephone. I say "difficulty" because Drouot does not provide good telephone connections; the house is only slowly moving its methods to accommodate twenty-first-century auction procedures. I spent far more than I should have, but I acquired most of the items I wanted in each auction, particularly the works relating to Saint-Exupéry that I had earmarked. The bidding in each auction was surprisingly lackluster, and since there were few people like me, bidding on their own account, I overpaid for nothing I bought. As a collector, I felt that this began to make up somehow for the items I had lost to Aristophil in the past, or for which I had overpaid thanks to Aristophil bidding against me. Among other items, I acquired in the Artcurial auction *Histoires Postale* some wonderful items relating to the life and work of Antoine de Saint-Exupéry—one of the corrected proofs of *Vol de nuit*, a fragment of the handwritten manuscript of *Terre des hommes*, and the handwritten manuscript of some chapters of *Pilote de guerre*.

I continue to feel sorry for those grandparents of France who invested with such enthusiasm into the dream of owning part of the great French literary heritage. Unfortunately, like all financial scams, when these things unravel it is usually the innocent and unwary who end up on the losing end. That maxim is certainly proving true in the case of the disposal of the collections of the late Société Aristophil.

Acceleration

COMPLETION OF THE CONNOLLY LIST

Farallon Restaurant used to be one of the most chic in San Francisco. The entrance, from whose ceiling hung large jellyfish made of blown glass, led to an elegant back room where more blown-glass fish and invertebrate sea creatures dangled from the ceiling or clung to the little fences and railings separating the ordinary diners from those favored customers who had penetrated the select inner circle. The seating in the back room rose in tiers: if you were one of the privileged few, you could be seated discreetly at the very back, on the highest level, at a booth or quiet table. During conferences held at the St. Francis Hotel across the street, it was almost impossible to obtain a table at lunchtime, because corporate executives booked these tables months, if not years, in advance.

Yet here I was, sitting at one of the best tables in Farallon, enjoying lunch with a colleague. It was January 2005, and the giant J. P. Morgan Healthcare Conference was in full swing. I had initiated the first of these meetings during my years at Hambrecht & Quist, and the first conference had been held in 1983. When Chase Manhattan Bank, later part of J. P. Morgan, acquired Hambrecht & Quist in 1999, it continued the tradition I had started, and the conference grew to become the largest health-care finance meeting of its kind. The first meeting I convened registered a total of 220 attendees and the conference showcased 20 companies. By 2005, the meeting was still being held each January at the St. Francis Hotel, but it now had to restrict itself to no more than 10,000 attendees, while it showcased between 400 and 500 company presentations. In addition to the registered attendees, the conference also attracted a large number of investors who were not registered at the conference, because the venue became the largest of its kind in the world for the financing of startup health-care businesses. Other in-

vestment banking firms, along with private investors and many venture firms, set up shop in the surrounding hotels and offices during the
conference in order to hear presentations from a selection among the
thousands of hopeful entrepreneurs who also came to San Francisco at
this time seeking funding, and who trudged around Union Square in
San Francisco in hopeful anticipation, slogging their way from meeting
to meeting, usually in the cold and the rain.

Things were going well for MedVenture Associates, and I was feeling tentatively happy about my career trajectory. At the end of 2004,
my partners and I had successfully raised a fifth significant venture
fund, and it had closed with $165 million of committed capital. This
meant we could fund a selection of the many investment opportunities that came our way—and even perhaps find a good investment
prospect among the business ideas being promoted by one or more of
the entrepreneurs currently treading hopeful paths among the Union
Square hotels. Other good things were happening, too. The aesthetic
laser company Cutera that we had backed when nobody else was interested had turned out to be a very profitable investment following its
successful IPO. In addition, MedVenture Associates had served as lead
investor for a diabetes diagnostic company, TheraSense, and the Med-
Venture funds holding that investment showed significant returns on
the invested capital when that company carried out a successful IPO
in 2001, followed by the sale of the company to Abbott Labs in 2004
for over $1 billion. As a result of all of these events, we had made a sig-
nificant profit for our investors at a time when the first technology dot-
com boom had come to a crashing halt. Although many investors in
other sectors were losing significant amounts of money as a result of
the dot-com bust, medical technology was prospering, and as a result
of our investments doing so well in that period of decline elsewhere, I
had found myself on the *Forbes* Midas List for the first time. The Midas
List, although somewhat superficial, was and remains a bellwether for
investment achievement. It lists, in descending order—based on the investment returns earned for investors in any particular fund—the top
one hundred private equity investors in the United States over the previous year. Everyone in venture capital feigns scorn for the Midas List,
but if they think they have a chance to be included, they nevertheless
eagerly assemble and submit the data the *Forbes* staff will analyze to
compile it. I had done the same thing, of course, and although I didn't
advertise that I had been selected, word had got around.

Chauvinism was not dead in the venture capital world. Shortly after the news came out about the Midas List, I was sitting next to an elderly but highly esteemed investor, Bill Draper, at a lunch meeting when someone came over to congratulate me on my inclusion on the Midas List. Bill, who overheard the words of congratulation, turned to me, his face registering genuine surprise.

"Would that Midas List be the same Midas List that my son Tim is on?" he inquired. He was another member of the generation that just couldn't fathom that women could succeed in the world of venture investing. I merely nodded assent and got on with my lunch.

However, the lunch at Farallon in January 2005 was different. Farallon was crowded with investors and senior-level corporate officials, and as I sat with my colleague, I felt like a very minor celebrity. One person after another came up to congratulate me. People turned in their seats to see what was happening at our table. At one point, as I looked up at the small circle of senior investors surrounding us, all of whom were genuinely happy for me, I was momentarily distracted by a small voice inside my head. "You'd better remember this moment," it told me, "because this is the highest career pinnacle you are going to reach. It's never going to be as good as this again. This is the top; you've gone as far now as you will ever go with this career."

It wasn't that I was prescient, but it seemed very unlikely that everything would come together in this way again, and, of course, it never did. That moment was indeed the high point of my career, but at least I recognized the fact at the time. To be truthful, since it was a career trajectory that had not been planned, the fact that it had gone well up until that time was surprising even to me. But I had worked hard, and this moment of recognition made all the hard work worthwhile.

My collecting activities, which always supplied my happiest hours, had also become more than prolific in those first years of the new century, especially once my auction addiction declared itself. In those years, there were a number of key sales in London, Paris, New York, and even Boston and Los Angeles. A number of significant collections, such as those of Roy Davids and Maurice Neville, came to the auction block in New York and London. In Paris, after the Ragazzoni sale, there was a continual stream of major sales of works related to surrealism, symbolism, and Modernism. I registered to bid at so many auctions that I nearly lost track of where I was bidding and when, but with funds at my disposal and a desire to complete my collection, I finally acquired all the books on the Connolly list. In fact, once I completed the list, I kept going, and now I was simply upgrading the quality of some of the items because I had the financial means at my disposal to do so.

My records from those years show that what I was earning on the one hand was being spent on the other on books and related material. Finally, after the years when I could only peruse the catalogs with longing, and had to make tough decisions about what to purchase, I was in the heady position of being able to afford most of the items of interest that came up in auction and dealer catalogs, although items priced in the six- and seven-figure range were still beyond my means. The only problem was that I was moving so fast in both my work and my collecting that I seldom really had an opportunity to spend time with a new acquisition and appreciate it as much as it deserved to be appreciated.

The auction world for Modernist items was moving almost at the same speed as my life as a professional investor, so it almost seemed as if completing the acquisition of works on Connolly's list had become like a commercial activity. Ticking off the final copies needed and finding a way to buy them, but with little personal investment in the decision, turned the completion of the list into a shopping expedition of sorts. I bid at auction from hotel rooms, from mobile phone connections, from my home, and from my office. I bid at all hours of the day and night—I remember once bidding at a Sotheby's auction at 2 a.m. from New Zealand, trying to stay awake throughout the course of the sale. In my spare time, I read dealer catalogs—at that point, dealers had not become as disintermediated by the Internet as they are today, so catalogs were still important records of dealer inventory. My collection grew and grew, and I was constantly expanding shelf space in the cabinets of my home office where the collection resided, in order to accommodate items that arrived in shipments from Federal Express or DHL or other couriers, although often I carried them home myself from one book fair or another.

It was during this period that I also became a critic of some of the titles on the Connolly list, and I began to question the reason for omission of other writers about whom I was enthusiastic. There were a number of books on the list in which I had little interest, so I had merely bought good examples of first editions and considered that part of the list complete. Among those names would be certain of the French writers—de Montherlant, Valéry, Michaux—whose works I bought in fine Livres d'Artistes bindings, although I never attempted to find reading copies of the works, either in French or English. Similarly, while I dipped from time to time into my copy of the nine volumes that made up the *Journal des Goncourt*, I never tried to find the best copy extant of the series. I had similar reservations about a few of the writers in English. I was not very interested in the work of Ivy Compton-Burnett, for example, and I thought Stephen Spender's poetry boring. My boat was bobbing up against the shore, because in truth, even though I was busy upgrading the Connolly titles in my possession, the collection was complete. The remaining interest in collecting resided in the fact that I was also expanding the collection laterally, acquiring, in addition to better copies of Connolly titles already in my possession, copies of related ephemera, such as authors' correspondence. I found the acquisition of key letters, drawings, and scraps of manuscript material to be strangely satisfying. I didn't know it at the time, but this expansion of the scope of my collecting activities would lead directly to my post-Connolly collecting world.

Sadly, there came a final moment when I knew that even collecting improved copies of Connolly books and associated material could no longer disguise the fact that the collection was complete. In the collection now were leaves of major manuscripts, perhaps the most important being a typescript page from the Circe episode of *Ulysses*, which I bought at Christie's in 2005. This acquisition, and the purchase of an excellent copy of Mallarmé's *Poesies*, in the limited edition of forty-seven examples on Japon paper, at an auction held by the house of Pierre Bergé et Associés to sell the library of the famous collector and auctioneer Pierre Berès, probably were the final purchases that completed the collection.

During this time, before I admitted that there was little more I could do to improve my collection of Modern Movement titles, I became increasingly interested in a new endeavor: finding material relating to writers whose work appealed to me personally, but whom Connolly had neglected. Some of these authors simply fell outside the limits of the timeline Connolly had imposed on the list, 1890 to 1950. But for others, the reasons were unknown. Those of interest to me who had been omitted included authors and poets such as Mervyn Peake, Malcolm Lowry, and, of course, Paul Verlaine.

At the Tajan sale in 2003, I had purchased a photograph of Paul Verlaine. It was an original print from an edition of four separate photographs, showing Verlaine drinking absinthe in a café, François 1er, in May 1892. The photographer was a mysterious chronicler of late nineteenth-century society who went by the name, probably a nom de plume, of Paul Dornac. In my photograph, Verlaine sits in the corner of his booth, almost shrinking from the camera, his glass of absinthe at his elbow. He looks worn and defeated. Perhaps he is contemplating the wreckage of his life; perhaps he has just had too much absinthe. It's a melancholy photograph, but I studied it again and again, because it brought an insight into the person who created that magical poetry, that word-music of the early symbolist movement which intrigued me so much. This could be a direction of collecting in its own right! In hindsight, it's clear that I really was more interested almost from the beginning of the Connolly collection in material that had a personal connection to the writers I revered and whose works I cherished. Books alone—even fine first editions in immaculate dust jackets, never had the same appeal, as my particular devotion to the copy of *The Great Gatsby* inscribed to Walter Bruington clearly showed.

I found, for example, that my Breton horoscope of Huysmans, which was not even close to being as important as, say, an inscribed copy of Breton's seminal work of surrealism, *Nadja*, was more fascinating to me than my copy of the book, even though the book was encased in a *Livre d'Artiste* binding. The horoscope was only incidentally related to Modernism, but Breton took enormous care over these horoscopes and clearly they were serious endeavors. As time went by in those early years of the twenty-first century, I found and purchased several books by authors in whom I had a deep interest that were not on Connolly's list. There was a battered copy of *Under the Volcano* that Lowry had dedicated to his wife Margerie, for example, and several copies of various books of the Mervyn Peake *Gormenghast Trilogy*, one of which was inscribed to Dylan Thomas. I suppose I had not yet admitted to myself that there was nothing more to be done with the collection of Connolly titles, but as time went on, the collection strayed further and further from the books of the Modern Movement.

Hubris

Without doubt, over the period of the so-called dot-com boom and for some years thereafter, I had conformed to every auctioneer's and dealer's idea of a perfect client. Dizzy with the purchasing power bestowed by my enhanced financial status, and not least owing to the fact that there was a lot on offer in those years, I had, by the early years of the new century, assembled a significant representative series of Connolly's Modern Movement books. My collection included signed copies of books as well as books with wonderful inscriptions—association copies linking authors to their contemporaries. I had a few manuscripts, examples of *Livres d'Artistes* bindings, and even some good English bindings. And, of course, I had significant books in some very fine dust jackets. Suddenly, it was not enough. Just as I had reached a dead end in my collecting all those many years ago before I began the project to assemble a representative group of Modern Movement titles, now I was at another dead end, because I had nowhere further to go with the books of the Connolly list.

It was strangely deflating to know, finally, that the list was complete. After spending over twenty years in the pursuit of the key works of Connolly's one hundred Modern books, the pure motive behind assembling the collection vanished. When the list was complete, the pursuit of better copies, closer associations, and related items lost its element of challenge—the excitement of finding a significant example of a major title needed for the collection was gone. I began to experience a certain fatigue with the project—Connolly fatigue, I called it. I had assiduously collected the titles of the list, and now the task was done.

Not only that, but I had by then developed my own opinions about Connolly's key books, and even had begun to disagree with some of his choices. For instance, when I thought about the French works on the

Connolly list, there was always in front of me that startling omission of Paul Verlaine's writing. I had by now spent so many years with Connolly, collecting the list of Modern Movement books, reading about Connolly, and discussing Connolly, that I felt familiar enough with his sometimes slapdash way of working to feel that the list included some writers whose presence might have been due to nothing more than Connolly's desire to get to that magic number of one hundred (or one hundred and eight, depending how one looks at the list). Some of the writers who had been included were distinguished, and in some cases, great, but I couldn't really see what their works added to the canon of the Modernist movement. In my mind, W. Somerset Maugham, Ivy Compton-Burnett, or even Katherine Mansfield belonged to a secondary list. These writers produced masterpieces of fiction, but I didn't think their works constituted Modernist writing. Modernism, to me, was T. S. Eliot, Ezra Pound, Mallarmé, Jarry, Joyce—writers who had taken literary expression into a new realm of ideas. I also thought some of the writers Connolly had chosen were simply not good enough to be on the list. My private opinion was that Stephen Spender was probably included merely because he happened to belong to the same social milieu as Auden and Isherwood. To me, the Modern Movement stemmed from Pound's observation, "Make It New," and I always looked at works I acquired from that viewpoint.

The idea of selling the collection never entered my mind at this stage, even though I worried about maintaining the condition of the books and manuscripts and about proper storage of the collection. The increase in value of some of my books mandated large insurance premiums, and with that increase in value, my pleasure in handling these now very expensive items had decreased. I was now continually concerned about somehow destroying the value of the books by inadvertently cracking a spine or splitting a page. At the same time, I was seriously concerned about how to conserve some very fragile items in the collection that had been published on paper that now threatened to disintegrate. The paper on which books were printed in the World War I and World War II eras was often of extremely poor quality, and it browned and flaked easily as it aged. Improper care by previous owners had taken its toll as well. The pages of my dedicated copy of *Ubu Roi*, Jarry's existentialist 1896 masterpiece, were now so fragile that I was afraid the tiny volume could disintegrate, so I never took it out of its bespoke case. I sent the *Ubu Roi* to an expert restorer in Chicago who suggested an unsatisfactory solution—conserving the pages separately by encasing them in sheets of plastic. What to do? I couldn't encase the pages of fragile books in plastic, like menus in cheap restaurants! The ownership of the collection was starting to become a big responsibility, which decreased the pleasure of ownership. This was something I had never anticipated. Plus—and this is important to reiterate—the collection was complete. I could keep adding better copies of books and related material, but this didn't have the same emotional impact for me.

At the same time that I was trying to solve the conundrum of what to do about my collection, the financial markets began once again to hurtle ahead like a runaway train. Few among us stopped long enough to reflect on what was happening in the markets in the early years of the twenty-first century. The Dow Jones Index, which reached a high of nearly 12,000 in 2000, fell to a low of about 7,500 in late 2002. From there it began to recover in a bull market that continued until the financial crisis of 2008, which brought everything to another crashing halt. During those few lean years up until 2003, what most concerned the majority of venture capital investors was how the aftereffects of the crash of the first Internet investing bubble were affecting the returns for their investment portfolios. Counterintuitively, it was in those few years that MedVenture Associates achieved its biggest successes. Although the firm had its share of losses from our dot-com investments in companies created during the Internet bubble, the funds were protected by the fact that we had continued to invest in new developments in the field of medical technology. The IPO of the diabetes off-fingertip monitoring company, TheraSense, occurred during the same period when we sold Spinal Dynamics, a company founded by a brilliant neurosurgeon from Seattle who had developed the first synthetic cervical disc implant. Since our funds had significant ownership of the stock of Spinal Dynamics, they made a good profit from that sale.

However, what we didn't realize at the time was that the crash of the first Internet bubble had created a fundamental dislocation in the venture capital investing markets that was going to affect all seed capital and medical technology funds adversely over the long run. Of course, in the business of early-stage investing in fields that are heavily regulated, such as medical technology, it takes a full investing cycle—at least five years—for a serious problem to declare itself. This is why we at first discounted the emerging competition in the medical technology investment field, which came from very large funds that had been raised to invest in Internet-related opportunities. Now that the cash in-

vested in those particular funds was lying idle—and once the partners
in those firms became aware of the ongoing success of medical technology investments—we found ourselves encountering unexpected
investment competition. Social media had not yet become a viable investment field, something that would later garner the attention of these
funds, so in the absence of other investment ideas, many of the same
huge funds that had once focused on investing in dot-com businesses
began to drown our small investment sector with the sorts of financings that had to be unproductive in the long term: large amounts of
money invested at valuations with which we simply couldn't compete. As a result, we had runaway inflation in the medical technology
sector—too much money was chasing after too few good investment
opportunities.

Still, nobody except a very few hedge fund investors had any idea
that a crisis was building that would obscure the magnitude of the market crash of 2000 and nearly bring down the entire world financial system. The public markets were recovering, and all seemed well once
again. The next meltdown of the markets was some years away, but the
size of the debt that was piling up in so-called safe institutions, such as
the large banks and federally backed loan agencies, was all the while
growing in the darkness. Everyone fishing on the banks of that river
of money rejoiced at the swell of the flood careening past, but without
stopping to consider that the high-water marks resulted directly from
the draining of the dams holding the water in the first place. The un-
regulated environment that led to the collapse of the financial markets
in 2008 with the implosion of the subprime mortgage market may still
emerge as one of the greatest financial scandals ever to hit the world
financial markets. However, despite fines being levied against a number of the banks involved in the scandal, in the end nobody paid with
jail terms. It's likely that this sort of financial disaster will happen again
sometime in some other form.

On a personal level, my alarm bells should have rung when our
housekeeper and her husband bought their second home. I vaguely
wondered how they could afford to do that, but I assumed that her husband was earning higher wages in his construction job than I thought
he was. I didn't think about what was happening in the mortgage finance markets. Certainly, construction was flying ahead with the demand created by those subprime mortgages. The story is well documented: many families were sucked in by these tempting mortgage
offers, where a house could be purchased with a loan that effectively

paid the down payment on a home, so that the buyer could acquire a mortgage to finance the purchase of the entire property. The hidden flaw was that these subprime loans had a sting in the tail. Although no interest was charged in the first two years, after those two years had passed the interest charges began to accrue, and there was a built-in formula that required interest to be paid on the whole loan from the time of acquisition. It was very bad; indeed, it was iniquitous—and except for a very few sharp-nosed traders on Wall Street, nobody had any idea that a great fall owing to this hubris was imminent. Most of the people who got trapped when the music stopped, those who lost their properties and their livelihoods, were at the lower end of the income scale.

I felt like a leaf on a pond during the first five or six years of the new century, in constant Brownian motion, rushing to and from meetings, traveling, participating on charitable boards—constantly engaged and constantly on the move. Our success led to increased investment opportunities, but the business had definitely become more challenging with the new competition that had emerged. During those years, when I seemed never to have a moment to myself, my book collection remained largely unvisited, the books and manuscripts lying silently in their bespoke glass cabinets in my home office. I had little to no time to spend with my collection now, and anyway, collecting rare books and manuscripts didn't have the same appeal. The auction catalogs didn't speak to me the way they had previously. How many copies of a Connolly item could be of interest when the list was complete? My schedule was now so demanding that I concentrated all my energies on work. When I look at old appointment calendars from those years, the state of activity they record makes me almost dizzy in retrospect. The fifth and what became the final fund was moving full steam ahead with its investment cycle. There were now five partners in the fund, none of whom, besides me, had any real investment experience. This was not ideal, but experienced venture capital investors were tied up in funds of their own, so the best one could do was to try to train people with a knowledge of health care in the arcana of venture capital investing. This was ultimately an impossible task. One needs years of experience and at least a full investment cycle to understand the subtleties involved in venture capital investing, particularly seed capital investing. My new partners did not have the benefit of this experience, and there was no solution: to gain the necessary confidence and ability required of a venture capital investor, each of my partners had to be free to go his or her own way. We were a fund of equal partners, and there were neither rules to enforce nor guidelines to point the way.

Other difficulties lay ahead. Not only had I raised a large seed capital fund with a team of partners largely inexperienced in the business of medical technology investing, but now MedVenture Associates was competing for investments with a whole new universe of venture funds that had bottomless assets at their disposal. These companies were prepared to pay unrealistic prices when they invested and could reward management with huge incentive payments in terms of both salary and stock ownership. The medical technology investment business threatened to become completely unprofitable for those smaller funds, like ours, that actually made the initial investments to create the companies in the first place. Management in our early-stage invested companies were often dazzled by the sums of money offered for new financings of startup companies, but those financings usually came with terms that, while favorable to management, almost penalized the seed capital investors. We early-stage investors were no longer being rewarded for the effort we had taken to create the businesses. To add insult to injury, the federal government embarked on a regulation spree for medical devices, and that added to the time and the cost of creating a successful new medical device product. What to do? I thought that if I put my head down and continued to work the way I always had, all would be well, but it wasn't. From being at the top of my game professionally, I was about to enter the most difficult few years of my investing career.

In the past, my book collection had provided solace no matter what was happening in the outside world. I could always open my book cabinets, take out books and manuscripts, and happily vanish into the world of my imaginary home. But now, the real world in which I spent every working hour became too exigent; by the middle of 2006, the business had become all-consuming, and it was impossible to do anything but attempt to continue driving the runaway train that had become my everyday working life and hope for the best. I had no time for anything but MedVenture Associates. Between caretaking past investments, doing diligence on and creating new ones, attending partners' meetings, and overseeing administration of the funds' activities, I had created Frankenstein's monster, and I had nobody but myself to blame. I was seriously overcommitted. At the peak of the activity, I participated as a board member on over a dozen startup ventures. This was no way to run a business in an environment that was becoming more competitive by the day. Just as suddenly as things had started to go well, now they started to take a turn for the worse, and we struggled to create value. My personal life shrank to nothing; my workweek had expanded to fill almost every waking moment. It couldn't go on like that.

As all of this was spinning round, I received a notice from my insurers in mid-2006 telling me that, owing to the value of my Connolly collection, they could no longer insure it. I couldn't find another company to write an insurance policy, and so now I had to worry about my collection being uninsurable. Our house stood on a hilltop next to a large state park, so fire was always a concern in the dry season. Moreover, the house was just isolated enough to be a target for thieves. Oakland, where we lived, had one of the highest crime rates in the United States. These things troubled me. The care of my collection had always been of great concern, because I had always been very aware that I was holding history, as well as literature, in those glass cabinets in my home, and that I had an unspoken obligation to keep the works in my possession safe and in the best possible condition. Now I couldn't even insure them! And this happened at a point when I just didn't have time to think about what to do about the insurance situation. In other circumstances, I might have made different decisions, but with such intense work pressure weighing on me every waking moment of the day, it now made sense—at least I thought so—to consider selling the collection. It would remove at least one item from my worry list.

Before going forward with a sale, I decided that first of all, I should consider donating the collection to a leading university. Since I was from New Zealand, it seemed appropriate that the collection should find a home in a New Zealand university, so I traveled to New Zealand to meet with the heads of some key libraries. The reaction to my proposal could not have been more disappointing. None of the discussions I had with different university libraries went anywhere. It's possible that nobody really understood the value of what I was offering to donate. Whatever the case, I had not anticipated such a lack of enthusiasm. I visited Victoria University in Wellington, the Turnbull Library, also in Wellington, which houses the Katherine Mansfield collection, and Canterbury University in Christchurch. The general reaction can be summed up in a single sentence: "Well, all right, if you insist. We'll take it." I never did get around to following up those first meetings, because I had no intention of allowing the collection to molder in the stacks of a provincial university library where it wouldn't be appreciated or properly cared for. There was only one choice left—to sell the collection, and, perhaps at a later stage, to start again.

I wondered whether I should call Sotheby's to see if it made sense
to ask Peter Selley to visit and examine my collection for a prospective
sale. Without giving myself a chance for second thoughts, I picked up
the telephone and called him.

"What do you think about selling my Connolly collection?" I asked.

"Let's talk," he replied.

Very quickly, it seemed, Peter came over from London and examined the books.

"Yes," he agreed. Sotheby's could do a good sale of this collection.

We signed the relevant agreements, and Sotheby's sent a team to
my house in California to pack up the books and send them over to
Sotheby's in Bond Street. I was on a sort of autopilot as the collection
was examined, appraised, and cataloged. I had mentally decided that it
was a necessary surgery, like an amputation of a limb that saves a life. I
hadn't thought at all about life after the sale—what I would continue to
collect, whether I would collect at all—but there must have been some
subconscious thought processes going on through it all. There were
signs of my reservations about the whole endeavor: first of all, I did
not send any of my very early collected items to the sale; secondly, I in-
sisted, over the objections of the specialists in the book department,
that the reserve prices for each book, shown by the low estimate in
the catalog descriptions, should remain high. I decided that if I was
going to part with my treasures, I would not allow them to be under-
priced. The pain of losing the books was going to be sharp enough—I
didn't need to feel that, in addition, they were being sold too cheaply.
The date of the sale was set for June 7, 2007, and it was exactly like entering a marriage about which one is unsure. Several times, I nearly
called off the sale, but I was prevented from doing so by the fact that it
would cost me a significant amount to change my mind. I had signed
a binding contract with Sotheby's, and besides, breaking that contract
would mean considerable loss of face. The calendar crept forward until
finally, as I realized with a certain sense of dismay, the day had arrived
on which I was about to sell my collection.

The Sale

Sotheby's produced a beautiful catalog for the sale, which has almost become a collector's item in its own right; I see copies listed for sale every now and again on AbeBooks, an online source for rare books and related material. The catalog, which emphasized the Modern Movement and its significance, was printed, like many of the French auction catalogs, on thick, high-quality paper, and the photography was superb. The pictures of different items—books, letters, manuscripts, and portraits—were cleverly integrated with the descriptive texts, so that each page drew you in, out of curiosity if nothing else. On the cover was a blown-up picture of the intricate *Livre d'Artiste* binding, made by the artist Rose Adler, of a privately printed copy of Apollinaire's *La Chanson du mal-aimé* (Song of the unloved). This book was one of the choice items in my collection, although it was not one of Connolly's selections. The title page of the catalog reproduced a watercolor by Apollinaire's onetime lover Marie Laurencin, an artist, who may have also had a relationship with Rose Adler. This small watercolor had been bound in with the text of *La Chanson du mal-aimé*. The book had always pleased me, owing to its many interwoven associations. In addition to the watercolor, there were handwritten notes by both Laurencin and Apollinaire that had also been bound in with the book itself. There was finally bound in a note from Pierre Bettencourt, the French writer and printer who had commissioned the publication, responding to Rose Adler that he had no further copies of the edition available. The tiny volume was listed as the first of twenty-five copies, and it had a distinguished provenance, having been in the collection of Colonel Daniel Sickles; afterward it had been in the Ragazzoni collection. I had bought the book in the Tajan sale in 2003.

There were some items I would have dearly loved to hold back from the sale. Katherine Anne Porter's copy of Hart Crane's *The Bridge* was one, because of the association created by those several photographs of Crane, taken in the garden of her house in Mexico and pasted with notations inside the front and back covers of the book. I fingered the typescript of *Decline and Fall*, but I knew that Sotheby's was adamant that the collection had to be sold in its entirety to justify the expense of a bespoke sale with a unique catalog. I swallowed hard and continued with the process. But it was too late anyway; the books were already at Sotheby's in London, the catalog had been printed and distributed, so there was no going back.

The items offered for sale in the catalog were not listed, as is usual in auction sales of rare books and manuscripts, in alphabetical order, but rather were presented as Connolly himself presented his one hundred key books in the catalog for the 1971 exhibition at the Humanities Research Center at the University of Texas at Austin, that is to say, in more or less chronological order, starting from the first book on the Connolly list in the catalog, which was Henry James's *The Portrait of a Lady*. The novelist Colm Tóibín had been commissioned to write an introduction to the catalog, and he produced a concise but critical précis of Connolly's list. All in all, it was a catalog designed for keeping and browsing, for the delight of anyone with an interest in either Cyril Connolly or the book that had started the whole collection for me, *The Modern Movement: One Hundred Key Books from England, France, and America, 1880–1950*.

In hindsight, I think that perhaps this was the last auction where a collection of Modern Movement titles could have been of significance as a bespoke literature sale, since interest in the Modern Movement seems to have diminished in recent years. Colm Tóibín, in his introduction to the catalog, almost said as much. He pointed out that in Connolly's time, it was generally accepted that Modernism in English literature had its roots in works of French writers of the early Modernist period, such as Rimbaud, Mallarmé, and Jarry, but he posited that a wide gulf exists today between the study of French and English writing, not least because French is neither spoken nor studied as much in English-speaking countries as it was up until the middle part of the twentieth century. Up to the time of Connolly's generation, educated people were very accustomed to reading in either French or English. Writers were preoccupied with "making it new," and Paris was the cradle for the evolving Modern Movement. The cross-Channel influences on style and content in literature that influenced the development of

Modernism in writing in the English language in the first half of the twentieth century would not be considered relevant today, where literary influences are globally recognized.

I had been sleepwalking throughout the entire process of cataloging the collection prior to the sale. Even when the collection left the house and was on its way to London, I didn't fully grasp the fact that my bookshelves had been emptied. The reason for my sangfroid was, primarily, that my work life was still churning on at a frenzied, unremitting pace. There was simply no room for anything but the business of MedVenture Associates. I was permanently tired, overscheduled, and longing to find ways to simplify my life. I felt nothing but relief that the stress of maintaining the collection was presumably behind me. All that was about to change.

I arrived in London shortly before the sale, ready to sell the collection; I felt that I could be objective, and I felt confident that I had done the right thing. What changed my attitude was the jolt I received when I finally viewed the collection the evening before the sale, at a small reception that Sotheby's held at its Bond Street headquarters. I was aghast! What was happening? Strange faces were eyeing my displayed treasures avariciously, and foreign hands were fingering the bindings and turning the pages of my priceless books. Ranged around the room, I saw my beloved books and manuscripts encased in tasteful little glass coffins. I felt they were crying out to me from their cases, looking to me to save them—but I could do nothing. It was all too late for that. *Alea iacta est*—the die is cast—I murmured to myself, and concentrated on photographing the books as they sat helplessly on display, abandoned by me to who knew what fate? At that point, if I could have gone back and stopped the process, I probably would have. But things had gone too far. I reminded myself sternly of the valid reasons for the sale and resigned myself to the prospect of divesting myself of the collection. After all, I had only myself to blame. It was I who had decided that it was time to move away from the Connolly list, and I who had concluded that this sale was the proper response to that decision. I realized, too, that I was anthropomorphizing the books in the collection to a ridiculous degree. But I couldn't help it. I felt as if I were about to participate in the sale of my children.

I thought of my ghostly and inappropriate mentor, William Beckford, because I had read about the agonies that he apparently had suffered on the occasion of being forced by debt to sell his possessions, including his library. Despite inheriting his great fortune, Beckford was in debt by 1822, and in order to pay his creditors he had been forced to put the great house of Fonthill Abbey up for sale. The sale of the abbey, together with some part of the great collections it contained, netted him the sum of £330,000, the purchasing power of which today would be close to £30 million. Beckford had amassed at Fonthill Abbey great collections of art, sculpture, books, furniture, tapestries, ceramics, porcelain, and other antiquities. The new owner of the abbey, John Farquar, a wealthy businessman, almost as eccentric in his own way as Beckford was in his, sold all the items he had bought along with the abbey in a great sale that was held at Christie's in 1823. What was notable was that Beckford himself had participated in both sales, and despite his personal debts, was a heavy repurchaser of many of his own effects. I completely understood and empathized with his desire to regain part of his property. But I was not going to participate in my own sale as a buyer, although, if truth be told, I thought about it!

When the auction at Sotheby's came around the day following the reception, Peter Selley, the specialist for the sale, sensed my heightened emotional state and sequestered me in an upstairs room with a closed-circuit television, so I watched the sale proceedings from that tiny, windowless room. I could see what was happening in the saleroom, but had no opportunity to burst in to bid on any item I felt was being sold below its true value. Peter was wise to put me up there, because I was in no condition to sit quietly by while the treasured items of my collection were sold. The austere surroundings matched my mood. Although it had a table and a few chairs, the room looked rather like I imagine a prison visitor's room would appear—dim, undecorated, and claustrophobic. The screen of the closed-circuit television had low resolution, so the picture was blurred, although I could hear everything that went on perfectly. My holding pen bore little resemblance to the elegantly decorated saleroom and had none of its sleek sophistication. I noticed that the saleroom was full, though, and the telephone banks had more than the usual number of phone specialists to take care of the phone bidders.

Auctioneers at the major English auction houses are not like general run-of-the-mill auctioneers, although they are certainly not as dramatic as most French auctioneers. They conduct the proceedings as politely as if they were at a discreet society gathering. The sale continues at a rhythmic pace, led by the smooth, even, impartial tones of the auctioneer as he or she leads the buyers through the items in the sale. My auction was no different. I sat in that tiny room with a copy of the catalog, watching my beloved books going under the auction hammer. My *Du côté de chez Swann*; my perfect copy of Hemingway's *The Sun Also Rises*; my annotated typescripts of Graves's *Good-Bye to All That*; and the manuscript of Evelyn Waugh's *Decline and Fall*. Who was buying these items, and where were they going to end up? Selling a collection is a strange experience—this thing, the collection, has come together to form a whole that represents something of meaning—in my case, the books of Connolly's one hundred key books of the Modern Movement. Now they would be dispersed—but in exactly what way? Some of the individual items would go to join other collections with different focuses. Perhaps they would be sold to collectors of works of particular writers, or perhaps collectors of literary high spots, or a great library, or some other type of institution wishing to augment a collection in a particular area. I never knew; the auction houses hold this information as tightly as governments in the past were able to hold state secrets.

I sat tensely for the several hours of the sale as the auctioneer methodically worked his way through the catalog, the knot in my stomach feeling like a billiard ball. I was so tense that I couldn't even swallow a glass of water. When an item achieved a significant premium to its estimate, I felt no sense of jubilation; when something did not sell for a premium, I shouted my disapproval at the closed-circuit television screen. When something failed to sell at all, I felt, above all, relief. It was all very contrary to how I had expected to feel. I paced the room, and I chewed a number of pencils to bits. I did not enjoy the process for one minute.

When it was over, Sotheby's deemed the sale a great success, despite the fact that nearly one-third of the items had failed to sell. The French items in the sale really belonged in a Paris auction house, but that would not have been possible, in view of the Connolly theme. Yet the fact that I was going to have one-third of my collection returned was a sort of solace. I was particularly pleased to note that the copy of *La Chanson du mal-aimé* would return.

As I left Sotheby's, I overheard Rick Gekoski telling a newspaper reporter from the *Daily Telegraph*, in his usual authoritative tones, "Of course, some of the items couldn't sell because they hadn't been in the collection for long, and she wanted too much money for them."

He was right about that. I had set the reserve prices high, and I had no regrets about this. It had been done intentionally. If someone didn't appreciate what he or she was buying, I didn't want to sell it to them.

However, I was too emotionally exhausted by the events of the morning to overtake him and correct him. Of course, his words were reported verbatim in the *Daily Telegraph* the following day, which didn't make me very happy at all.

The next day, it was back to business as usual at Sotheby's, while I evaluated the ruins of my collection and tried to plan ahead. I felt as if I had taken a hacksaw and carved off the main branches of a beautiful tree, leaving only a few spindly wisps to sway in the breeze. Although before the sale I had objectively decided that I was done with book and manuscript and literature collecting, and that the sale would bring my many years as a collector of such to a close, exactly the opposite happened. That morning after the sale, I understood that I would never be finished with collecting, because a collector is in some ways an addict, and like an addict, I now felt the pain and panic of withdrawal. There was no pleasure in cataloging those items that had failed to sell, and that would therefore be returning to me. It was now not a collection, but a stub of a collection, with neither meaning nor focus. What had I done? All the reasons I had given myself before the sale about why it was time to sell now meant nothing. Lack of insurability? I could have found insurance if I had tried hard enough. Simplification of my life by divesting of material things? How stupid—it was the collection that supplied a refuge in times of stress. I had been just so caught up by the pace at which things were proceeding in my corner of the world of venture capital that I had failed to consider rationally the consequences of selling my collection. What a fool I had been! In my process of rationalizing why it was necessary to sell the collection, I had failed to take into account the reasons why I should keep it. I had completely misjudged the very personal meaning the collection had for me, and I certainly had not understood what I now knew—that I belonged to the tribe of collectors, and being of that tribe makes collecting the inescapable vocation of a lifetime. Collecting had been part of what had made me happy over all those years—from the day I bought that first, still-cherished copy of "A Song for Simeon"—but now I had only the shreds and remnants of the collection to take back to California, where the earliest books of the collection remained on nearly empty shelves in my study.

I panicked. Sotheby's had a sale that same week that featured some volumes of Russian literature and poetry. Even though I scarcely knew her work at that time, I registered to bid and acquired two volumes of the poetry of Anna Akhmatova, one of which was at least historically important. It was a volume of her *Six Books: Poetry*, published in 1940 in Leningrad and inscribed by the author:

> To dear Knasa for being faithful to my poetry
> Akhmatova, 1945, 21 October

The identity of Knasa has not been established, nor has the depth of his or her relationship with Akhmatova. What is certain is that the book was published at the beginning of World War II and that Akhmatova gave it to Knasa at the end of the war. The time frame therefore encompasses the entire dreadful time of the Siege of Leningrad, which they had both miraculously survived. Even so, I had no intention of beginning to collect Russian poetry. I think those purchases were merely a first indication that I was, in some way, going to continue to be a collector of Modernist literature.

The End of the World?

Quite unexpectedly, the timing of my sale in June 2007 proved to be strangely prescient; indeed, more than one person asked me later if I had somehow suspected that the financial markets were shortly to collapse when I made the decision to sell the collection. Certainly, there were a few advance signs of the impending crisis. Alan Greenspan, head of the Federal Reserve of the United States, had cautioned timidly about "irrational exuberance" in the financial markets and warned against financial bubbles, but at the same time he had expressed optimism about the fluid way in which the financial markets were moving. What could go wrong? By the time mid-2007 rolled around, the financial world was moving at increasingly dizzying speeds. The indices peaked in October of that year, but before that it appeared that each month brought new highs in the markets. A new billionaire was being celebrated in the financial pages every day, and many of them were partners in hedge funds.

In the world of technology, a new form of Internet investing was emerging: just as the success of online search engine businesses such as Yahoo and Google and online commerce companies such as Amazon and eBay had defined the first wave of Internet investing, venture funds were taking the first steps into the social media investing that would define the second wave. (When, a number of years later, the first of these companies went public, it was clear that the world of venture capital investing would never be the same again.) The crisis in venture investor confidence caused by the technology meltdown that had occurred at the time of the changing millennium now seemed like a distant nightmare, and the river of money funding these new venture-backed companies appeared to have turned into an unstoppable torrent. However, the new financial bubble was not only occurring in the venture world,

but in all of the financial sectors, and the investing fever was being fueled by ever-increasing amounts of debt—most of it subprime debt.
Something had to happen, and something did.

Like most of my peers in the financial business, I went about my
business unconcerned about the larger global picture. My worries
were not only confined to the ones that affected my small corner of
the venture capital world, because owing to the loss of my collection,
my personal life also felt out of balance. Even though I had neglected
my collection during the past few years of frenzied activity, now that
it was gone, I was missing it. I found time to try to find a new mode of
collecting, to fill the hole left by the sudden end of a meaningful activity that had been part of my life since those long-ago days in London,
but I was mostly unsuccessful. In my search for new directions, I went
down a number of very blind alleys. I made a desultory pass in the direction of collecting world literature and literary high spots, but these
efforts went nowhere. I bought and for a time, I owned one of the recognized world literature high spots—the best existing copy of Shelley's
famous poem *Queen Mab*—but I took little interest in the book. I tried
other areas, too—plays and playwrights, for example. Flailing about, I
bought a definitive set of the collected plays of Harold Pinter and his
early poetry in first editions, brought the collection home, and immediately took a dislike to the whole endeavor.

This speaks to that which is unknowable about collecting in the first
place. Why collect what one collects? After all, *Queen Mab* is a masterpiece, and Pinter was one of the bedrock playwrights of Modern English theater. Perhaps, after all, my Connolly collecting had been more
deeply bound up with that sense of home, which had been such a significant part of my early years, than I had acknowledged. Pinter and
Shelley did not live in that place, but T. S. Eliot and many of the English
authors from the Modern Movement list did, and they were as familiar to me now as distant relatives. But that was all over now; the collection had been dismantled. I thought back longingly to the days and
evenings when the companions of my invented home of long ago had
helped me through so much. If only the books of my collection were
still with me! I knew almost viscerally that I had to find a new collecting direction; I simply wasn't happy living without collecting books
and related items.

And increasingly, I needed that connection, that familiar security
blanket, because the global financial crisis was now at hand. The world
had been rapidly changing in those months immediately following the

sale of my collection, but I had been so focused on the activities of MedVenture Associates that I'd had no inkling that the financial bubble was finally about to burst. No one had had any idea that this would result in a financial crisis of global magnitude. For me, the consequences of the financial meltdown would prove to be of far graver import than the reckless sale of a collection of Modernist books. Selling my books had been a folly that was my problem alone; the shadows that were building would shortly threaten the future existence not only of my business but also of many small financial businesses in unrelated fields.

Over the course of 2007, the merry-go-round of Wall Street ebullience continued in full swing, but the daily financial headlines started to build a wall of worry concerning the long-term viability of the subprime mortgage lending market. I didn't take much notice: mortgage lending seemed a far cry from investment into startup companies in the medical technology field. A few outliers among the economic experts had appeared on financial news programs from the end of 2006 onward, warning that the collapse of the housing bubble could cause a failure of the world banking system. Still, nobody I knew in the financial world was paying any attention. In fact, I noticed so much building going on in areas around the San Francisco Bay Area— suburban communities that appeared almost overnight, built by giant construction companies—that I just assumed this building orgy was an indicator of economic strength. In retrospect, I see that it was really a symbol of economic folly and blindness. These same suburban communities became ghost suburbs when the markets imploded.

Alan Greenspan continued to announce that all was well. He had assumed almost mythic status as a living embodiment of the principle of free markets. But despite his prognostications, on October 12, 2007, after the Dow Jones Index peaked at just over 14,000, the markets began a retreat that lasted until March 2009, when the index finally bounced off the bottom at just over 6,600. The market sell-off was initially triggered by the failure of Countrywide Loans, one of the companies that had been heavily involved in the sale of subprime mortgages and the packaging of these mortgages. Other, smaller loan companies had failed during the year, but Countrywide was a larger company, and its failure was the first to cause people to sit up and take notice. After that, events came thick and fast: it was a catastrophe, and it brought the world financial system to its knees before it was done.

The US government "suggested" that Bank of America, the nation's largest bank, purchase Countrywide Loans to save it from bankruptcy, and later Bank of America was also forced to buy the giant brokerage firm of Merrill Lynch for $50 billion. After that, the investment bank Bear Stearns, which also had an overexposure to subprime, was forced onto J. P. Morgan, and the world watched in horror as respected financial institutions collapsed overnight. Employees of Lehman Brothers were pictured on the nightly news in September, with their possessions in cardboard cartons, leaving buildings that had housed their offices earlier that day, but were now closed. The mortgage giants Fannie Mae and Freddie Mac were taken over by the government, which also had to finance companies like the insurance giant AIG, which had insured many of the subprime loans against failure; later on, the government also came to the aid of bellwether companies such as General Motors and Chrysler, which also threatened to collapse. How could I be concerned about the sale of a book collection when the world felt like it was coming to an end?

I had no idea how the financial collapse would affect business at MedVenture Associates in the long term, but I knew it would not help in the short term. Of particular concern was the potential fate of our fifth and largest fund to date, which was still in its investment phase and was also nurturing a number of very thirsty embryonic investments. Our business model was no longer viable in the new environment, because our tiny startup companies lost access to the investment capital they needed to finance the clinical testing necessary to prove out their business models. Almost overnight, the venture financing environment changed from one where too much money was chasing down venture deals to one where little or no new funds were available to finance the startup of early-stage medical technology ventures. There just wasn't that sort of risk capital money available anymore; in that environment, nobody wanted to invest in a new medical technology that might take up to ten years to prove out its concept. Our institutional investors, whose portfolios were reeling from the downturns in the stock market and the collapse of the bond markets, began watching our portfolio progress more keenly, but they did not allow us to change our investment strategy as we requested, although it would have been the sensible thing to do under the circumstances.

This was a recipe for disaster, because there was a knock-on effect from the lack of available financing, which meant that we had to make hard choices in our portfolios about which companies would be fed with our limited capital and which we could sacrifice. We obviously had no funds to spare for new investments. Other investors, sensing opportunity, offered capital for further financings at below-market valuations, which sometimes we had to accept. As a result of this sea change in our business, things began to go from bad to worse for Med-Venture Associates. In fact, things became so difficult that I didn't expect the business to be able to recover from the blows inflicted. The fallout effects of the financial catastrophe were raining down on us like a heavy tropical thunderstorm. From maintaining a frenetic pace to keep up with the competition, and invest in the best of the many business opportunities presented to us, we were, almost overnight, plunged into a world where our main goal was to nurture the most promising of the businesses in the existing portfolio while letting the others die off. A physician breaking the news of a terminal illness to a patient could not have felt worse than I did on the several occasions when I had to tell the management of an invested company that we would no longer back that investment. Very quickly, this meant that a number of the early businesses in our portfolios began to wither on the vine.

MedVenture Associates was not alone—the entire early-stage medical technology investment business now entered into a severe decline. The river of money had run dry, and such capital as was available was not to be diverted to the kinds of companies we had financed. The main problem was this. Our investors made money from the returns on the successful investments made by MedVenture Associates. The companies that successfully developed products could usually count on carrying out an IPO to raise funds for commercialization. It was at this point that our institutional investors would be distributed shares in the newly public company, which generally meant a good profit on the overall investment. Sometimes, a company might be bought by a larger business before its IPO, but that was all right, too. Having both of those routes to exit from a deal ensured good returns on investments made. But now, with the financial crisis at hand, it was impossible to take our little companies public, and the larger companies, sensing the dilemma, began to offer less and less cash or stock to acquire our fledgling businesses. They could do this because of the overall increase in the backlog of starving venture-backed medical device companies. Often, a company had no choice but to take a low offer in order to raise money to survive. It was a perfect storm. From being overcommitted, owing to the pace of business opportunities, I was suddenly flung backward into a role of trying to find ways to raise money to keep the companies we had chosen to nurture in our portfolios afloat. Since we were only a seed capital fund, we had to find co-investors for later rounds of financing, and increasingly, those funds came with a huge penalty for the earlier investors, rather than a reward in the form of an increase in valuation.

Work became a treadmill, where every day, we expended useless energy going nowhere as we tried to find money to finance the companies in the portfolios. Small businesses are like living organisms: money feeds development, and without access to proper funding, the embryonic companies die. There were too many funerals for those companies; even though we had some good successes, we knew that our remaining investment funds could never be profitable with the small number of survivors that we chose to nourish with our depleted funds.

Throughout this period, I didn't even have the solace of my book collection. How I longed to be able to disappear again for long spells of time into that home of my childhood and encounter once again those imaginary friends I had made in my youth. Each time I looked at the bookcases, I mourned anew those items that were lost to me forever. It was a feeling that was hard to shake, and one that would remain with me for some time. It wasn't just a collection of books I had sold. Part of my being had been among the volumes in that bookcase, and now I felt wrenched into pieces. I had destroyed my dreams of home.

All those days chasing down books in catalogs, at auction sales, and in dusty bookshops in order to find material by the authors represented on the Connolly list, some of them writers with whom I had a ghostly personal relationship—it was all gone, thanks to my folly in selling the collection. I remembered how the early books had comforted me during that grim Christmas alone in the house in Wembley Park. But where were my key volumes residing now? Other than those first purchases I had made nearly forty years previously, only the stub of my Connolly collection remained in my bookcases, as well as a number of random items that were of little interest to me. It was imperative that I find a new collecting focus.

New Horizons

Despite the random and unsatisfactory nature of my purchases in the first few years after my sale at Sotheby's, I was, without acknowledging it, taking the first small steps toward creating a new and different sort of collection based around Modernism. The Modernist authors were just too much a part of me by now, and nothing else seemed to connect in the same way. In addition to the items I had bought in a panic after the sale of my collection, I started acquiring items that actually related to those particular Modernist authors. But this embryonic new collection was not that of Connolly's Modernism: I was starting to buy items that I alone, with no reference to a list or advice from others, personally thought of as exceptionally interesting, and of course these were items relating to the lives as well as the works of these particular authors.

One of the first of these purchases was a fantastically inscribed copy of Mervyn Peake's *Titus Groan*, which I acquired even though I already owned a copy of the *Gormenghast Trilogy*. Inside the front cover was a drawing of Lady Groan, one of the key characters in the books. I also bought a letter James Joyce had written to Archibald MacLeish, which I purchased from the Boston-based auction house of Skinner; it was not an important letter, but the association between the two writers was interesting. At the same auction, I acquired a rather prim letter Virginia Woolf had written to a fan who had been less than enthusiastic about *Mrs. Dalloway*. I even began to consider portraiture and caricature, and purchased at Sotheby's a portrait of James Joyce by the famous American photographer Berenice Abbott. In themselves, none of these items showed an emerging core of a new collection, but in buying them I felt that I was somehow back on my own turf. Suddenly, without the constraints of the Connolly list, the possibilities seemed limitless. There was a sort of controlled randomness to what I was now starting to collect, but it was generally pointing in one direction. I was finding my way again, and my second collection of literary Modernism began to build.

I am a strong believer that, in life, you have to create your own luck, and so I set out to put my world in order again. It was time to close out my activities in the world of venture capital. I doubted that my partners and I could do more than rescue the investments of the later MedVenture Associates' funds; the heady days of profitability that we experienced with the early funds were no more. In light of the dismal outlook, I didn't have the heart to continue trying to grow the business after the financial collapse, and so I decided simply to manage the re-maining funds to their conclusion. I would not try to raise further cap-ital. In my personal life, meanwhile, instead of winding things down, I was now once again starting to contemplate seriously the creation of a new collection. I had found my own voice, and this time, I was de-termined to build a new collection relating to the Modernist authors who appealed to me and me alone, and I would make it as significant as I could. No longer for me only those pristine, dead first editions. I wanted letters, manuscripts, writings scribbled on the backs of menus, drawings, posters, photographs—things that could connect me per-sonally to these writers and their times.

In my final years collecting the Connolly list, as I gained confidence in my own opinions, I had found works that were too interesting and desirable to be missed. Of particular interest were choice items of-fered at auction from the collections of Roy Davids, who sold these at Bonham's auction house in London in five sales carried out over a number of years, the first taking place in 2005. Roy Davids was, for many years, head of the book department at Sotheby's, which rightly should have sold his collection. However, Roy and Sotheby's were not able to agree on terms, and in the end, Bonham's attained the rights to the sale. Roy Davids had assembled a remarkable collection; for me, of most interest were the many items of ephemera relating to the work of significant twentieth-century English writers that he had acquired over his many years of collecting. He had been able, by virtue of his position at the podium at Sotheby's over those many years, to acquire, in addition to inscribed first editions, such association items as por-traiture, photographs, and some manuscript material of a number of the Modernist writers in whom I had a keen interest. He was also very learned and wrote his own catalog copy describing the material he was presenting for auction. Sadly, he had a series of strokes after the final sale of his collections and was never able to enjoy the rewards from his collecting labors over all those many years.

I bought a number of items of ephemera relating to Modern Movement authors in the first sale in 2005. In addition to literature and letters, the catalog contained descriptions and photographs of a significant number of literary portraits. In the past, I had not thought about literary portraits as collectible, but I found myself drawn to a number of these, not usually relating to their value, but more to what they could tell me about the literary figures who appeared in the photographs. Some of the more interesting photographic records were not even formal portraits. Of great interest was a set of two photographs I acquired at the first auction, which had been taken of E. M. Forster in India, during the time of his service as secretary to Tukojirao III, the Maharaja of Dewas State (1900–1937). One of the pictures, dated from 1912 or 1913, showed Forster playing a game called *jubbu* with eight others, including the Maharaja, in the palace courtyard at Dewas; the other showed him in 1921, again with the Maharaja, along with several of his children and some employees in the palace courtyard. In the second portrait, Forster, rather surprisingly, sports a large turban. I think the photographs have an association, as yet undetermined by scholarship, with a contemporaneous series of nine letters and one card in my possession, which I acquired through Sotheby's in 2000. Forster had written these letters to Syed Ross Masood, the dedicatee of *A Passage to India*, mostly between 1907 and 1913; Masood was one of the great unrequited loves in Forster's life. Both of those Forster items had been offered in my Sotheby's sale in 2007, but fortunately for me, neither of them had sold. Pondering where to take my new collection, I now began to look at these Forster items in a new light. Was there a connection between the photographs and the letters? Certainly, the first of the photographs had been taken at the time of Forster's infatuation with Syed Ross Masood, so was the Masood family on friendly terms with the Maharaja? The Masood letters I had acquired also included a later, but voluminous, correspondence between Syed Ross Masood and his wife. Although these letters did not reference Forster, I knew the letters not been studied for any further family connections. Perhaps the letters might indicate the standing of the Masood family in the state of Dewas, including their relationship to the Maharaja's family, and through that, with Forster himself. Those portraits and letters showed that it was still possible to acquire items of literary ephemera that could contribute to the study of the lives and associations of the writers of

Modernism. But I still hadn't made the connection that actually, what ownership of such items as those Forster photographic portraits and the series of Masood letters showed was that yes—even I could still create a Modernist collection that had interest and even scholarship value. Not everything had disappeared into great libraries and private collections. When I looked at the few items I had started to purchase and studied those items that had been returned as unsold by Sotheby's, I knew that these seemingly unrelated items could form the core of a new and more personal and important collecting direction.

What finally set me on my way with a new focus for my collecting efforts were the later sales of the Roy Davids collection. In early 2011, Bonham's carried out the second sale. Although nothing offered in this sale could be termed either a high spot of literature or an immaculate copy of an important first edition, it contained the kinds of items in which I continued to have the greatest interest—letters, photographs, art, and manuscript drafts from English writers of the early to mid-twentieth century. When I looked over the catalog, I felt that familiar tremor of excitement and anticipation that I used to get during the heady days of my early collecting, when I was first assembling the Modern Movement collection and had noticed a particularly interesting item coming up for sale. Nothing in the Roy Davids sale in which I had an interest was estimated at a price beyond my budget, so I went to London and registered to bid at Bonham's.

The exhibition of the Roy Davids collection before the sale was for me the final moment of awakening. When I viewed the letters and manuscripts exhibited in the display cases, I experienced that same visceral feeling of excitement that I remembered experiencing many years earlier, before I had even bought that first book that started my collection. It happened at the British Library, when it was still at its former location as part of the British Museum, and it occurred owing to the unexpected discovery of a small display of works by such iconic British writers as Jane Austen and John Keats. There is something particularly fascinating about viewing the actual handwriting of a writer in whom one has an interest. Looking at that letter or manuscript, you feel as if you are part of the conversation of that moment. The next day, I bought quite heavily at the Roy Davids sale—works by Jean Cocteau, T. S. Eliot, Ford Madox Ford, Robert Graves, Thomas Hardy, James Joyce, D. H. Lawrence, Anthony Powell, Evelyn Waugh, and W. B. Yeats. There was nothing that would be considered a high point, and mostly, I bought letters, but I also splurged a little on certain portraits and photographs of exceptional interest. Connolly would not have approved, but I was happy with my purchases. My budget remained under control, and what I bought was, for the first time since I had sold my collection, interesting to me as a collector.

Not everything I bought that day related either to Modernism or to writers and poets of the one hundred key books. I bought some of the items of literary ephemera just because they were of the period and they appealed to me. For example, as companion pieces to a portrait I already owned of Gertrude Stein, taken by the novelist and photographer Carl Van Vechten, I purchased a set of three rather wonderful pictures of Gertrude Stein and Alice B. Toklas taken during a road trip. The centerpiece of the triptych was a photograph taken in Venice, in St. Mark's Square: amid a flock of pigeons, Gertrude Stein sits stolidly on a step while Alice B. Toklas flutters ineffectively above her, like one of the many pigeons surrounding them. I also bought a signed caricature in pen and ink of John Steinbeck, drawn by a friend of his, the Swedish artist Bo Beskow. Apparently it was drawn the evening before Steinbeck's acceptance speech at the Nobel Academy in Stockholm. Steinbeck has a glass of orange juice in his hand, and he has noted that fact on the drawing in pencil. I felt that it brought me closer to Steinbeck than reading a copy of *Cannery Row* was ever likely to do.

In homage to Siegfried Sassoon, I also bought two desk seals that had been engraved in relief with those famous "SS" initials that accompany so many of his personally signed works. One of these is of carnelian and the other of lapis lazuli; both are elegant and made to order for Sassoon. In later of the Roy Davids sales, almost as if I were buying family heirlooms, I purchased an eightieth birthday book that had been prepared for Sassoon by a band of devoted friends. In this book, many artists and writers—as well as religious figures—had competed to provide ever wittier and more extensive entries. Over the course of his long life, Sassoon had been connected with practically every significant writer of his generation, and the birthday book showed how loved and appreciated he remained. I admired in particular his conscientious objection to the indiscriminate killing of young men in the trenches toward the end of World War I. One of my acquisitions was the draft of his famous poem "Atrocities," which he wrote from Craiglockhart Hospital, where he had been sent in 1917, perhaps to recover from shellshock, or perhaps because of his increasingly pacifist writings, which were inconvenient to the authorities. The poem was altered by the censors before publication, but here was the draft, the true uncensored version:

> You bragged how once your men in savage mood
> Butchered some Saxon prisoners. That was good!
> I trust you felt no pity when they stood
> Patient and cowed and scared as prisoners should.
>
> How did you kill them? Speak, and don't be shy.
> You know I love to hear how Germans die,
> Downstairs in dug-outs. "Camerad," they cry:
> Then squeal like stoats when bombs begin to fly.
>
> I'm proud of you. Perhaps you'll feel as brave
> Alone in no man's land, when none can save
> Or shield you from the horror of the night.
> There's blood on your hands—go out and fight.

By way of comparison, here is the censored version, taken from *The War Poems of Siegfried Sassoon*, W. Heinemann, 1919:

> You told me in your drunken, boasting mood,
> How once you butchered prisoners. That was good!
> I'm sure you felt no pity while they stood
> Patient and cowed and scared, as prisoners should.
>
> How did you do them in? Come, don't be shy:
> You know I love to hear how Germans die,
> Downstairs in dug-outs. "Camerad!", they cry;
> Then squeal like stoats when bombs begin to fly.
>
> And you? I know your record. You went sick
> When orders looked unwholesome: then, with trick
> And lie, you wangled home. And here you are,
> Still talking big and boozing in a bar.

Nothing in this new collection related, but in a way, it all related. But what was this new collection about? I suppose it all went back to those distant days of childhood, when I read works by these authors and assimilated them into my dreams of home, that faraway place of country gardens and civilized conversation. I thought of that first purchase of "A Song for Simeon," for instance. The poetry was important, and the limited edition and its bespoke lithograph entrancing, but what had attracted me above all, what had caught my attention so that I paid half a month's salary for the book, had been T. S. Eliot's signature. It was the signature in the book that I had stared at during those long-ago lonely nights in London when I still had to find a job and a career path. Connectedness to the past—letters, inscribed books, manuscripts, photographs, and portraits—it had never been only about the literature. It had been about this lost world where the literary giants of the early twentieth century lived and wrote and mingled. My private and secret home of the imagination. Connectedness was important. During the days when I was assiduously collecting Connolly's list, I had assembled over time a small library of biographies of the Connolly writers who interested me the most, and I was delighted when I made discoveries about new connections among them. Now I began consciously to seek letters by authors of the period written to or about each other, or even manuscripts or scraps of manuscripts where an author might offer a critique of another's work. This was not going to be a collection bounded by a list: the only limitation on this new collection was going to be what came to market, what I believed to be interesting and important, and what I could afford.

In the first days after the dramatic sale of my Connolly collection, I hadn't expected that collecting would ever again play a significant role in my life, and I certainly wasn't expecting to find much material outside what had come up at the Roy Davids sales. But I was wrong.

Only a few months after the second Roy Davids sale, I began to notice that a number of auction catalogs were offering significant collections for sale, and that my own field was well represented in these sales. In all my years of collecting, I had never seen such an embarrassment of riches offered at auction. Each of the three major auction houses in New York carried out significant bespoke sales. Material relating to the life and work of such great authors as William Faulkner, F. Scott Fitzgerald, Ernest Hemingway, and Joseph Conrad were just some of the names that came up in key sales. The French sales were robust and were mining even richer ground—Guillaume Apollinaire, Paul Verlaine, Jean Cocteau, Marcel Proust, Joris-Karl Huysmans, Stéphane Mallarmé, Arthur Rimbaud, and Alfred Jarry. The French material was of higher quality and even more significant than some of the English and American writing that suddenly was available at auction, and later, owing to the collapse of the Société Aristophil, the prices were even somewhat more approachable. These were happy developments, but concerning all the same, because I could not perceive a reason behind this sudden trove of first editions, letters, minor manuscripts, and other items by or about Modernist authors that were turning up at auction. Sometimes, I had three or four catalogs simultaneously under review for sales that were being held merely weeks apart.

The first thought that came to mind was naturally a cynical speculation that perhaps I was witnessing the end of collecting. Perhaps collectors everywhere were divesting themselves of their collections because they thought we were facing the end of the printed word, and somehow I hadn't received the message. It's true that computers have spelled the end of handwritten draft manuscripts, copies of which were always deemed important, since, among other things, they provide insight into the developing thought processes of major authors and their most important works. Yet, if handwritten manuscripts are now things of the past and draft material only available on computer hard drives, that fact should only increase the value of written draft manuscripts, as these items become not only important from the point of view of literary content but also begin to have historical significance for future generations.

In the end, I concluded that the sudden appearance of so much material at auction was due in part to the fact that a number of family collections—such as those of F. Scott Fitzgerald and William Faulkner—which had been inherited by the offspring of these authors, were now in the process of being broken up. The third and fourth generations, the grandchildren and great-grandchildren, simply didn't have enough interest in their famous ancestors to keep the items in the family, especially since many of these items were now of considerable value. Scotty Fitzgerald, the daughter of F. Scott and Zelda Fitzgerald, for example, had owned a number of her father's letters and manuscripts, and she had treasured them. But these things did not have the same emotional connection for the third generation, so off to auction they went. Similarly, the great sale of William Faulkner's items at Sotheby's in New York in 2013 included many items of personal significance. Among other treasures that I acquired in that sale was a tiny, framed, unpublished poem that Faulkner had composed when he was twenty. It is carefully written on a sheet of paper in elegant script underneath a charming drawing, which is also in the hand of Faulkner. The poem and drawing had been for Estelle Oldham, Faulkner's great love at the time, when she was to be married to Cornell Franklin. Both frankly allude to his sense of loss that she has married another:

> And Pan through anguished pipes doth blow
> His sudden heart in one wild strain
> Fond and tremulous and low;
> For springs he cannot know again,
> For springs before the world grew old,
> For blond-limbed dancers lemon-clad
> From vales and hill-tops fiery cold—
> A world fantastical and sad.

It's an important item on many levels, not only that of the poem itself. The illustration shows Pan piping, seated on a rock. Standing near him, but somehow remote nevertheless, is a slender nymph, whose modesty is shielded by a stand of willow reeds. The style of the drawing is reminiscent of Aubrey Beardsley, while the text of the poem has some relation to Faulkner's first published long poem, *The Marble Faun*. For Faulkner there was a happy ending to this story, since Estelle's marriage to Cornell Franklin ended in divorce, so that Faulkner was able to marry her after all.

The fact that I could find and acquire items like this so easily convinced me even more that I could assemble a meaningful collection of letters, manuscripts, drawings, and photographs that would somehow reflect the movement of Modernism but also provide insight into the personalities and lives of the writers of the Modern Movement and others of the period. Of course, I never expected to be able to assemble a collection that would in any way resemble the great Modernist collections in libraries such as the Ransom Center at the University of Texas at Austin. Yet, in thinking about building a new collection, I remembered an article I had read in *The New Yorker*, only a few days after my Sotheby's sale. Written by the journalist D. T. Max and published in *The New Yorker*'s edition of June 11, 2007, it was titled "Final Destination," with a subtitle inquiring "Why do the archives of so many great writers end up in Texas?" Writing about the vast collections of author archives residing in the Ransom Center, which was still making acquisitions, the article pointed out something I hadn't considered. According to D. T. Max, who had spent time at the Ransom Center, "usually, the only person to have read the entirety of an archive is the author, and the authority on its contents is the scholar who has studied it the most." He went on to say that at all libraries with major archives, the archives usually sit side by side on shelves in cavernous basements—like rows of coffins in a crypt—waiting for a scholar to come along to breathe for a moment some life into their contents. The implied conclusion was that a collection does not have to be vast to have meaning. Sometimes size is overwhelming, and it's actually more significant in the end to be able to spend time with a small but choice collection that you know, love, and have learned from. This is the sort of collection that I now longed to build.

Much of the material I began to purchase had not been offered previously at auction and was new to literary scholarship. Some of the literary associations in the letters and drafts of poems I managed to acquire were astonishing. One of my favorite moments came when I bought through Bonham's an unpublished series of nearly one hundred letters that Clive Bell wrote to Lytton Strachey. These letters, which were unknown to literary scholarship, provide an insider's view of the Bloomsbury Group by one of its members who has not been seriously considered until recently. The Bloomsbury set thrived on mutual cohabitation and collaboration, so that even today younger readers are fascinated by the stories of their lives as well as by their art and their literary and critical output. Various members of that charmed circle—Virginia Woolf, in particular—are of interest. Clive Bell's correspondence with Lytton Strachey over the years from 1906 to 1931, which is now part of my collection, speaks in familiar terms of the complicated lives of the members of that group. There is significant as yet undocumented scholarship in those letters. Bell, for example, returns repeatedly to the subject of Virginia Woolf's fragile health, and discusses other Bloomsbury contemporaries from Cambridge, such as Maynard Keynes and Leonard Woolf. Some letters date from Bell's years at Cambridge and contain rather unguarded comments about his contemporaries, including Rupert Brooke and the explorer George Mallory.

Of course, there continued to be a steady flow of those exquisite French catalogs, which made me positively avaricious—I always wanted to acquire some of the items of literary ephemera that were so lavishly described and illustrated in those wonderful pages. Some years after the sale of my Connolly collection, I participated in a Sotheby's auction in Paris where I was able to acquire a lithograph that had been issued at the time of the publication of Verlaine's first book of poetry—*Poèmes saturniens,* (or *Poems Under Saturn,* in the translation by the American poet Karl Kirchwey)—in 1866. The poem "Chanson d'automne" appears in that book of verse, which was published when Verlaine was only twenty-two years old. The lithograph, by the illustrator and lithographer Jules-Barthélemy Péaron, shows Verlaine handsome, rugged, and energetic—with a mane of hair flowing freely—riding a horse energetically around a grotesque arena under a starry night sky. The audience members, the horse, and Verlaine himself are depicted as skeletons or creatures with the heads of beasts. To me, it demonstrated that Verlaine had not always spent his life submerged in a fog of alcohol and drugs; at least in his early life, he had been a man of energy as well as inspiration. That poster was personally inscribed to the writer and poet Anatole France, who had first been a friend, but was later an enemy, of Verlaine; nevertheless he was later on discerning enough to appreciate that Verlaine's poetry would live on in posterity, as the quotation in an earlier chapter attested (see "The French Modern Movement: *Du côté de chez Swann*").

Items such as these appeared in catalogs and at auction from time to time, as many of the writers of the Modern Movement circle knew one another, socialized together, and even critiqued one another's work. There was, for instance, that well-known circle in Rye that included Joseph Conrad, Henry James, and Ford Madox Ford. Conrad and Ford even coauthored several books, although they were not very successful, and have not survived in print much beyond rare book collecting circles. I was intrigued to find such significant associations among writers of Modernism.

The search to find material whereby one could learn more about the authors behind the printed word was becoming richly rewarding. One can read biographies, and visit places of significance to an author, but in the end, nothing compares to the thrill of owning something that has been part of a writer's personal history. Other collectors obviously agree with this sentiment. That specially dedicated copy of F. Scott Fitzgerald's classic *Tender Is the Night* previously owned by Maurice Neville, which contained a long inscription dedicated to Zelda Fitzgerald's psychiatrist, sold in 2016 at auction for $175,000—over four times the auction estimate.

A book collection is like a living organism: one purchase can irrevocably affect the balance of the rest of the collection in unexpected ways. When one embarks on a search for collectible material related to authors of interest, and is able to unearth, for example, significant personal correspondence, or a scratchy piece of paper containing a draft of a famous poem, these items can come together as a wondrously interesting whole. My experience with collecting items related to Ford Madox Ford, for example, continues to alter my perception of the man and his work. Until several years ago, particularly owing to the troubled personal history that I knew was hidden behind the copy of the limited American edition of *The Good Soldier* I owned, which was inscribed to Stella Bowen with the letter to her as dedication, I had thought of Ford Madox Ford as an overly confident writer with a weakness for women. After I became more interested in literary letters, I purchased at auction a long letter Ford had written to the British man of letters Gerald Bullett in 1933. By that time, Ford was depressed about his place in the literary world and how he would go down in posterity. He wrote to Bullett, in part:

> I have for years been writing—for American and a little for French consumption—an immense series of works attempting to render our own times. America, and to a lesser extent France have, thank goodness, consumed them in sufficient quantities to keep me going on a Mediterranean terrace where I continue to work.... Occasionally, one English publisher or another has published one of these books in London. Six months after he has written to tell me that that book has sold from two to a hundred copies, that he has lost a thousand pounds over it and that his imminent appearance in Carey Street is all my fault.... I gather that the English public does not like my work.

> (*Carey Street is a euphemism for bankruptcy, from the street where the Bankruptcy Court used to be located in the nineteenth century.*)

This letter shows how the perception of literary value can change over time, because today Ford is enshrined securely in the literary pantheon of the Modern Movement.

Ezra Pound, who always discerned genius, understood the importance of Ford's work. Some years ago, I purchased some letters Pound had written in the 1930s. One of the letters, written to a former lover, Charlotte Teller Hirsch, offered some insights into Pound's views on writing—he compared what he called her "impossibly bad" writing style and lack of talent with the style of leading Modernist writers. Among his comments was this one:

200

F. M. F's apparent simplicity and lack of style is the result of such a
tremenduous [*sic*] amount of technique that it is no use offering it as
a model.

Pound had been silently involved in improving the work of many of the
writers of Modernism, particularly some of its key poets and writers,
such as Eliot, Joyce, Hemingway, and Yeats. Pound himself, of course,
was discredited by his treasonous broadcasts from Italy during World
War II. However, I always felt that his fragile mental health was responsible for many of his actions, and I began to take a strong interest in his
work and life. His reputation as a cornerstone figure of the Modern
Movement has been somewhat rehabilitated in recent years. What fascinated me the most about Pound was the interest he took in helping
his compatriots refine their poetry—and yet he was generous enough
not to take credit for it. Eliot's *The Waste Land* might never have become a Modernist masterpiece without Pound's silent editing and corrections. Pound's influence on Modernism was key: it probably was
what enabled Modernist literary thought to earn its credentials. Indeed, it is Pound who is often quoted as the originator of the thesis of
Modernism—"Make It New"—which may be one of the most debated
pronouncements in Modern literary analysis.

Here, for example, is Ernest Hemingway writing about Pound in
a letter from my collection, written in 1933 to Arnold Gingrich, the
founder and editor of *Esquire*:

> I've read every word he ever wrote and still believe the best is in the
> cantos. . . . [T]here is some Christwonderful poetry that no one can
> better.

These examples demonstrate what I cherish so much about my present
collection. Above all, with a focus now firmly set on items that explore
Modernism from the viewpoint of letters between authors, along with
literary portraits, manuscript material, and related ephemera, I am now
assembling something that is developing into a more personal collection than my previous one, when obedience to the dictates of the Connolly list dominated my collecting activities.

The world of collecting continues to be a key component of my
personal life. I enjoy the auctions, the chase of the rare and unexpected
and underappreciated, and I am grateful for the acquaintance of so
many book dealers and others in the world of books who have over the

years become my friends. It is still thrilling to acquire a new item, and I appreciate the catalogs that describe, item by precious item, the collections that others have made, but that are now being offered to new caretakers. On that score, I continue to admire the 2007 Sotheby's catalog that accompanied the sale of my Connolly Modernist collection, and that, coincidentally, was an inspiration for me to write this memoir in the first place. Although selling a collection allows a new generation of collectors to cherish the items which you yourself have assembled, and gives them meaning and life in a different format, I learned my lesson with the sale of my Connolly collection. I am not good at selling. Probably no true collector is good at selling, unless posthumously. Anyway, now that I am uncoupled from Connolly and his list, there is a wide menu from which I can select items that appeal to me personally. My task is to buy judiciously so that each new purchase contributes to the coherence of the collection as a whole.

Epilogue

THE POINT OF IT ALL

I ask myself questions about my lifetime passion of collecting works of these Modernist authors who have been my silent companions for so many years. Do the works I have collected mean anything to anyone except me? Who cares about Modernism in literature, and more particularly, who cares about the lives and times of the writers and poets of the past? What's the point of the faded handwriting or typescript in an author's letter, and does this really tell us anything about the people who wrote these letters and documents? Does reading the originals of manuscripts, letters, and other documents bring us any closer to the individuals who wrote them? Do the works in my collection teach us anything that we don't already know about the development of Modernist literature and thought? In a digital age, what matters now to posterity?

I think back on how collecting shaped my life. In the beginning, in those far-off, lonely days in London, and during my early times in California, the writers of World War I poetry and their friends and colleagues were my friends. They lived in that imaginary world of home that I constructed and that gave me so much comfort. It was my parallel universe, in a sense, but I do believe that everyone who has ever lived on this planet exists in the same blink of the cosmic eye—that, in a metaphysical sense, there is no such thing as time. Bearing all of this in mind, it's easy for me to imagine my literary friends residing somewhere in a cosmic bubble, continuing to go about their business, just as they did on earth. It's a flight of fancy that I enjoy, although it goes no further than that. It does not address the larger question of whether there is any meaning for posterity residing in the collection of papers, letters, manuscripts, photographs, and other miscellany that I have collected over a lifetime.

There's a side to assembling this collection that has nothing at all to do with the search for items related to Modernist thought and writing. Sometimes, an item catches my attention only because it reminds me of the days when my imaginary world of home dominated my literary choices. Sometimes, an acquisition can provide an interesting example of literary scholarship while at the same time triggering a sort of literary Pavlovian response in memory. Both of these sentiments probably were reflected in my purchase of two drafts of the legendary poem "Tarantella" by Hilaire Belloc, who, although a writer of the late nineteenth and early twentieth centuries, could by no means be considered a writer of Modernism. Belloc was a true Edwardian.

I acquired these drafts at a third sale of significant items from the Roy Davids collection, which was held at Bonham's early in 2013, just over a year after the second sale. That sale confirmed for me that what was now important to me in collecting was not just works exploring the Modern Movement in literature, but works and other items relating to the potential for revelations in scholarship in the material I was acquiring.

"Tarantella" was written by the same Belloc who authored *Cautionary Tales for Children*, which I had read as far back as the days when my family lived in that tiny flat in Broken Hill when I was a very young child. This was the book that talked of "Matilda who told dreadful Lies and was Burned to Death," or young Jim, "Who ran away from his nurse and was Eaten by a Lion." It is hard to think of these books as collections of children's poetry, but the Edwardians had a unique sense of humor and understanding of children. Being an impressionable child, I had always thought of Belloc as a sort of stern Edwardian great uncle who obviously wasn't particularly fond of children.

I went to Bonham's on a rainy afternoon to look at the presale exhibition. It was large, and I found the usual assortment of bibliophiles and dealers peering through the glass of the cases arranged around the room, viewing the literary treasures that were about to go under the hammer. The literary portraits, clustered densely on backgrounds of black sacking, looked down on us distantly from the high walls. I had a list of what I wanted to see and began to search for the item of most interest to me, a daybook in which Siegfried Sassoon had written thoughts and scraps of poetry over a period of several years in the

1920s. I was in no hurry, so I ambled around, delighted to view letters and poetry with the handwriting and characteristic signatures of so many old friends, as I had come to think of them. The room was as quiet as a library reading room.

There was a case near the entrance that seemed to be attracting a good deal of quiet attention, so I lined up, rather as one does to view a painting at a crowded exhibition, to wait for my turn. There were two items in that case: the first was the Sassoon daybook I had been seeking, and next to that was a sheet of paper with lopsided writing—clearly the draft of a poem of some sort. I leaned in closer to read the handwriting. "Hilaire Belloc," I exclaimed to myself, because this was not one, but two early drafts of Belloc's poem "Tarantella." Even though Belloc was not really of literary interest to me, I had met him often over the course of my childhood. I had not only learned to read from Belloc's *Cautionary Tales*, among other works, but I knew "Tarantella" well from my schooldays. In my time, and probably for years before that and years after, the poem was a staple of English poetry classes in schools.

The draft is written, as so many of these poetry fragments are written, on a darkened and frail sheet of paper. Actually, the manuscript I bought at that auction contains two working drafts, and the written lines are replete with scratch-outs and doodles. Obviously, this was not the final and fair copy of the poem, but a real working draft, which is of much more interest—to me, in any case. It provides a better idea of the workings of the creative mind than a first edition, or even a perfect handwritten copy of the final version. Looking at the poem in its case took me straight back to my high school days in South Africa, to that same Herschel School in Cape Town where I had languished over my last three years of high school, that same boarding school for young ladies where most of our teachers were the wives of retired Anglican clergymen, unschooled in training young minds and incapable of inspiring us. I remembered the deadly dull experience of that school almost viscerally, and how I sat in the back row in my classes daydreaming of freedom. Yet, as I have acknowledged, I did leave Herschel with a thorough grounding in English literature and poetry. I remember vividly that our English classes belonged to late morning, when the African sun was nearly at its highest, so that shafts of sunlight, made visible by the myriad dust particles hanging in the air, drifted lazily through the high-paned windows toward the scrubbed wooden planks of the floor. We sat and sweltered in the heat of the dim room, longing for release. There is a stillness to a hot Cape summer day, and a stagnant air that produces a lethargy so profound that one can only sit and yearn for sleep.

Our English teacher, Mrs. Clark, was the wife of a practicing, rather than retired, Anglican clergyman. Not that it made any difference. She was tiny and earnest. Her teaching method involved endless backward and forward pacing before the blackboard, all the while teetering on impossibly high stiletto heels. She had no imagination and taught words, not meaning. She was, like the rest of them, an uninspired teacher, but those heels gripped the attention! It made me wonder how long she could maintain balance. She always carried a pointer, which I mentally compared to the balancing rod carried by tightrope walkers. My guess is that she had no formal teacher training, but at Herschel that didn't matter, because nobody expected any of us to have serious careers. Since I was always bored in class, sitting at my desk in the back gave me the best opportunity to do something else—read, write, or simply daydream. It really was hard to stay awake.

"Tarantella" came as a welcome surprise that particular morning. Suddenly, I'm sure without being aware of it, Mrs. Clark was pacing in time to the words of the poem, the click of those enormously high heels creating the sound of an accompanying castanet instead of their usual irritating click-click-click. I sat up and listened. Immediately, I loved this poem. I loved the speed of the lines and the crisp way in which the words told the story, whether you understood it or not.

> Do you remember an Inn,
> Miranda?
> Do you remember an Inn?
> And the tedding and the spreading
> Of the straw for a bedding,
> And the fleas that tease in the High Pyrenees,
> And the wine that tasted of the tar?

> (All quotes from *The Oxford Book of Modern Verse, 1892–1935*, chosen by W. B. Yeats)

"Tarantella," as a poem, is quite different from Belloc's usual writing. I've sometimes wondered if it was an attempt to emulate Mallarmé and the symbolists, because the poem relies on the flow of the words to convey meaning, rather than on the meaning of the words themselves.

The poem tells a story, but it's an ambiguous story that leaves itself open to interpretations of mystery and secret romance. You don't even have to know the English language to get caught up in the hasty music of the words:

> And the cheers and the jeers of the young muleteers
> (Under the vine of the dark verandah)?
> Do you remember an Inn, Miranda,
> Do you remember an Inn?
> And the cheers and the jeers of the young muleteers
> Who hadn't got a penny,
> And who weren't paying any,
> And the hammer at the doors and the Din?
> And the Hip! Hop! Hap!
> Of the clap
> Of the hands to the twirl and the swirl
> Of the girl gone chancing,
> Glancing,
> Dancing,
> Backing and advancing,
> Snapping of the clapper to the spin
> Out and in—
> And the Ting, Tong, Tang, of the Guitar!

I asked one of the staff to take the poem out of the case so I could hold it and look at it more closely. I had never aspired to collect Belloc's work; on the other hand, I could not escape his influence. During his lifetime, he was an extraordinarily prolific writer. He died in 1953 and did not slip into relative obscurity for some time, but what remains of his reputation today resides mostly in his poetry. I hadn't thought about Belloc for years, but there was that special personal connection with him.

Standing there, I decided against buying the draft of "Tarantella." Although the poem is well known, I considered that it held little appeal as an item of scholarship, and I did not add the lot number to the items on my want list. When the auction was held several days later, the bidding was brisk. There were many collectors and dealers in the room, and the telephone bank was larger than usual. Several bidders were participating online, so the progress of the sale was slow. Because the order was strictly alphabetical, the Belloc items came up early on, and "Tarantella" inspired a rash of bidding as the price crept up to the reserve. As the bidding started, I found myself gazing at the picture of the draft in the catalog, which was balanced on my knee, and of course, I knew what I had subconsciously known since the viewing—I wanted to buy that poem. With a sigh of capitulation, I raised my paddle and competed until the lot fell to me.

Like most of the purchases I never intended to make until the bidding began, "Tarantella" did not disappoint. I never regretted the purchase for an instant. A few years later, when I acquired the final handwritten draft of the poem—the one that Hilaire Belloc sent to his publisher—from the bookseller Bertram Rota, I was able to add context to that series of drafts. Along with the poem, Belloc had sent his publisher a letter:

> Here, then, is the Tarantella. It would only go on being tortured if I kept it and it is a happy release.
>
> Yours,
> HB
> I shall see a proof

So it's true, then, that Belloc revised the poem and carried it around until he finally gave it to his publisher in frustration.

After that third sale of the Roy Davids collection, my new collecting direction was clearly set; actually, it had probably been waiting in the wings for some time, and once I recognized it, of course, it all made perfect sense. It was only natural that, of the items sold in my Sotheby's sale, I did not mourn the pristine copy of *The Great Gatsby*, or the perfect copy in dust jacket of Hemingway's *The Sun Also Rises*. Instead, I grieved for Katherine Anne Porter's copy (a second edition at that) of Hart Crane's *The Bridge*, with the photographs and comments that she had pasted into the book relating to one of his visits to her home in Mexico. I continued to miss the Duchess of Clermont-Tonnerre's copy of *Du côté de chez Swann*, with Proust's inscriptions to her and the letters he had written inserted into the copy of the book. It wasn't the literature I missed: it was the fact that those books had provenance and association, and that the inscriptions and letters and photographs brought a personal touch to the key volumes themselves. When I had owned them, they became part of my life, and I became part of that long-ago world.

The circle closed in that key moment of understanding. The tiny collection that had sustained me during those lonely early days in London had become, brick by brick, room by room—with each new acquisition of a Connolly title—the material embodiment of that dream of a home which had eluded me all of my life. In building my Connolly collection, I had created my own parallel imaginary world to which I could retreat when the noise of the real world became too overbearing. With the sale of the collection, I had willfully destroyed this place— but happily, all was not lost, because I had now discovered a path back. I was now engaged in the process of building a bigger and better collection, one, moreover, that relied only on my own judgments and choices. I was buying items by and relating to authors who were not on the Connolly list, because adherence to the Connolly list didn't matter anymore. In auction catalogs, it was not only books that I looked at, but also letters and manuscripts and portraits. Once again, I had direction and focus, and of most importance, enthusiasm about collecting, because I was on my way to building something that was new, different, and ultimately more satisfying. My business world might never be the same again, but now I had something to sustain me. In business language, I had finally found the perfect mission statement for a new collection, and as a result, collecting had begun again in earnest. And this is how it has continued with the process of creating this second and more significant collection. As an added bonus, this time around I have finally found not only my imaginary home once again, but, in chasing down and acquiring these more personal—and personalized— examples of works by and about Modernist authors, to me it seems as if I have also found a real vocation.

Appendix

List of books presented in order in exhibition catalog for *Cyril Connolly's One Hundred Modern Books from England, France and America, 1880–1950. An Exhibition: March–December 1971*, The Humanities Research Center, The University of Texas at Austin

I present this list in the order used for the exhibition at the University of Texas at Austin because I used the catalog as my guidebook and reference over the years when I collected the books on the list. Some of the authors are represented with more than one of their works, so the list technically consists of more than 100 titles—108, to be precise.

1.	Henry James, *The Portrait of a Lady*	1881
2.	Gustave Flaubert, *Bouvard et Pécuchet*	1881
3.	Auguste Villiers de L'Isle-Adam, *Contes cruels*	1883
4.	J. K. Huysmans, *À rebours*	1884
5.	Charles Baudelaire, *Oeuvres posthumes*	1887
6.	Arthur Rimbaud, *Les Illuminations*	1886
7.	Stéphane Mallarmé, *Poesies*	1887
8.	Guy de Maupassant, *Bel-Ami*	1885
9.	Edmond and Jules de Goncourt, *Journal des Goncourt*	1887–1896
10.	J. K. Huysmans, *Là-Bas*	1891
11.	Alfred Jarry, *Ubu Roi*	1896
12.	Henry James, *The Awkward Age*	1899
13.	André Gide, *L'Immoraliste*	1902
14.	Joseph Conrad, *Youth*	1902
15.	Joseph Conrad, *The Secret Agent*	1907
16.	Henry James, *The Ambassadors*	1903
17.	George Moore, *Memoirs of My Dead Life*	1906

18.	J. M. Synge, *The Playboy of the Western World*	1907
19.	E. M. Forster, *The Longest Journey*	1907
20.	Norman Douglas, *Siren Land*	1911
21.	D. H. Lawrence, *Sons and Lovers*	1913
22.	Guillaume Apollinaire, *Alcools*	1913
23.	Marcel Proust, *Du côté de chez Swann*	1913
24.	W. B. Yeats, *Responsibilities: Poems and a Play*	1914
25.	Thomas Hardy, *Satires of Circumstance*	1914
26.	James Joyce, *A Portrait of the Artist as a Young Man*	1916
27.	Ford Madox Ford, *The Good Soldier*	1915
28.	Norman Douglas, *South Wind*	1917
29.	Percy Wyndham Lewis, *Tarr*	1918
30.	T. S. Eliot, *Prufrock and Other Observations*	1917
	T. S. Eliot, *The Waste Land*	1922
31.	Paul Valéry, *Le Jeune Parque*	1917
	Paul Valéry, *Charmes*	1922
32.	Guillaume Apollinaire, *Calligrammes*	1918
33.	Gerard Manley Hopkins, *Poems*	1918
34.	Arthur Waley, *One Hundred and Seventy Chinese Poems*	1918
35.	Ezra Pound, *Lustra*	1916
	Ezra Pound, *Hugh Selwyn Mauberley*	1920
36.	Wilfred Owen, *Poems*	1920
37.	Lytton Strachey, *Eminent Victorians*	1918
38.	D. H. Lawrence, *Sea and Sardinia*	1921
39.	Aldous Huxley, *Crome Yellow*	1921
40.	Katherine Mansfield, *The Garden Party*	1922
41.	W. B. Yeats, *Later Poems*	1922
42.	James Joyce, *Ulysses*	1922
43.	Raymond Radiguet, *Le diable au corps*	1923
44.	Ronald Firbank, *The Flower Beneath the Foot*	1923
45.	E. M. Forster, *A Passage to India*	1924
46.	Wallace Stevens, *Harmonium*	1923
47.	E. E. Cummings, *Tulips and Chimneys*	1923
	E. E. Cummings, *Is 5*	1926
48.	F. Scott Fitzgerald, *The Great Gatsby*	1925
49.	Ernest Hemingway, *In Our Time*	1924
50.	Ernest Hemingway, *The Sun Also Rises*	1926
51.	André Gide, *Si le grain ne meurt*	1924
52.	William Plomer, *Turbott Wolfe*	1925
53.	W. Somerset Maugham, *The Casuarina Tree*	1926

54.	Virginia Woolf, *To the Lighthouse*	1927
55.	André Breton, *Nadja*	1928
56.	W. B. Yeats, *The Tower*	1928
	W. B. Yeats, *The Winding Stair*	1929
57.	D. H. Lawrence, *Lady Chatterley's Lover*	1928
58.	Evelyn Waugh, *Decline and Fall*	1928
59.	Henry Green, *Living*	1929
60.	Ernest Hemingway, *A Farewell to Arms*	1929
61.	Robert Graves, *Good-Bye to All That*	1929
62.	Jean Cocteau, *Les enfants terribles*	1929
63.	Ivy Compton-Burnett, *Brothers and Sisters*	1929
64.	Hart Crane, *The Bridge*	1930
65.	T. S. Eliot, *Ash-Wednesday*	1930
66.	Ezra Pound, *A Draft of XXX Cantos*	1930
67.	Edith Sitwell, *Collected Poems*	1930
68.	Antoine de Saint-Exupéry, *Vol de nuit*	1931
69.	William Faulkner, *Sanctuary*	1931
70.	Virginia Woolf, *The Waves*	1931
71.	Edmund Wilson, *Axel's Castle*	1931
72.	T. S. Eliot, *Selected Essays 1917–1932*	1932
73.	W. H. Auden, *The Orators: An English Study*	1932
74.	Louis-Ferdinand Céline, *Voyage au bout de la nuit*	1932
75.	Aldous Huxley, *Brave New World*	1932
76.	Nathanael West, *Miss Lonelyhearts*	1933
77.	André Malraux, *La condition humaine*	1933
78.	Dylan Thomas, *18 Poems*	1934
	Dylan Thomas, *Twenty-Five Poems*	1936
79.	F. Scott Fitzgerald, *Tender Is the Night*	1934
80.	Henry James, *The Art of the Novel*	1934
81.	Marianne Moore, *Selected Poems*	1935
82.	Henry de Montherlant, *Les jeunes filles*	1936–1939
83.	Henri Michaux, *Voyage en Grande Garabagne*	1936
	Henri Michaux, *Au pays de la magie*	1941
84.	Jean-Paul Sartre, *La nausée*	1938
85.	Louis MacNeice, *Autumn Journal*	1939
86.	Christopher Isherwood, *Goodbye to Berlin*	1939
87.	James Joyce, *Finnegans Wake*	1939
88.	Graham Greene, *The Power and the Glory*	1940
89.	Arthur Koestler, *Darkness at Noon*	1940
90.	W. H. Auden, *Another Time*	1940

91.	Stephen Spender, *Ruins and Visions*	1942	
92.	T. S. Eliot, *Four Quartets*	1943	
93.	George Orwell, *Animal Farm*	1945	
94.	Albert Camus, *L'Étranger*	1941	213
95.	Albert Camus, *La peste*	1947	
96.	Dylan Thomas, *Deaths and Entrances*	1946	
	Dylan Thomas, *New Poems*	1943	
97.	John Betjeman, *Selected Poems*	1948	
98.	Ezra Pound, *The Pisan Cantos*	1948	
99.	George Orwell, *Nineteen Eighty-Four*	1949	
100.	William Carlos Williams, *Paterson* 1, 2, 3, 4, 5	1946–1958	

Index